South America's National Parks
A VISITOR'S GUIDE

South America's National Parks

A VISITOR'S GUIDE

William C. Leitch

The Mountaineers/Seattle

The Mountaineers: Organized 1906 ". . . to explore, study, preserve, and enjoy the natural beauty of the outdoors."

4 3 2 1 0
5 4 3 2 1

Published by The Mountaineers
306 Second Avenue West, Seattle, Washington 98119

Published simultaneously in Canada by Douglas & McIntyre, Ltd.,
1615 Venables Street, Vancouver, B.C. V5L 2H1

Published simultaneously in the UK and Europe by Moorland Publishing Co., Ltd.,
Moor Farm Road West, Ashbourne DE6 1HD, England

Manufactured in the United States of America

Edited by Miriam Bulmer; maps by Steven R. Holloway
All photographs by the author
Cover design by Elizabeth Watson; book design by Barbara Bash
Cover photograph: Mount Fitzroy, Los Glaciares National Park, Argentina. Insets: **top,** giant toucan, Iguaçú National Park, Brazil; **left,** guanaco, Torres del Paine National Park, Chile; **right,** Magellanic penguins, Punta Tombo, Argentina; **bottom,** nine-banded armadillo, Los Glaciares National Park, Argentina.
Frontispiece: Mount Fitzroy from Lago Capri, one of the finest wilderness campsites in South America. Page 5: swaying palms, gentle breezes, clear waters, and glistening beaches, Morrocoy National Park, Venezuela.

Library of Congress Cataloging in Publication Data

Leitch, William C.
    South America's national parks : a visitor's guide / William C.
Leitch.
        p. cm.
    Includes bibliographical references.
    1. South America—Description and travel—1981—Guide-books.
2. National parks and reserves—South America—Guide-books.
I. Title.
F2211.L45 1990
918.04'38—dc20   90-35389
                                                          CIP

ISBN 0-89886-248-5 (paper—US)
ISBN 0-89886-259-0 (cloth—US)
ISBN 0-86190-447-8 (paper—UK)

This book is for Angela

⊡ ACKNOWLEDGMENTS

During the years I spent visiting parks and reserves in every corner of Latin America, I subjected scores of field staff to a relentless barrage of questions about this and about that. With few exceptions, they responded with boundless good will and great forbearance. To these staff and their supervisors—members of the park services of Argentina, Bolivia, Brazil, Chile, Colombia, Ecuador, Guyana, Paraguay, Peru, Suriname, Uruguay, and Venezuela—I owe a great debt. Thanks also to Susie Baldwin, without whom the book could not have been written, to Chris Field, Greg Kroll, Tom Lemke, and others who reviewed sections of the book and offered many helpful suggestions, and to Karen Leitch, for her patience and help. Errors or omissions are, of course, entirely my own responsibility.

▣ CONTENTS

ARGENTINA

1. El Palmar
2. Laguna Blanca
3. Nahuel Huapi
4. Lanín
5. Los Alerces
6. Península Valdés
7. Bosques Petrificados and Cueva de las Manos
8. Perito Moreno
9. Los Glaciares
10. Tierra Del Fuego

BRAZIL

11. Tijuca
12. Itatiaia
13. Aparados da Serra
14. Iguaçú/Iguazú
15. Das Emas
16. Amazonia

CHILE

17. Lauca
18. Fray Jorge
19. Los Paraguas and Conguillío

20. Payehue
21. Vincente Perez Rosales
22. Torres Del Paine

COLOMBIA

23. Puracé
24. Isla del Salamanca
25. Tayrona

PERU

26. Paracas
27. Pampa Galeras
28. Huascaran

SURINAME

29. Brownsberg
30. The Coastal Reserves
31. The Inland Reserves

VENEZULA

32. Henri Pittier
33. Morrocoy
34. Sierra Nevada

NUMBERS REFER TO PARK LOCATIONS SHOWN ON MAP

Caribbean Sea

North Atlantic Ocean

㉔ ㉕ ㉝ ㉜
　　㉞

GUYANA
VENEZUELA   SURINAME
　　　　　　㉚
COLOMBIA   ㉙ FRENCH
　　　　　　㉛ GUIANA
㉓

EQUATOR

ECUADOR

⑯

㉘

BRAZIL

PERU

㉖ ㉗

⑰

BOLIVIA   ⑮

PARAGUAY
　　　　　⑪
　　　⑫
⑭

ARGENTINA

⑬

①

URUGUAY

⑱

CHILE

②
⑲
　④
⑳
　③

South Pacific Ocean

㉑ ⑤ ⑥
　　⑦   South Atlantic Ocean

⑧
⑨

㉒

⑩

9

▣ PREFACE

People need parks; parks need people.

It sounds like a chicken and egg problem, and in some measure it is. Park managers need to have people visit their parks in order to justify budgets adequate to protect the resources that bring the people to the parks in the first place. To be sure, this is not an easy notion to embrace in the United States or Canada, where many park managers are trying to figure out how to keep a flood of visitors from adversely impacting a park's features, but in South America the number of people who visit parks is of paramount, indeed decisive, importance.

The fact that some tourists will spend good hard dollars to visit a park or reserve to see unusual flora and fauna is not lost on park managers or politicians. One country, Suriname, has in fact deliberately developed its park and reserve policy so as to exploit that possibility. But the key to success is the number of visitors.

When tourists visit a park in the United States they sometimes unwittingly increase the manager's problems, but when tourists visit most South American parks they help the manager solve his greatest problem: lack of money. They enable him to tell his supervisors that park visitations are on the increase and he needs additional funds to hire more staff to respond to visitor needs, construct a center to help visitors interpret and understand what they are seeing, hire more staff to protect wildlife from poachers, send staff to training programs, construct and maintain trails, and so on.

In this fashion, every time someone visits a South American park he or she makes a tiny contribution to that park's welfare, and to the national park movement itself.

And that's one of the main purposes of this book: to let travelers know where the principal South American parks are and what is in them, so they can enjoy themselves, and, at the same time, make their own small contribution to the future.

⚏ FOREWORD
by Michael Frome

On my first trip to South America I saw a land that was whole. That image is still vivid: of the unbroken forest, a "jungle," if you wish, endless and so thick my crewmates and I could barely see the streams flowing from mountains and highlands to join other streams on their journey to the sea. In those days I was a young navigator in the Air Force (then the Army Air Corps), flying a transport mission across Venezuela, the Guianas, and the broad delta of the Amazon, eastward to the Brazilian bulge in the Atlantic, and from there to Africa. It was 1944, when most of South America might have been considered as a national park without the name.

That was almost fifty years ago, a brief flicker of time, but since then the world has turned upside down. All across the planet, seemingly impenetrable strongholds of nature have lost their defenses. In the four decades I have worked to recover those defenses by fighting for parks and reserves, I have learned that virtually anything set aside and saved reflects human restraint and deliberate design, the best side of modern civilization. For this reason I'm pleased to contribute introductory words for William Leitch and his useful, pioneering guidebook to the national parks of South America, fittingly published by The Mountaineers as part of its mission "to explore, study, preserve, and enjoy the natural beauty of the outdoors."

North Americans actually know little about the great continent to the south, as compared with the Caribbean, or Europe, or even Africa. Yet South America is a composite of wonderlands, extending 5,000 miles from the tropics almost to Antarctica. The Andean Cordillera, the longest continuous mountain range in the world, embraces forty-five peaks rising above 20,000 feet. Angel Falls, in the Guiana Highlands of Venezuela, is the highest waterfall in the world. Iguaçú, the chain of falls along the border Argentina shares with Brazil and Paraguay, is higher than Victoria, twice as wide as Niagara, bordered by virgin forests bright with flowering plants, birds, and butterflies. At the southern tip of South America, the Strait of Magellan recalls the Inside Passage to Alaska and the Norwegian fjords, with their snowy peaks and glaciers, rocky headlands, clouds and mists, and a life-community where whales, porpoises, and penguins outnumber people.

One part or another of South America provides home and habitat to marmoset and monkey, giant armadillo and anteater, the world's tiniest deer, maned wolf, mountain tapir, mountain lion, jaguar, ocelot, llama, and vicuña—plus bird life that includes the black-necked swan, cacique, condor, quetzal, flamingo, parrot and parakeet, toucan, trogan, and hundreds of species of dazzling and bizarre butterflies.

The survival of these species is no accident. Today these natural treasures of South America are located primarily within national parks, much like the treasures of the United States, and of countries all over the world, established through the initiative of individual citizens and the response of governments to their concern. The first national park in South America, as a case in point, was set aside in Argentina in 1903, from lands in Patagonia donated by Francisco "Perito" Moreno, who devoted his life to preserving Argentina's wild landscape. Where he began, others followed. In 1958, George Fulda, an executive of an Argentine travel agency, organized the Friends of the National Parks. In time he was joined by Dr. Maria Buchinger de Alitz, a professor of natural resource policy, who on a Guggenheim Fellowship had studied national parks in the United States. She then became a prime mover in organizing continent-wide seminars on natural areas and tourism.

South American parks are not as well developed as those in our country, and they are different, in general much more primitive, and for the most part, poorly financed and understaffed. For these reasons, North Americans are well advised not to carry preconceived expectations with them to South America.

Leitch carefully points out that visitors are often on their own, obliged to create their own park experiences. The serious parks traveler will consider this an advantage rather than a liability, reading in advance and preparing carefully. *South America's National Parks* will prove invaluable with its details on climate and weather, visitor facilities, historical aspects, and glossaries of useful Spanish, Portuguese, and Dutch phrases.

The author and I believe that increased nature tourism will encourage countries to safeguard their treasures. Certainly Amazonia is worth more in its natural state to the eight countries sharing the river basin than if it was deforested and industrially developed. In 1978 I visited the Amazon mainstem at Manaus, 850 miles upriver from the Brazilian coast. I was astonished to find stretches of the river near the city lined with steel plants, power plants, microwave stations, logging mills, alcohol and petrochemical complexes, and storage plants. In places it looked more like the Hudson River at Hoboken than a jungle river. On the other hand, I also saw pink freshwater porpoises, birds and fish, and lovely *Victoria regia,* the lovely, meter-wide water lilies that symbolize the lush Amazon forest—a rain forest with more types of plants, flowers, trees, birds, butterflies, reptiles, and mammals than any other forest on earth.

As scientists warn, stripping the Amazon forest cover can drastically alter the world's climate. Tourism can help to save it. Nevertheless, if tourism is an appropriate goal, it must be quality tourism worthy of the resource. That is what national parks are all about: protecting the setting and adjusting visitor use accordingly.

Members of the Mountaineers and others who read this book will want it that way and can help make it so. This book will help readers to appreciate the sense of place, the purpose of place, the spirit of natural sanctuaries still largely undefiled. Once, at Rotorua, in New Zealand, an American woman told me how she had turned up the air conditioning and kept her windows closed all night to shut out the sounds and smell of the geysers and other thermal features. She might as well have stayed home.

The way to see the national parks of South America—or national parks anywhere—is to travel simply, take nature as it comes, exult in it, and support the preservation of whatever can still be saved.

🔲 INTRODUCTION

For more than 200 years, legions of foreign travelers have journeyed to South America to see the sights of the Green Continent. Early on, travelers such as Charles Darwin went to out-of-the-way places, and they went the hard way—on foot, by horseback, in canoes. Gradually, the travelers became tourists, and an odd pattern established itself: the tourists went only to cities—Rio de Janeiro, Buenos Aires, Lima, Quito, Santiago, and a few others, with perhaps a daring expedition to a festival in a small town or to such tourist lodestones as Machu Picchu and Iguazú Falls. As a result, few tourists realized that South America possesses a treasury of national parks that offers precisely what most travelers seek: outstanding scenery, unusual wildlife, a wide choice of recreational opportunities, and the tang of adventure.

This scenario has changed dramatically in recent years. The backcountry has been discovered, and modern travelers are shifting their interests to South America's hinterlands. Rural transportation has improved; trips to Patagonia, the Llanos, and Tierra del Fuego no longer require an expedition. Inevitably, with the arrival of modern transportation much of the romance—and discomfort—of travel in South America has disappeared: one can now drive an air-conditioned rental car through the heart of the Amazon Basin.

These changes have brought many of South America's national parks within easy reach, and with the growing international awareness of the importance of national parks in developing countries, they are quickly becoming primary destinations for discriminating tourists.

South America is no longer a sparsely populated continent pushing back a wilderness frontier. Modern technology and an insatiable demand for natural resources are tremendously accelerating the modification of the South American landscape to suit commercial development. Few South American countries have instituted wilderness preservation systems; eventually, the only areas in which wildlands will receive effective protection may be those areas incorporated into parks and reserves. Consequently, the importance of South American national parks rests not only in their growing role as tourist attractions and centers of interest to students of natural history, but in their maintenance as repositories of wilderness. If South America's wildlands are to survive the tumultuous decades to come, it will be in that continent's national parks and reserves.

South America claims more than 160 national parks and reserves. A few are nearly ideal; many exist only on paper. Unfortunately, it is not possible to describe them all between the covers of one book. Accordingly, I have made difficult choices about which parks to describe and which to disregard. Those choices are based primarily on the following criteria:

◆ **Would a reader experience an area as a park?** Many parks included in this book meet criteria established by the International Union for the Conservation of Nature and Natural Resources (IUCN), but not all of them. Some South American countries bestow the title "national park" on small, scenic areas popular for family outings. Essentially regional recreational sites, they offer little to the foreign traveler and have been included only if they possess features of outstanding interest. ("National park" is only one of many terms used by South American bureaucracies. "Ecological reserve," "nature reserve," "floristic reserve," and several other titles are also used to describe what are essentially parks. As in this country, valid political reasons may exist for calling a park something else. I have therefore included a few areas that are parks in every sense but their title.)

◆ **Can a reader get there?** There are South American parks that have most of the natural features that would satisfy a visitor, but are virtually inaccessible to the average traveler. If a long expedition or great expense for aircraft or river transport is required to visit a park, it is not described in this book.

◆ **Is other information available?** A few parks, especially those located on remote islands, such as Easter Island or the Galapagos Islands, are excluded because they are well described elsewhere.

◆ **Does a park represent a major South American region?** A few parks have been excluded because other parks better represent a particular region. The parks in this book represent every major South American biotic region: tropical and temperate rain forest, desert, savanna, cordillera, altiplano, seashore. Collectively, they offer visitors an astonishing variety of flora, fauna, scenery, and adventure.

Travelers wandering through South America's national parks today have fresh opportunities to scrutinize the features of this continent's immensely rich natural history. I hope that those readers with a yen to roam through the jungles, deserts, steppes, and mountains of South America will first derive satisfaction from roaming through these pages, and then set out for the Green Continent.

With the southern Andean ice cap as backdrop, a guanaco watches over his territory in Torres del Painee National Park, Chile.

🌀 1
SOUTH AMERICAN
GEOGRAPHY AND FAUNA

Understanding South America's natural history requires understanding the continent's geography. Mother Nature seems to have tried out all her geographical tricks in South America before applying them elsewhere. Indeed, the word "diverse" most appropriately characterizes the landforms, climates, and vegetational zones encountered here. And what superlatives: the world's longest mountain chain (the Andes) divides the world's driest desert (the Atacama) from the world's most vast jungle (the Amazon Basin) from which flows the world's largest and longest river (the Amazon) and so on.

But South America is not merely a land of dramatic extremes. Climate and physiography interact to produce an endlessly varied series of contradictory landscapes, each more surprising and unlikely than the last. Chile, for example, contains territory where rain has never been recorded as well as lands that endure an annual deluge of over 18 feet of rainfall. Peru and Bolivia possess bleak, windswept plains so high as to approach the upper limits of permanent human habitability, as well as vast reaches of low-lying forests, which even today are not fully explored. In Colombia, a traveler can stand on a glacier in the northern Andes and glimpse through the thin haze a distant strand of beach washed by warm subtropical seas.

South America's size and location account for much of its complexity. At its widest point, the continent is nearly as wide as North America. Longitudinally, it stretches nearly 5,000 miles south from the sunny Caribbean Sea to the icy waters of the South Atlantic Ocean, which only narrowly separate it from Antarctica. With more than 65 degrees of latitude, the continent is subject to climatic regimes whose interplay with landforms results in a bewildering mosaic of distinct vegetation zones.

The geography seems confounding, but a clear pattern of landforms can be discerned. Reduced to its simplest elements, the continent comprises three mountain masses with their associated plateaus, and five vast plains that seldom exceed 2,000 feet in elevation. On this basis, South America can be divided into nine major regions: the Andean Cordillera, the Brazilian Highlands, the Guiana Highlands, and the Altiplano, all mountainous regions; and the Llanos, the West Coast Plains, the Amazon Basin, the Gran Chaco, and Patagonia, all plains regions.

⊡ THE MOUNTAINOUS REGIONS

Andean Cordillera

The most prominent mountain mass is the Andean Cordillera, the longest continuous mountain chain on earth. The chain runs the length of the entire continent, rising abruptly from the Caribbean and disappearing into the restless Antarctic waters. For most of its 4,500 miles, the Cordillera parallels South America's west coast, separating a narrow coastal plain from the rest of the continent. In the extreme south, this coastal plain disappears, and the Cordillera itself forms the sea-battered west coast of the continent's southern tip.

The entire Cordillera is studded with conspicuously high peaks. This string of peaks begins with Pico Cristóbal Colón, which reaches nearly 19,000 feet at the edge of the Caribbean. The chain marches southward in a nearly uninterrupted procession of high mountains to the rugged snowcapped peaks that overlook the turbulent Strait of Magellan. More than forty-five of these mountains exceed 20,000 feet. Parks of alpine character are well represented throughout the Cordillera, especially in Peru, Chile, and Argentina.

Dozens of Andean peaks are in the classic cone shape of a volcano. At least twenty-four live volcanos brood in Chile, and every country on South America's west coast has a share of these dangerous, smoking giants. Volcanos are centerpiece attractions in a number of Cordilleran parks, including Parque Nacional Lanín in Argentina and Chile's Parque Nacional Puyehue.

Because of its great length and, in places, width, the Cordillera embraces four significant subzones. In the northernmost subzone, the Andes divide into three distinct ranges, rich in live volcanos, and separated by deep, humid valleys. The three ranges converge in southern Colombia to form a single massive chain of mountains that thrusts southward through the center of Ecuador. The mountains of this Ecuadorian subzone are densely forested. Only the highest ridges and peaks are treeless.

In the next subzone, the Andes again divide into parallel ranges divided by deep valleys. Southward, the ranges diverge, eventually becoming widely separated by extremely high, arid plains. This complex of mountains and high plains, up to 400 miles wide, sweeps through southern Peru and Bolivia into northern Chile and Argentina. This is the region of the Altiplano, a stark combination of high, windswept grasslands, lakes and salt flats, and snowcapped mountains. For nearly 2,000 miles, the mountains of this subzone are all but treeless. Thin, isolated patches of scrub and cactus predominate; forests flourish only in the low, moist valleys.

In the next subzone, the Andes again converge to form a single narrow chain of peaks. Here, the Cordillera thrusts up its highest peak—Aconcagua, at 22,834 feet the highest point in the western hemisphere—but from this point southward, the Cordillera gradually begins to lose elevation. Forests again appear on the slopes at low elevations.

In the southernmost subzone, the coastal plains that separate the Andes from the Pacific disappear, and the mountains meet the sea. The inundated Cordillera forms Archipelagic Chile, a narrow maze of islands, glacier-carved fjords, and ragged peninsulas. The mountains extend south, make a sharp eastward hook at Tierra del Fuego, and sink into the foaming sea. This section of the Andes is a wild and remote region of thick forests, low continental icecaps, and heavy rainfall. Two national parks, Chile's Torres del Paine and Argentina's Tierra del Fuego, superbly represent this spellbinding and seldom-visited zone.

Altiplano

The series of high plateaus associated with the central Andean Cordillera is known as the Altiplano, one of the world's great highlands, rivaled only by the tablelands of Tibet. Not the single high plain that its name suggests, the Altiplano is a discontinuous series of plateaus and basins of varying size and elevation, separated from each other by mountain ranges or deep canyons. These plateaus extend from southern Colombia to northern Chile and Argentina, but reach their highest elevations and broadest extents in Peru and Bolivia.

In the southern Altiplano, the plateaus often take the form of enormous, gentle depressions through which are scattered a number of large lakes. Famed Lago Titicaca—deep enough for steamships—is one of these, but most of the lakes are little more than vast flooded marshes that disappear completely in dry years. Many basins lack outlets, and are floored with salt flats or weird saline lakes such as Bolivia's Laguna Colorada, a remote Altiplano lake as red as tomato soup, and nearby, pea-green Laguna Verde.

The sheer height of the Andean plateaus is astonishing. Those of the Bolivian and Peruvian Altiplano *average* 12,500 feet, several plateaus in Peru exceed 14,000 feet, and one lofty plain in southwestern Bolivia lies at 16,800 feet.

At such elevations, temperatures may drop below freezing at night during any season; winter brings bitter, subzero cold to many of these plateaus. Yet because of the rarefied atmosphere, sunshine is unusually intense: puddles on the shaded side of an Altiplano village street may be frozen solid while vendors work in shirtsleeves on the opposite, sunny side of the street. In the southern Altiplano, light rainfall is limited to a few summer months. Fierce, dessicating winds rage out of the Cordillera, sweep across the rolling plains, and raise enormous black clouds of dust.

Life is difficult for plants and animals alike under such conditions. Altiplano vegetation is sparse and tough, primarily coarse grasses and hardy, low shrubs. This plant association is quite distinct from the relatively lush growth characteristic of the moister highlands of Colombia and Ecuador.

Despite the harsh climate and forbidding landscape, a unique and austere beauty imbues the Altiplano, a quality of scenery unlike any other region of South America. Among the several national parks located in this fascinating zone are Puracé in Colombia, Pampa Galeras and Huascarán in Peru, and Lauca in Chile.

View of a small part of Iguaçú Falls from the Argentine side of the river

Brazilian Highlands

High furrowed plateaus form the second prominent mountain mass on the South American continent—the Brazilian Highlands. They differ from the Andes in two important respects. First, they were ancient when the Andes were born. Composed in part of Precambrian granites and schists, they are among the oldest known rocks, at least 500 million years old. Second, they are not as high as the Andes—only a few peaks exceed 8,000 feet—and do not modify climate as dramatically as the towering wall of the Andes.

The humid coastal margins of the Brazilian Highlands support a dense tropical forest, but the lack of high inland mountains to force rain from the moist trade winds has resulted in formation of an arid plateau. The bulk of the northern Brazilian Highlands is desert, over which is scattered a dry forest of thorny scrub, the *caatinga*. *Caatinga* means "white forest" in an Indian dialect, and the phrase accurately describes the appearance of these leafless trees during the dry season. Erratic rainfall accounts for the formation of a desert so surprisingly close to the dense forests of the Amazon Basin. In many areas only cactus can survive the frequent droughts. A few humid zones and valley bottoms support groves of palms and other trees, but the hillsides are covered with open, dry forests or the diabolically spiked plants of the *caatinga.*

Distinctly richer vegetation covers the southeastern half of the Brazilian Highlands. While not excessive, rainfall is distributed evenly throughout the year, and because humidity is always high the area supports the largest expanse of tropical rain forest in South America outside of the Amazon Basin. These forests are not as luxuriant as those of the Amazon, partly because of soil and climatic factors, but principally because for several centuries much of the forest has been overexploited by man. Fortunately, in recent years the Brazilian government has instituted regulatory measures and has created reserves in an attempt to halt the destruction. Although much of the forest has been destroyed, a great deal remains, and several parks are located in this intriguing zone, among them Brazil's Itatiaia and the national parks established on the Brazilian and Argentine sides of Iguazú Falls.

The southwestern corner of the Brazilian Highlands is a good example of the tropical savanna. In this area, a region of headwaters for both the Amazon and Paraná river systems, the continuous tropical forests give way to scattered clumps of tall trees, thickest in valley bottoms and near water. Patches of tall grass and sedges appear and soon predominate as the zone merges into the seasonal marshlands of the northern Chaco. Located near the center of the continent, this transitional zone divides humid lowland forests from grasslands, and links the Brazilian Highlands to the Andean Cordillera.

Guiana Highlands

The third and smallest South American mountain mass, the Guiana Highlands, borders the Venezuelan Llanos and the Brazilian Highlands through which the Amazon River winds its way to the sea. The Guiana and Brazilian highlands form the bulk of South America's prominent eastward bulge into the Atlantic Ocean.

Geologically, the Guiana Highlands are related to the Brazilian Highlands: both are composed in part of ancient crystalline rocks that predate the appearance of the Andes by several hundred million years.

The plateaus of the Guiana Highlands are relatively low. On the west, the plateaus reach 4,000 to 5,000 feet of elevation, interrupted by deep canyons cut by the numerous rivers that feed the Orinoco River system. The world's highest waterfall, Angel Falls, plunges 3,212 feet into one of these canyons. But the great majority of the Guiana Highlands comprise monotonously flat or rolling plateaus little more than 1,000 feet high. A few isolated mountains rise to 8,000 or 9,000 feet from these low tablelands. The most prominent and best known of these mountains is Mount Roraima, located at the intersection of the borders of Brazil, Venezuela, and Guyana.

Where undisturbed by man, tropical rain forests flourish on these highlands. In the Venezuelan sector of the zone, sections of savanna and grasslands of the Llanos extend like fingers into the forests. Along the Atlantic coast, a belt of grasslands from 10 to 30 miles wide separates the forests from the sea.

Devil's Island lies at the edge of this region, and the highland's reputation for having a hostile, if not lethal, climate may stem from the literature and myths associated with the now-dismantled penal colony. The reputation is not quite deserved. Hot, but not unbearable temperatures prevail during the day, but nights are relatively cool. Humidity, however, is always high near the coast. Days during which the humidity dips below 90 percent are rare.

Until recently, lack of easy means of transportation has nearly isolated this region from the rest of the continent. In addition, perhaps due to its fearful reputation, travelers seldom visited the region. Indeed, many sections of the highlands remain largely unexplored. The region is unspoiled, an excellent reason to visit the splendid parks of Suriname and southeastern Venezuela.

⌷ THE PLAINS REGIONS

The Llanos

The great expanse of plains drained by the Río Orinoco and its numerous tributaries is the Llanos. The northernmost of South America's plains regions, the Llanos' 360,000 square miles occupy most of central Venezuela and northeastern Colombia. Extensions of the Andean Cordillera lie to the west and north; to the south, the Llanos gradually rise and merge into the plateaus of the Guiana Highlands.

Low, almost perfectly flat alluvial plains, most of the Llanos is grassland and savanna. Deciduous gallery forests grow along many of the waterways, and clusters of several types of palm trees are characteristic of the region.

Seasonal ponds and lakes dot the Llanos throughout, for the plains are inundated each year when the numerous rivers overflow their banks. Flat terrain and a high clay content in the soils inhibit drainage, converting the grasslands into vast swamps during the rainy season. Construction and maintenance of roads are difficult under such conditions. Few roads penetrate the Llanos.

The climate of the Llanos has two distinct seasons: the rainy season, April to October, when the rivers flood much of the countryside; and the dry season, when the same areas may suffer extreme drought.

Western Coastal Plains

The coastal plains of western South America, cramped into the narrow shelf between the Andean Cordillera and the Pacific Ocean, can be divided into three major subzones.

The first, extending from the Panamanian isthmus to southern Ecuador, is hot, humid, and verdant. Numerous short streams drain off the heavy rainfall, and make road building difficult. In the northern sector of this subzone, tropical rain forest predominates, while to the south much of the forest has been replaced by plantations devoted to production of cacao, bananas, and sugar cane.

In northern Peru, however, this belt of greenery abruptly ends, transformed by the effects of a quixotic cold ocean current into a narrow desert—the Atacama—that stretches southward for nearly 2,000 miles. The largest subzone, and in many respects the most interesting, the Atacama region is the smallest of the world's great deserts—a mere 140,000 square miles—but the driest of them all. In northern Chile, fearsome areas exist in which no rainfall has *ever* been recorded. Other parts receive rainfall so slight as to be of no biological significance. Iquique, Chile, for example, records one third of an inch of rainfall in an average year.

A few widely separated streams wind through the Atacama from the Andes to the sea. Where landforms permit irrigation, croplands in valley bottoms form ribbons of rich green across the desert. But between these fertile oases, the landscape is grim and lifeless, for in many areas lack of rainfall prohibits growth of any plant life whatsoever. Here the desert floor is paved with a dusty, baked amalgam of sand, gravel, cobbles, and boulders.

Despite the Atacama's forbidding aspect, desert, sky, mountains, and seacoast combine in a potent visual mixture to create areas of spectacular scenery. Peru's exquisite Reserva Nacional Paracas embodies most of the characteristics of this unsettling region.

Ocean-going steamers can reach Manaus, and beyond. Local traffic moves up and down the river in the smaller riverboats in the foreground. Amazonia National Park, Brazil

Rainfall slowly increases to the south, and the Atacama begins to lose its harsh grip on the terrain near central Chile. Sparse patches of grass and drought-resistant shrubs appear, and soon merge into scrub forest. Near Santiago, Chile, the coastal plains acquire the distinctively Mediterranean character produced by abundantly wet winters and dry summers. This area, South America's California, is densely populated and intensively cultivated.

The first of Chile's thick beech forests begins to appear near Concepcíon. Farther south, moderate to heavy annual rainfall sustains the vast forests that cover this southernmost extreme of the coastal plains. This zone of abundant rivers, large lakes, wild forests, and dramatic alpine scenery contains several of Chile's finest national parks.

The coastal plains of South America's west coast sink into the Pacific at the Gulf of Ancud, near Puerto Montt, Chile. For the remaining 1,000 miles of coastline to the south, the wild, rainswept peaks of the Andean Cordillera drop nearly straight into the sea.

Amazon Basin

Abundant rainfall, warm temperatures, and high relative humidity combine to form the world's largest remaining expanse of tropical forest—the rain forests of the Amazon River Basin, or Amazonia. This immense plain—over 2.7 million square miles—occupies about one third of Brazil and large portions of Venezuela, Colombia, Ecuador, Peru, and Bolivia.

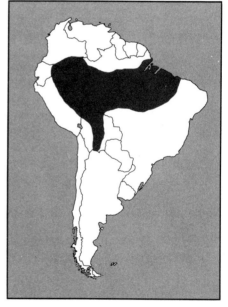

Amazonia is flat and low. The river port of Iquitos, Peru, more than 2,300 miles from the Amazon's mouth, lies only 330 feet above sea level. Once the river or one of its 18,000 tributaries enters the basin from surrounding highlands, they drop only one foot in each seven miles. More than 50,000 miles of the river and its tributaries can be navigated.

Because many rivers here regularly overflow their banks, the basin has been, until recently, roadless. With frantic speed, however, an aggressive Brazilian government has forged a network of roads into the basin. Two north-south roads are finished, and several others are near completion. Despite the steady advance of highways through the rain forests, much of Amazonia remains largely unexplored.

The heart of Amazonia is hot and wet year-round. An average of 80 inches of rain pours into the basin each year, and torrential thunderstorms may occur at any time of year. Because of its size, a single dry or wet season cannot be defined for

Amazonia. In the north, for example, the rainiest months are from May to September, while the southern part receives most of its rainfall from October to April.

While hot, Amazonia is not intolerable. At Belém, near the mouth of the river, the average daily high reaches 88 degrees Fahrenheit, but at night the temperature drops to a pleasant 72 degrees. At Manaus, 850 miles upriver, the daytime temperature may near 90 degrees, while evening temperatures fall to 75 degrees. Experienced Amazon River travelers keep a light sweater handy. Relative humidity, however, is always high, and near the coast often approaches 100 percent.

The combination of abundant rain, stable high temperatures, and high humidity creates ideal conditions for lush growth. The forests here include giants that exceed 300 feet. Most, however, reach from 150 to 180 feet at maturity, and form a dense upper canopy that effectively shades the forest floor. Thus, although dense thickets are common, most Amazon jungles are not the impenetrable tangles of legend, movies, and popular literature. They may be more accurately described as fairly open understory associations of young trees and shrubs adapted to low levels of light intensity.

Gran Chaco

The wild, empty region that occupies portions of Bolivia, Brazil, Paraguay, and Argentina is known as the Gran Chaco.

Deciduous scrub forests that form nearly solid thickets cover half of the Chaco, while the other half is composed of open, grassy savannas. A few sluggish, unnavigable rivers drain the Chaco, periodically overflow their banks, and convert vast areas of low-lying ground into swamps. These swamplands are usually dotted with Caranday palm trees, from which enterprising farmers extract a valuable wax. But these palms, and the quebracho tree, a source of tannin, are the only natural resources of commercial value in the entire region. Less than 1 percent of the Chaco is under cultivation.

The Chaco is favored with a warm and mild climate, although summer temperatures skyrocket in the southern parts of the region. Indeed, the highest temperatures in South America have been recorded in the Argentine Chaco. Most of the rainfall occurs between November and February, and although the eastern Chaco receives sufficient rainfall for agriculture, precipitation drops off sharply along the region's western margins.

Because of the lack of natural resources and poor communication networks, the Chaco remains one of the most sparsely populated regions in South America, with a population density of less than one inhabitant per square kilometer. In South America, however, wildlife proliferates where people are scarce. *Chaco* itself is an Indian word meaning "an abundance of animal life," and areas as yet unsettled still support ocelots, jaguars, tapirs, anteaters, peccaries, and many other mammals. Because of the swamps, bird life is equally rich; storks, ibises, rheas, and many species of shorebirds and waterfowl prowl the swamps and savannas of the Chaco.

Pampas

Eastern Argentina, south from the Paraná to the Río Negro and west to the foothills of the Andes, is a huge grassland interrupted only by scattered patches of scrubby woodlands. As in the Ukraine and our own Grain Belt, the Pampas, one of the world's great grasslands, has the deep, rich soils required for high yields of cereal grains. Breadbasket of South America, the region is densely populated; what is not under cultivation supports large herds of cattle.

The Pampas consists almost entirely of loess and alluvium, finely eroded materials carried by wind and water from the Andes, and deposited in layers up to 1,000 feet thick. Obscuring normal landscape features, these layers formed a flat plain several hundred miles across, which in spring is covered by a vast carpet of lush green grass. The alluvial deposits are not quite thick enough to completely bury two small mountain ranges in the western Pampas and another in the southeast. The wooded slopes of these western ranges are the only significant forested elevations in nearly 300,000 square miles of treeless Pampas.

Rainfall, moderate throughout the year, is heavier near the Atlantic coast, and decreases markedly further inland. Argentines describe the northeastern Pampas as humid, and the western Pampas as dry.

The utterly flat Pampas landscape does not lend itself to formation of dendritic drainage patterns. Furthermore, Pampas soils contain a high content of fine clays that form layers impervious to water. As a result, innumerable marshes and shallow lakes cover the plains of the eastern Pampas. These waters provide such excellent habitat for shorebirds and waterfowl that ornithologists include the area among the world's great bird-watching regions.

Patagonia

The wedge of low, semiarid steppes that stretches south from the Pampas, and east from the Cordillera to the South Atlantic is Patagonia. A sparse population and broad, treeless vistas lend the Patagonian landscape a sense of limitless space, of splendid and lonely isolation. Monotonous expanses of flat steppes, covered with a sparse growth of low, hardy shrubs, separate Patagonia's few communities from one another. The fly fishermen who have journeyed here for the region's outstanding trout fishing will testify that Patagonia's reputation as one of the windiest regions on earth is warranted. Fierce gusts regularly lash the rivers.

Rainfall is light, for the incessant west winds that sweep over the steppes lose most of their moisture when they cross the Andes. Aridity tends to increase eastward across Patagonia, and low desert-like benches overlook the Atlantic. A few broad valleys have been carved into the plains, but dust blows from the river beds for most of the year. Only a half-dozen vigorous rivers reach the sea along the thousand miles of Patagonia that lie south of the Río Negro. Despite, or perhaps because of such austere characteristics, Patagonia has always exercised a peculiar and irresistible fascination for travelers, and probably always will. Sunrises and sunsets tend to be spectacular. When the wind does not stir up great clouds of dust, the atmosphere, lacking tropical haze and the smudge of industrial effluents, is uncommonly clear.

Thousands of square miles of gravel and cobble overlie the steppes, alluvial material eroded and spread eastward from the heavily glaciated southern Cordillera. Other areas are covered by immense lava flows. Eroded caprocks of black basalt overlie the low, steep-sided mesas common throughout Patagonia. Isolated cinder cones are scattered over the landscape in the volcanic areas. Some of the world's finest petrified forests lie near Jaramillo in central Patagonia, a further result of volcanic activity.

In the extreme south, the bleak steppes gradually merge into densely forested foothills of the southern Cordillera. First, small clumps of trees appear; then, long green ribbons of beech forest extend into the grassy plains. Forests soon predominate, and lakes and rivers begin to appear. The steppes end at the kelp-strewn beaches of the Straits of Magellan. Across the straits lies Tierra del Fuego, the southernmost of the earth's settled regions, and beyond, Antarctica.

A few of Patagonia's parks are located in the arid plains along the Atlantic coast, but most lie in the mountainous western margin of the region, where the mixture of glaciers, forests, mountains, and enormous lakes results in landscapes of outstanding beauty.

INTRODUCTION TO THE FAUNA

Wildlife is such an important aspect of the parks of South America that a brief introduction to the continent's fauna is appropriate.

The story begins several hundred million years ago, when the world's continents were united in a single great land mass called Pangaea. This giant continent began eventually to split up into smaller units, and it is believed that about 135 million years ago, South America split away and began the long westward drift that formed the gap we now call the South Atlantic Ocean. In this manner began a period of geographical isolation that was to last for over 130 million years.

The Age of Fishes and the Age of Reptiles came and went during this immense period of isolation, and finally the tiny, efficient animals destined to rule the Animal Kingdom—the mammals—made their first tentative and inconspicuous appearance. During the isolation, a host of preposterous animals evolved in South America. Most became extinct, but a number of bizarre forms survived, among them many of the most interesting of the animals found today in South America, such as armadillos, anteaters, and sloths.

A common animal in Los Glaciares National Park, Argentina, is the three-banded armadillo, Pichy ciego *or* peludo, *which can become an armored softball at will.*

In the meantime, a slow but decisive struggle for survival was taking place in the rest of the world between marsupials—pouched mammals—and the more efficient placental mammals. The marsupials lost the struggle, and practically disappeared from all of the continents except Australia, which, like South America, had been isolated from the northern hemisphere for eons. Only in South America did the two types of mammals evolve and develop together. Today, only South America and Australia possess significant numbers of marsupials.

The development of strange animals in South America might have continued undisturbed up to the present day but for a geological event with profound and, for some species, catastrophic effects. Between two million and three million years ago, Central America rose from the sea, and a land bridge connecting the Americas was born. In geological and zoological terms, South America's isolation ended in the wink of an eye.

In slow but inexorable waves, placental mammals crossed the new bridge from North America and fanned out into ecological niches throughout South America. Hoofed mammals and members of the raccoon family were among the invaders, but the most ominous new arrivals were the successful and efficient predators: the cats, the canines, and the mustelids (weasels, otters, and skunks).

These deadly new arrivals soon swept the marsupial carnivores into extinction. Most of the herbivorous marsupials also disappeared. The placentals from the north established themselves in the niches formerly occupied by marsupials, and the invasion was complete. Today only a few opossum and shrew-like forms survive to represent South America's once diverse population of marsupials.

South America's present fauna, then, is a curious mixture of the old and the new. Included among the old residents is an assortment of about sixty-four species of marmosets and monkeys, together called New World monkeys. These animals are generally smaller than the Old World forms. They are more strictly arboreal, and many have prehensile tails, a characteristic unique to South American monkeys. Although a few species are distributed from Colombia to southern Brazil, most are found in the Amazon Basin, where they range in diversity from the delicate, chipmunk-like pigmy marmoset to the heavy-bodied howler monkey, a placid vegetarian that has developed the spine-tingling roar of a primeval flesh-eater.

The edentates—armadillos, anteaters, and sloths—are a particularly interesting group of old residents. Armadillos, which range in size from the 5-inch fairy armadillo to the 100-pound giant armadillo, are widespread throughout the continent. Some twenty species populate a variety of habitats, from grasslands to humid tropical forests. Three types of anteaters are found in South America. The giant anteater, the size of a large dog, is a creature of the open savannas, while the smaller lesser anteater is found only in dense forests. The squirrel-sized silky anteater is strictly nocturnal and arboreal. Two types of sloth, one with two claws on its forepaws, the other with three, are found in South America. Both are arboreal vegetarians, at home among the highest branches of the canopy.

Many rodents are among the old residents. They inhabit virtually every type of habitat found in South America, and are found at elevations from sea level to over 16,000 feet. Guinea pigs (which are neither pigs nor from Guinea), chinchillas, and nutrias are well known in North America, but most South American rodents, such as vizcachas, capybaras, agoutis, pacas, and maras, are unfamiliar to outsiders.

The groups of animals that are "new" South American residents are more diverse than the endemic species. The cat family is represented by mountain lions, jaguars, ocelots, and a number of smaller cats. Among the canines are several species of foxes and one wolf, the maned wolf. Smaller predators include skunks, otters, weasels, and raccoons. However, only one species of bear, the spectacled bear, is native to South America.

All of the hoofed mammals found on the continent today are descendants of invaders. Deer are widespread, from the rare and shy pudú, the world's tiniest deer, to the familiar white-tailed deer. Three species of peccaries (one discovered as recently as 1974) and two types of tapirs live in the South American rain forests. The domesticated llama of the Andean Highlands and several of its relatives are believed to have evolved from a single camel-like ancestor that crossed the land bridge and later became extinct in North America.

Because birds have light skeletons that do not readily fossilize, little is known about how birds evolved and populated the continent. Many birds achieved modern characteristics in early geological history, however, so it is likely that they were already a diverse group by the time the land bridge formed. Since then, they appear to have become even more diverse, for no continent has a greater number of birds species than South America, sometimes called the Bird Continent.

South America's animals benefit greatly from the continent's parks and reserves. Several species were pulled back from the brink of extinction in recent decades only by the most vigorous and concerted actions of governments and conservation interests. Today many animals—among them the mountain tapir, giant armadillo, maned wolf, and pudú—are losing ground, and for the majority of these and other animals, their last sanctuaries are the parks and reserves.

The good news is that almost every South American bird or animal can be found somewhere in a national park or reserve. Travelers who delight in watching strange new birds and animals have reason to rejoice, for if they select parks in diverse regions, they will see most of the continent's delightful wildlife.

ᛒᛒᛕ 2
SOUTH AMERICAN NATIONAL PARKS: THE VISITOR'S PERSPECTIVE

South American national parks are situated in mountains, deserts, jungles, and steppes. They border tropical seas and seas cold enough to float icebergs. There are parks of the savanna and parks of the high altiplano. On both sides of the Andes, a long chain of parks encompasses smoking volcanos, advancing glaciers, and remote continental icecaps. They support a variety of wildlife unfamiliar and therefore particularly fascinating to foreign visitors. Visitors can also see waterfalls, hot springs, lakes, rivers, snowcapped peaks, deeply cut gorges, petrified forests, and—*sometimes*—visitor centers, park rangers, and nature trails.

For several reasons, North Americans have certain ideas of what a national park ought to be. They expect a national park to be a large tract of land with outstanding natural features, popular with the public, where visitors can expect to find facilities for specific types of recreation, education, and accommodation as well as a staff of professional personnel hired and trained to protect park resources and to assist the public.

In general, the rest of the world shares this vision of national parks with North America. However, few nations can afford the expense required to sustain such a high standard of park development and maintenance. Progress is being made, but for the sake of perspective it is essential that visitors to the parks of South America not carry their expectations with them, for while foreign visitors will find in great measure features associated with parks, there are also surprises.

ᛕ PARK DEVELOPMENT IN SOUTH AMERICA

At the close of the nineteenth century, only a handful of national parks existed, most of them in North America and Australia. Today, more than 1,500 national parks are scattered over the globe in more than 100 countries. Most were created during the surge of interest in parks that began soon after World War II. As each country developed its own park system, considerable confusion resulted, for areas designated as parks also served such disparate functions as nature reserves, playgrounds, hunting preserves, picnic sites, research stations, and so on. It soon became clear to international observers that the interests of conservation would be better served if criteria could be developed that were acceptable to all nations.

The International Union for the Conservation of Nature and Natural Resources (IUCN), working under the auspices of the United Nations, undertook this task, and by 1969 had worked out a definition of a national park, as well as several conditions

The Refugio Frey, on Cerro Catedral, Nahuel Huapi National Park, Argentina

that could serve as the basis for the establishment of such a park. The conditions were: (1) the territory had to be of a size in excess of about 2,500 acres; (2) it must offer scientific, educational, or recreational interest or contain natural landscapes of great aesthetic value; (3) effective measures must prevent as far as possible human exploitation and illegal occupation; (4) these measures must be taken by the highest official authority in the country; and (5) visiting must be allowed.

These are rigorous conditions, and yet by 1975, eighty-nine parks in twelve South American countries satisfied the criteria. By 1982, the IUCN had broadened its definitions of protected areas, and the total number of South American parks had grown to 131, along with twenty-two managed nature reserves and eleven biospheric reserves.

One hundred thirty-one parks may not seem remarkable compared to the sixty-four national parks shared by the United States and Canada alone, but considering that the national park movement gained momentum in South America only during the last three decades, the numbers are phenomenal.

The numbers are also somewhat misleading, for as mentioned earlier, many of the parks are not what most people would experience as a park. One South American country, for example, has a national park that covers only 7 acres, and another park that includes a gambling casino and swimming club. Other South American countries tend to minimize the diversity of their park systems by locating several parks within the same biotic province; one country has done this with twenty-one parks.

Argentina is generally credited with creating the first national park in South America—Nahuel Huapi—established from lands donated to the government in 1903. As is so often the case in conservation matters, the efforts of one determined man were largely responsible for the establishment of this remarkable park. Francisco P. Moreno, nicknamed "Perito" (Ace), was a government surveyor with a flair for exploration. He fought vigorously for many years to have this and other parks set aside, and is today honored as the father of Argentina's excellent system of national parks.

Chile became the next South American country to establish a national park, with the creation in 1926 of Parque Nacional Vicente Pérez Rosales, comprising over 500 square miles of forested mountains in the Andes of southern Chile.

During the next decade, Argentina and Chile each created several additional parks, and Ecuador, Brazil, and Venezuela established their first parks. By 1940, South America had eighteen parks, and a firm foundation had been laid for future development. Growth was slow and steady until the 1960s. Then began an unprecedented acceleration, during which parks sprang up practically overnight all over the continent. Brazil, for instance, created eight parks in a single year (1961), bringing nearly 1 million acres of land into her park system. Chile, in 1967, also set aside over 5,500 square miles of land for future park development, and in 1981 set aside ten managed nature reserves. Colombia created nineteen national parks (at least on paper) in 1972.

Erratic Development and Lack of Funds

During these decades of rapid growth, however, parks were often created faster than money could be found to develop and administer them. As a result, many South American parks were—and still are—parks in name only, lawfully designated tracts of land neatly crosshatched on government maps, but with not so much as a sign on the site to inform a visitor that he or she has arrived at a park.

These phantom parks are sometimes the result of bureaucratic whim, but not always. Visitors should be aware that park systems in South America are in a highly dynamic phase of development. New parks are constantly being created, and parks long established by law, but effectively ignored for many years, are being developed in stages as funds become available. This erratic development accounts for the often surprising inconsistencies observed from one park to another, even within the same country, where a half-day's journey may take a visitor from a superbly developed and managed park to a nearby park that appears utterly abandoned and is being ravaged by poachers and illegal settlers.

In general, South American parks are poorly financed. Governments struggling to solve critical social and economic problems are understandably reluctant to spend large sums of money on projects that, in the short run, appear to be nonessential or politically unrewarding. A number of interrelated effects result from this chronic shortage of funds. Parks are often inadequately staffed. It is not uncommon to find that one or two underpaid, untrained staff are given a horse, a pistol, and orders to protect all of the flora and fauna in 3,000 to 4,000 square miles of park or reserve, a nearly impossible task that sometimes costs them their lives. Park staff are poorly paid in many countries, and are often poorly trained for their tasks. Many park rangers, struggling to cope with a public just becoming aware of the park concept, function as guards rather than managers, and spend much of their time trying to keep livestock, hunters, woodcutters, and even settlers outside park boundaries.

Lack of funds often means that parks are poorly surveyed, and that park resources are seldom completely studied and inventoried. Many park personnel know very little about the wildlife and natural history of the parks that employ them. Printed material on park resources and attractions is not usually available, and even simple maps are seldom handed out to visitors.

With a few exceptions, South American parks do not yet enjoy mass popularity. Therefore, though park attendance is increasing each year, South American parks are seldom crowded. This also means, however, that South American park services are not nearly so visitor-oriented as their North American counterparts. Education and interpretive programs and facilities are rare. Park trails are seldom well marked, and, though shown on park maps, seldom well maintained. Secondary access roads to park attractions may be in appalling condition.

Despite these difficulties, a strong national park movement is well underway throughout South America today. The problems are not insurmountable, and the overall outlook is excellent. Most South American parks now have visitor facilities that range in style from rustic shelters to luxury hotels. Argentina and Venezuela provide intensive training courses for aspiring park rangers, and other countries are likely to follow suit. Perhaps most important, an environmental sensibility, that critical underpinning for any successful park movement, is slowly developing within the South American public.

Of paramount importance for the future is the fact that substantial tracts of land are indeed being set aside for parks. Over 120,000 square miles of national park lands had been set aside in South America by 1982, and considerably more land is set aside today. More parks are needed, of course, but the main problem now facing South American conservationists is to bring parks already established by law under effective administration—which often means adequate protection—as soon as possible. In all South American countries, the pressures of resource exploitation are increasing apace, and the danger is acute that fragile park resources may be irretrievably degraded before protection can be achieved.

Fortunately, South America's potential for park development is vast, and if conservationists can win the race against resource exploitation, mankind will inherit an enduring and superb natural legacy.

▣ THE PARK VISITOR AS EXPLORER

Every foreign visitor to a South American park is to some degree an explorer. Because the parks are not yet as visitor-oriented as those of North America, serious visitors are often on their own, obliged to create their own park experience. The obligation is by no means unpleasant, and can be a refreshing contrast to the ready-made, uniform, and overregulated "park experience" often offered up by North American park services. It simply means that visitors wishing to obtain more than a cursory impression of a South American park must exercise some initiative, for they often may lack the advantages of convenient transportation, maps, field guides to flora and fauna, trails, and park personnel who speak their language.

In South America, even the scantiest preparation can spell the difference between a successful and an unsuccessful visit. A small map, the correct Spanish phrase, or a picture of an animal in a book may enable a visitor to obtain the precise information required for his or her purposes. Much of the information a visitor is likely to need is provided in this book, but readers are urged to seek additional information from the sources described in the "Selected Bibliography."

Language

Language is the most obvious concern of foreigners. Although Dutch is the official language of Suriname, and Spanish and Portuguese are the principal languages of South America, one need not learn them to visit South American parks any more than one needs to learn seven or eight languages to tour Europe. Nevertheless, a relatively small investment of time spent in language study will return great advantages. A basic traveler's vocabulary will save time, money, and frustration, and a vocabulary specialized in accordance with your interests will be helpful. Few rangers at the numerous Patagonian parks, for example, will recognize either the English phrases "southern lapwing" and "Chilean cedar," or their respective scientific names, *Vanellus chilensis* and *Austrocedrus chilensis,* but the smallest child will eagerly point out a "tero-tero" or a "ciprés" to a curious visitor.

English frequently works. Bilingual officials often work at headquarters for South American park services—invariably located in the capital cities. Regional and local park officials occasionally speak some English.

A short glossary at the end of each park description lists Spanish, Portuguese, or Dutch words and phrases that may prove useful at a particular park. Obviously, the glossaries cannot be exhaustive; specialists will have to refer to other sources for more complete information. A master glossary keyed to translating from English is located at the back of the book.

Although much has been written about South America, only a handful of recent books printed in English deal extensively with its natural history. A few of these books, ranging from technical to popular works, are listed in the "Selected Bibliography," and should be secured in advance of your trip.

Information on specific parks is difficult to obtain in English from any single source. The park services of several South American countries, however, publish descriptive pamphlets in Spanish, Portuguese, or Dutch (occasionally in English) that contain some basic information sought by most park visitors. Park services will usually send information to prospective visitors in response to written requests. Titles of particularly useful pamphlets and booklets are also provided in the "Selected Bibliography." Addresses of South American park service offices are listed in "Additional Information." Be advised, however, that numbers of these publications are limited, and when supplies are exhausted, they may not be replenished.

Safety

Is it *safe* to tour South American parks?

Will you be bitten by snakes or spiders, contract tropical diseases, get caught in revolutions, be kidnapped by drug smugglers (*narcotraficantes*), get lost, die of thirst, be robbed or cheated or eaten by piranhas or crocodiles?

Well. . . if you are extremely foolhardy or appallingly unlucky, some of these disasters may come your way, yes, but that is highly unlikely. If you drink water everywhere, flaunt your bankroll, tromp around barefoot in snake country, or try to buy narcotics, you will eventually run into trouble, but if you are that careless, you'd better not get out of bed. Revolutions do occur, and tourists do get robbed, but these problems are not unique to South America; from the perspective of tourists they are problems usually associated with cities, not the countryside. In general, South American parks are far safer than South American cities, where you have to cope with drivers who are among the most aggressive in the world.

I have experienced no serious trouble during the years I have lived and traveled in South America, but I cannot provide you with formulas for touring a continent unscathed. There are none. I can, however, offer a few general suggestions that will help you to make your own way safely through South America.

First, your own common sense will keep you out of most difficulties. Conduct yourself as you would in New York City or Los Angeles. Don't make deals with strangers in dark alleys. Make certain you know how much you will be charged for any service from taxi rides to currency exchanges *before* accepting those services. If there is rioting in the streets, stay in your hotel room.

Second, seek information from travelers who have just returned from the next place on your own itinerary. You will meet them everywhere, and information exchange has become expected travel etiquette in South America. You will quickly learn that there exists a circuit that travelers follow through the continent. The circuit is based upon such information as dates of festivals; hotels and pensions that offer particularly good value; certain train or boat trips that are cheap, scenic, and efficient; organized tours that are not the usual herd experience; and so on.

Third, obtain and take with you a book called *The South American Handbook* (see the "Selected Bibliography"). It is expensive, but for unsurpassed practical information, it is more current, comprehensive, and reliable than any other other guide to South America.

Etiquette

If you intend to visit several parks within one country, you would be wise to begin your tour with a visit to park service headquarters in that country's capital city. Such visits are by no means necessary or expected, but they are considered to be courteous, and are more customary practice in South America than elsewhere. A visit not only indicates good manners, but helps to indicate to park staff the level of interest shown by foreign tourists in certain parks. There are also practical reasons for courtesy calls. Park staff may be able to suggest which parks will most likely satisfy your interests. You may be given printed information and maps that have not yet been distributed to individual park offices. In some instances, it is customary to provide visitors with letters of introduction to park directors. These letters are again matters of courtesy, but they may help to ensure that you can make use of overnight accommodations, enter protected areas, and so on. For a few parks or reserves, you must obtain authorization from park service headquarters prior to your visit.

Similarly, it is considered courteous, although not necessary, to visit a park director upon your arrival. Directors and their staff are always glad to meet visitors interested in their parks, can tell you where to go to see wildlife or other attractions, and like to be assured that you intend to collect nothing but photographs. If you are planning difficult climbs, float trips, or hikes into protected areas, you may need authorization from park staff. It is not uncommon for directors or staff to offer to show you around a park themselves.

Hazards

South American parks present foreign visitors with a few hazards to which they may be unaccustomed, but with proper planning they can be dealt with effectively.

If you plan activities that could be dangerous, such as mountain climbs, whitewater river trips, long-distance backpacks, scuba diving, and so on, be advised that if you get into trouble, you cannot usually count on a speedy rescue. Difficult terrain, poor road networks, and poor communication facilities do not allow for efficient search and rescue. You must be as self-sufficient as possible, and accept the risks.

Health hazards are usually related to water or insects, not food. As long as your food is cooked or canned, it will be safe; salads are risky in every country but Argentina. In every country but Argentina, it is imprudent to drink tap water or from streams. Either purify your water, drink bottled mineral water (*agua mineral*) or purified water (*agua purificada*), which is available almost everywhere, or drink beer. Rely on park staff or local residents to warn you about any hazard but water; they may have immunities to microorganisms that would knock you flat in a day.

Several insects in the tropics carry diseases: malaria, yellow fever, river blindness, chagas' disease, schistosomiasis, and others. In almost all populated areas and almost all national parks and reserves, the diseases have been nearly eradicated. You should be concerned only if you intend to visit areas in which the diseases are endemic. Even though the chance of contracting these diseases is remote, take the safe course and obtain the following immunizations prior to departure: tetanus/ typhoid, yellow fever, and gamma globulin (for hepatitis). Consult your doctor about the best current prophylactic medicine for malaria.

You are more likely to be bothered by biting or stinging insects than by disease-carrying insects, so take plenty of insect repellent with you. Also try some of the local

Bugs tend to be big in the Amazon Basin. Amazonia National Park, Brazil

repellents, which can be very effective. If local residents use mosquito nets and your hotel provides them, you should use them.

Snakes are far more rare than is popularly believed. You will be lucky to even see one. But don't tempt fate; in snake country wear good boots.

Do not swim in tropical rivers or lakes until you have checked out local customs. In a few places, there may be electric eels, stingrays, piranhas, giant catfish, or crocodiles, any of which could be dangerous.

Clothes

If you plan to visit parks in several countries, you must outfit for all conditions of climate and weather, plain and simple. Take warm clothes for temperate and Altiplano parks, light clothes for the tropics. Include long-sleeved shirts and long pants for tropical climates for protection from insects. Cotton, not acrylic, fabrics are best for hot climates. For parks in any climates, include lightweight rain gear. Take sturdy boots that are already broken in, and don't forget a good hat and sunglasses.

Hiking and Camping

Trails in many parks will not be as well marked as you would like, and terrain can be confusing, particularly in tropical parks, so bring a compass. Don't eat those strange but appealing fruits and berries unless locals do.

Backpacking shelter in the tropics is a question of priorities. Tents can be oppressively hot, and because they are on the ground they must be very well screened to keep out bugs and other creatures. Hammocks are cool and keep you out of range of things that creep, but they won't protect you from rain, and screened hammocks are bulky and clumsy. Best buy a hammock and a separate mosquito net, and take your chances with rain.

Hitchhiking

Hitchhiking is an acceptable means of travel in all South American countries and generally safe, although customs vary from country to country. In parts of Bolivia and Peru, for example, a hitchhiker may be accepting a ride. Competition for rides can be intense during university holidays and weekends in many countries. Traffic is light in some remote regions, where determined hitchhikers must be prepared for delays of two to three days. It helps to dress neatly. Except as otherwise noted, hitchhiking should be avoided in Colombia. Single women hitching alone should exercise the same prudence they would use anywhere else.

William C. Leitch

A Note About Safety

Safety is an important concern in all outdoor activities. No guidebook can alert you to every hazard or anticipate the limitations of every reader. Therefore, the descriptions of parks, roads, trails, routes, animals, and natural features in this book are not representations that a particular place or excursion will be safe for your traveling party. When you visit any of the parks or follow any of the routes described in this book, you assume responsibility for your own safety. Under normal conditions, such excursions require the usual attention to local travel restrictions, traffic, road and trail conditions, weather, terrain, the capabilities of your traveling party, and other factors. As the publishers of this book, we do not advocate hitchhiking; visitors who travel by this means do so at their own risk.

Some of the countries described in this book have experienced political and economic turmoil in recent years. Political conditions may add to the risk of travel in South America in ways that no one can predict. When you travel, you assume this risk, too, and should be aware of ongoing political developments that may make travel difficult or impossible. Keeping informed on current conditions, local laws and customs, and exercising common sense are the keys to a safe, enjoyable visit to the countries and parks described in this book.

The Mountaineers

⫘ 3
ARGENTINA

Imagine a country one third the size of the United States, but with one tenth of its population. Endow it with splendid scenery, a wide variety of landforms, and a remarkable range of climatic regimes. Finally, distribute the country's million square miles over 32 degrees of latitude—nearly half the length of South America.

These features characterize Argentina and explain in part why it has the most diverse, well developed, and attractive system of national parks in South America.

Argentina possesses in abundance the natural raw materials for a network of parks. One third of Argentina comprises forestland. Traveling south along the Andes, the tropical montane rain forests of northern Argentina give way to desert scrub and to coniferous forests, which in turn merge into the beech forests of southern Patagonia and Tierra del Fuego. Northern and central Argentina are drained by one of the world's great river systems—the Paraná—and enormous glacial lakes jut into the steppes of Patagonia from the Andes. Over 2,000 miles of the east front of the volcano-studded Andes lie within Argentine territory, and the Atlantic Ocean washes 1,600 miles of its wild, often desolate coastline. Like California, Argentina is characterized by topographical extremes: the highest point in the western hemisphere, Mount Aconcagua (23,080 feet), as well as the lowest point in South America—a bleak salt marsh 131 feet below sea level—are located in Argentina.

Physical features alone, however, do not create parks. People do. And that the Argentines take their parks seriously is suggested by the motto of the Argentine Park Service: The conservation, maintenance, and growth of national parks is an operating principle of national security.

Argentina has a long-standing tradition of national parks—the oldest in South America. The lands that became the first national park on South American soil were formally set aside in Argentina on November 6, 1903. The tradition has sustained its vitality to the present, for despite recurrent political upheaval, both professional land managers and an increasing sector of the Argentine public recognize the value of preserving natural features for future generations as well as the dangers represented by thoughtless exploitation of natural resources.

The commitment of the Argentine government to its system of national parks is reflected in part by the relative abundance of park-related activities. In general, Argentine parks provide the public with more visitor services and printed materials than any other South American parks.

Argentina is also the only country on the continent that maintains an academy devoted to the training of park personnel. As a result, visitors to most Argentine parks can expect to meet *guardaparques,* smartly uniformed park rangers entrusted with protecting and interpreting park resources.

Argentina has such diverse parks and reserves that a visitor could spend several profitable weeks exploring the parks of this country alone. In such an event, the trip should start at the headquarters of the Servicio Nacional de Parques Nacionales (Argentine Park Service) in Buenos Aires. Located at Santa Fe 690 in a central, fashion-

BOLIVIA

BRAZIL

CHILE

Pacific

Ocean

PARAGUAY

Asunción

Iguaçú

Iguazú

(14)

San Miguel de Tucumán

Resistencia

Río Paraná

Laguna Mar Chiquita

Córdoba

(1) El Palmar

Mendoza

Rosario

URUGUAY

Santiago

Montevideo

Buenos Aires

Río de La Plata

ARGENTINA

Bahía Blanca

Mar del Plata

(2) Laguna Blanca

Atlantic Ocean

(4) Lanín
(3) Nahuel Huapi

(5) Los Alerces

(6) Península Valdés

Comodoro Rivadavia

(7) Bosques Petrificados
& Cueva de las Manos

(8) Perito Moreno

(9) Los Glaciares

Falkland Islands

Strait of Magellan

(10) Tierra del Fuego

Miles   500

Km   500

able section of the city, the headquarters are housed in an ornate, three-story, turreted building far more Parisian than Argentine in style and design. Travelers who intend to visit several parks should describe their plans and ask for descriptive brochures of the parks. Printed materials are usually in short supply, but it pays to ask. Staff are friendly and helpful. Usually someone can be found who speaks English.

Argentina's park system has grown rapidly in recent years. Argentina can claim to have parks from one end of the country to the other, for in its extreme northeast corner Parque Nacional Iguazú joins the boundary of Brazil, while in the extreme south Parque Nacional Tierra del Fuego, the world's southernmost park, borders the Beagle Canal, not far from Cape Horn. Most of Argentina's parks are located in Patagonia, but if long-range development plans are carried out successfully, nearly every Argentine province will eventually have at least one national park.

At present, Argentina has eighteen national parks; eleven of the most interesting are described below. They are organized more or less from north to south. Iguazú, a border park shared with Brazil, is described in the chapter on Brazil.

EL PALMAR:
Palms on the Pampas

North-central Argentina is pure pampas, the breadbasket of South America—a treeless, undulating steppe under intensive cultivation. Nearly every square inch of the region grows something for human consumption or is grazed upon by domestic livestock, mainly cattle.

It is therefore a pleasant shock for visitors to come upon a small island of untamed vegetation in the midst of this sea of carefully husbanded agriculture. This island is a national park that has been set aside to save a tree.

In Spanish, the word *palma* means "palm tree"; a *palmar* is a grove of palm trees. In 1966, about 21,000 acres of pampas on the shore of the Río Uruguay were set aside to protect and perpetuate a representative community of *palmares* that were well on the way to extinction by the time the threat was recognized and dealt with. El Palmar provides visitors with a delightful combination of pampas plant and animal life that might otherwise have been lost forever.

At the turn of the century, stately groves of Yatai palm, *Syagrus yatay*, grew throughout the region of the pampas near the Río Uruguay and its tributaries, creating a savanna-like zone within the normally treeless steppes. The origin of the *palmares* is not well understood. Some botanists believe that palm seeds were carried here by local rivers, some believe that the palms were cultivated by early Indian inhabitants. A few believe that the palms are relict species of a floristic community that survived from much earlier geological periods because of the favorable sandy soils found in this region.

While the palms may have survived geological upheavals, they nearly failed to survive an ecological factor introduced by humankind: cattle. Settlers quickly recognized that the region would support enormous numbers of cattle. Only recently, however, did systematic surveys reveal that the *palmares* throughout the region were declining, and that virtually no young seedlings were appearing to replace the dying stands, for the cattle grazed on the young palms as readily as on the lush grasses.

Fortunately, the park, a former cattle ranch (*estancia*), was set aside in time to permit seedlings to appear, and the future is now bright for the Yatai *palmares*. Ironically, the uniform age of the trees in the park is one of the factors that lend the *palmares* their striking appearance. As in desert landscapes, the character of the *palmares* alters during the passage of the day. The palms may be rose-colored when backlit by the light of daybreak or sunset, or spooky when enveloped in the warm mists common in the mornings. Most of the palms are from 150 to 200 years old (about the time cattle raising began in the region) and about 40 feet high, topped with graceful 6-foot fronds.

The *palmares* are distributed in groups over grassy, rolling terrain through which several small streams (*arroyos*) flow to the immense Río Uruguay. The edges of the *arroyos* and the river are sites for yet another classic floristic regime, the gallery forest. As the name implies, these forests form in narrow bands along stream courses, where moisture and humic soils permit them to compete successfully with grasses. The uppermost canopies of these forests sometimes close over the top of the *arroyos*, forming the galleries through which the streams pass. A host of subtropical trees and shrubs make up gallery flora, the most conspicuous of which is the aromito or espinillo, a thorny

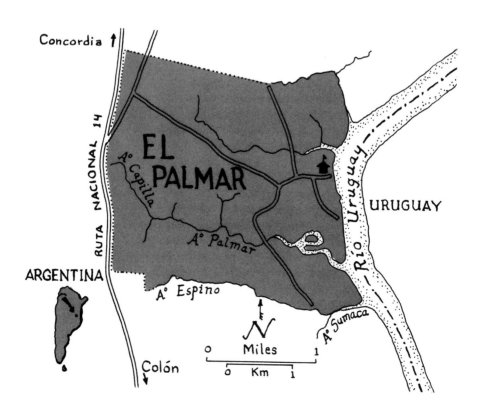

A typical grassland palmar at El Palmar National Park, Argentina

acacia tree (*Acacia caven*) distinguished by round clusters of fragrant yellow flowers.

Because of its relatively open character, El Palmar is indeed one of the better parks in which to observe the wildlife characteristic of this region. The combination of grasslands, *palmares,* watercourses, and gallery forests provides habitat for a host of birds and wildlife. About 40 miles of roads cross the park, but the best way to see wildlife is to hike through the *palmares,* walk quietly along the many watercourses, and concentrate your walks at dawn and dusk, when wildlife is most active. With respect to wildlife observation, I wish to reemphasize the importance of walking. Wildlife is abundant in El Palmar, but if you do not keep the same hours as the animals, and get away from roads, you will see only a small portion of the park's fauna.

Caution: Wear boots and thick pants, and watch where you step. Three species of venomous snakes have been identified on park lands. They are so shy that you are not likely to see them, but you should be aware of their presence.

El Palmar is a good place to see capybaras (*Hydrochoerus hydrochoerus*). The animal is rare outside parks and reserves; it is hunted for food in some areas, and for its hide, which produces exceptionally soft leather much in demand for gloves, purses, and saddle parts. Capybaras are the largest and, to my eye, most bizarre of the rodents. They are brown, and although related to guinea pigs, resemble fat, blunt-nosed rabbits

Domesticated capybaras make good pets. El Palmar National Park, Argentina

with short ears. For rodents, they are huge, up to three feet long, and they can weigh 150 pounds. They prefer to live near water, and feed on both aquatic and terrestrial plants. They are well adapted to their semiaquatic life-style—their feet are somewhat webbed and they swim well. Walk near streams to see them. Capybaras live in small groups, and have acute hearing but poor eyesight. If you sit quietly you should be able to watch a group go about its business for as long as you like. If you are lucky, you may also observe two other rarer, semiaquatic animals along the streams: the river otter (*Lutra platensis*) and the muskrat-like nutria (*Myocastor coipus*).

One of the most common and entertaining animals in the park, especially abundant near established campsites, is the pampas vizcacha (*Lagostomus maximus*). Rabbit-sized gray creatures with short, tufted ears, pampas vizcachas, unlike their Andean cousins, are strictly nocturnal. They betray their presence with piles of grass, twigs, and other debris deposited near the openings of their burrows. Take care—like packrats, they are said to steal small shiny objects left lying about campsites. Though nocturnal, vizcachas are easy to see, for they are not shy in lamplight. Indeed, it can be rather unnerving to be under the scrutiny of scores of blinking orange eyes reflecting the light of a campfire. Vizcachas are also easy to hear; they hop about squeaking and scolding each other throughout the night.

Foxes, skunks, ferrets, raccoons, and wild boars inhabit the park, but are rarely seen. Jaguars and pumas have not been seen in years, and are probably no longer in this area. Birds are also abundant in the park (Río Uruguay is sometimes called *Río de los Pájaros*—River of Birds), and easily observed in both grasslands and forests. The most numerous are monk parakeets (*Myiopsitta monachus*), foot-long gray-and-green birds that fly about in huge, noisy flocks. Look in marshy areas for giant woodrails, great egrets, snowy egrets, whistling herons, white-tailed herons, wattled jacanas, and Maguarí storks. In grasslands, look for the spot-winged pigeon, common gallinule, southern lapwing, crested caracara, red-winged tinamou, campo flicker, and ovenbird. In the forests along the watercourses, you will find Brazilian ducks; neotropic cormorants; red-headed, white, and golden-breasted woodpeckers; and three different kingfishers.

The most conspicuous of El Palmar's birds is the rhea, called ñandú (nyan-DOO) and sometimes avestruz. Ñandús are popularly considered South American versions of the African ostrich. Actually, they are only distant relatives of ostriches, and are more closely related to the flightless birds of Australia—kiwis, emus, and cassowaries—further evidence for the theory that Australia and South America were once united in a single continent.

Ñandús are smaller than ostriches, about 4 feet high, weighing from 40 to 60 pounds, but they appear enormous to anyone who sees these birds for the first time. They are ungainly in appearance, but their periscope-like neck is well adapted to life on the flat plains; they can outrun a horse and maneuver cleverly over broken terrain. Their camouflage is flawless; when they hold still, they appear to vanish. They invariably flee when threatened, but can be dangerous when cornered because of the sharp claws on their powerful legs. Avoid being kicked by a ñandú.

Running ñandús are a most comical sight. They lean forward like roadrunners, alternately flap their ostentatious but quite useless wings, and dash helter-skelter across the plain like creatures out of a cartoon.

Ñandús live most commonly in family groups made up of a male, five or six females, and several young birds. They dig shallow nests in the ground, where females lay from two dozen to three dozen large eggs (up to 5 inches across). The males incubate the eggs, and guard and raise the young.

Ñandús were once found throughout the plains areas of central and southern South America, but their range has been reduced as a result of habitat loss and hunting. The breast meat is especially prized, but the birds were also hunted for skin, feathers, and from horseback for sport. Most ranchers now protect the birds, and populations are stable or increasing.

Two species of ñandús inhabit South America. The bird found in El Palmar is the greater rhea (*Rhea americana*), which inhabits lowland plains in eastern and central Brazil, Uruguay, Paraguay, eastern Bolivia, and Argentina as far south as the Río Negro. The second, smaller species is the lesser rhea or Darwin's rhea (*Pterocnemia pennata*), which inhabits the Andean highlands of Peru, Bolivia, Chile, and Argentina, and most of Patagonia, including Tierra del Fuego, to which the bird was introduced.

Visitor Facilities

El Palmar is one of the few Argentine parks that contains no private holdings or settlers. Since the park occupies land that was once an *estancia,* all facilities are centered around the old ranch house and outbuildings on a high bluff overlooking the mile-wide Río Uruguay. Facilities include park headquarters; a small visitor center; a small, but well-stocked store; a free campground; and a pay campground with hot showers, modern sanitary facilities, and wash tubs. Camping in the park is restricted to these campgrounds. No hotel accommodations are available in the park, but visitors who do not camp may find lodgings in the nearby town of Concordia.

Two main gravel roads lead to different sections of the park, one to Arroyo Palmar and a second to Arroyo Loros. These roads also cross several smaller *arroyos* full of wildlife. No long trails are maintained, but the countryside is open enough to hike without need of trails.

As in most smaller Argentine parks, the staff are enthusiastic and well informed about the park and its features. They are friendly, patient with language difficulties, and eager to help curious visitors. Descriptive brochures and maps are sometimes available.

Recreation

Bird-watching, wildlife observation, and walks among picturesque 200-year-old *palmares* are the primary recreational opportunities for visitors.

El Palmar was the first Argentine park situated relatively close to large population centers. As a result, the park is used by large numbers of city dwellers. Although hunting and fishing are prohibited within the park, visitors camp, picnic, swim in the Río Uruguay, and sunbathe on its sandy beaches during summer months.

Climate and Weather

El Palmar's climate is unusually benign; the region enjoys nearly perpetual spring. As a result, the park is open year-round. The average temperature is about 65 degrees Fahrenheit, and ranges from 54 degrees to 76 degrees. About 45 inches of rain falls during the year; May through September are the driest months.

A lightweight sweater may be needed for some evenings. Biting bugs are relatively scarce in the park.

Location and Access

El Palmar is located in the province of Entre Ríos in northeastern Argentina. The literal meaning of *entre ríos* is "between rivers," and this province so rich in agricultural resources lies between Río Uruguay and Río Paraná, which together form one of South America's great river systems and empty into the estuary of the Río de la Plata. The park lies adjacent to the Río Uruguay between the towns of Concordia and Colón on Argentine Ruta (Route) 14. Uruguay lies across the river from the park.

Visitors who choose not to camp can stay in Concordia, a quiet but colorful river town of about 60,000 people located 35 miles (58 kilometers) north of the park. The town has a dozen small hotels and several pleasant restaurants. Check at the Tourist Office on Plaza 25 de Mayo for information about hotels, car rental, organized tours to the park, and public means of transport to the park. Hitchhiking to and in the park is feasible. If you go by taxi, ask for a group rate.

El Palmar lies only 225 miles (360 kilometers) northwest of Buenos Aires, and can be reached from the capital (via Concordia) by bus or plane. Visitors can also take an 8-hour train ride from Buenos Aires to Concordia (Pullman, first class, and second class are available), and then take one of the regularly scheduled buses to the park entrance. Bus service is likewise available from Colón.

Glossary

bosque galería	gallery forest
carpincho	capybara
carpintero	carpenter (woodpecker)
estancia	large ranch
Intendencia	park headquarters
jabalí	wild boar
lobito de río	river wolf (river otter)
loro	parrot
Martín pescador	kingfisher
ñandú	rhea
zorro	fox

The stately black-necked swan of Patagonia, Cygnus melancoryphus

◧ LAGUNA BLANCA:
Swans on the Steppes

Only two reserves have been set aside in the western hemisphere for the express purpose of protecting swans. One is Red Rock Lakes National Wildlife Refuge in southwestern Montana, established to protect the trumpeter swan, and the other is Parque Nacional Laguna Blanca in northern Patagonia, established in 1945 to protect the cisne de cuello negro, the black-necked swan (*Cygnus melancoryphus*).

The *laguna blanca* (white lake) is a large shallow lake that provides the combination of features essential for the survival of these birds: excellent habitat and a location sufficiently remote to ensure that the birds will not be unduly disturbed. Situated on austere Patagonian highlands just east of the Andes, the park is in a region typical of Argentina's precordilleran steppes, a harsh land from the perspective of humans, but admirably suited for swans wherever there is water.

A short but high mountain range—the first intimation of the Andes—lies to the west, but a few parched hills provide the park with its only vertical relief. The park's volcanic origin is somewhat masked by sedimentary strata laid down by ancient seas, but evidence of more recent vulcanism is plentiful. The sandy ground is strewn with cobbles of pumice and basalt, and outcrops of black basalt to the south of the lake are practically unweathered. The lake itself may have been formed when a lava flow blocked two small streams that flowed through the area.

The swans of Laguna Blanca are large, but timid. Excellent swimmers, they have a short, low cry. Black-necked swans are relatively common in temperate South America, with a range as far south as Tierra del Fuego, but travelers will be impressed by the large flocks of birds to be seen in Laguna Blanca.

One other swan is native to South America, the coscoraba swan (*Coscoroba coscoraba*). The distribution of the two swans overlaps, but bird watchers are not likely to confuse the two species: the smaller coscoraba has black-tipped primary wing-feathers and a pink bill; the black-necked swan has a distinctive ebony neck, and a ruby-red caruncule at the base of its bill.

Male and female black-necked swans look alike, although the male is somewhat larger. Nesting begins around November. The birds construct their nests in thickets of rushes or sedges not far from the water, where the female lays four or five creamy white eggs, and incubates them for about thirty-five days. The cygnets are pearly gray for the first two weeks of their life, with lead-colored bill and feet, but snowy-white down soon begins to appear, and by the age of three months, their definitive plumage has developed.

Black-necked swans feed on vegetation, including algae, and small arthropods. There are no fish in Laguna Blanca, probably because of the lake's high alkalinity, but the lake is rich in plankton. The alga nostoc is the most noticeable phytoplankton; the lake is often filled with round pale green colonies of this plant, some nearly the size of golf balls.

While swans are the most striking birds on Laguna Blanca, other waterfowl are even more abundant. The swan population may vary from a few hundred birds to more than 2,000, but several thousand coots (*Fulica* sp.) are almost always in residence. At least three species of grebes visit Laguna Blanca, of which the silvery grebe (*Podiceps occipitalis*) is the most common. Ducks and sheldgeese are abundant. Several species of

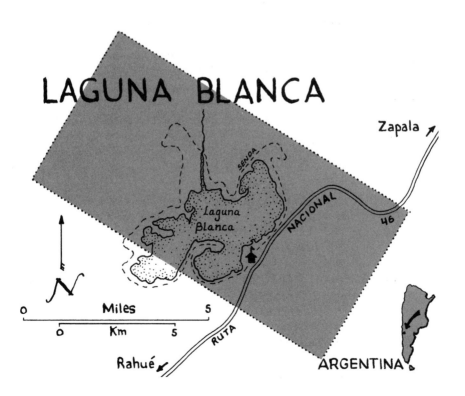

gulls and herons have been sighted at the lake, and a few dozen flamingos are usually on the lake.

The vegetation in the park is typical of the Patagonian steppe. All plants are xerophytes; there are no trees in the park. Shrubs tend to be low, and are formidably spined. Sturdy boots, not tennis shoes, are required footwear.

Visitor Facilities

There are no overnight accommodations at Laguna Blanca. The town of Zapala, 21 miles (34 kilometers) to the east of the park, has several hotels, however. A park ranger occupies a small cabin near the road at the southeast corner of the lake, and will direct visitors to a small campsite on the lake's edge. Drinking water may be scarce, and campers are cautioned to seek sites that are well sheltered from wind.

Two miles (3 kilometers) to the west of the ranger's residence, a modern combination visitor center and restaurant has been constructed, but is not yet opened. The facility is admirably situated atop a massive lava outcrop overlooking the bird-filled lake.

Recreation

Bird-watching is the primary recreation offered by this park. A good spotting scope is invaluable.

A formation of yellowish limestone that forms outcrops in several parts of the park may be of special interest to naturalists, for it is rich in marine fossils. Bivalves and ammonites of the Upper Jurassic Period are the most common remains.

Archaeologists have confirmed that the northeast shore of the lake was once the site of intensive pottery manufacture. Shards of pottery—Mapuche in origin (the Mapuches are descendants of Araucarian Indian tribes of Southern Chile and Argentina)—are strewn along the shore in this area. Artifacts of preceramic origin may also be found, including arrowheads, fleshing tools, and pestles manufactured from bone splinters, obsidian, and flint.

Climate and Weather

The climate is dry, with hot summers and cold winters. Temperatures may exceed 110 degrees Fahrenheit in summer, and drop well below freezing in winter. Even in summer, however, nights can be chilly. The most dramatic climatic features are the notorious Patagonian winds, which sometimes roar across the plains unabated for days on end, and have shaped the vegetation and landforms throughout the park. Visitors should bring good heavy parkas for protection from these wild blasts.

The best month to visit the park is February, when the largest numbers of birds may be seen. Cygnets are most likely to be seen with the adult birds from late February through April.

Location and Access

Laguna Blanca is remote, with few signs of human life in the vicinity of the park. Yet the park is relatively accessible by public transportation.

The park is located in the province of Neuquén, 21 miles (34 kilometers) southwest of the town of Zapala. Ruta 46, a well-maintained road, connects Zapala with Aluminé, a small town near the northern tip of Parque Nacional Lanín.

The Ferrocarril Roca (Roca Railroad) connects Zapala with Buenos Aires. Visitors can then reach the park from Zapala by bus or taxi.

Glossary

alfarería	ceramic pottery
hembra	female animal
macho	male animal
Mapuche	descendant of Araucarian Indian tribes of southern Chile and Argentina
picadera	tool-making site
punta de flecha	arrowhead
raspador	scraper
Tehuelche	pre-Columbian Indian tribe of Patagonia, now extinct

🎮 NAHUEL HUAPI: Something for Everyone

When certain Pleistocene glaciers retreated from the steppes into the fastnesses of the Andean Cordillera of northern Patagonia, they left behind an enormous, irregularly shaped lake. The lake is deep, but the vagaries of glacial sculpture left a narrow island anchored in the center of the lake. Centuries ago, the Mapuche Indians, a tribe that fiercely resisted the incursion of Europeans onto their lands, gave this island a revealing name: Nahuel Huapi (Tiger Island). Much later, a man named O'Conner rechristened the island, giving it a much less imaginative name: Isla Victoria (Victoria Island).

O'Conner's name stuck. The island is still called Isla Victoria. But the original name also stuck, and has been given to the entire park of which this spectacular lake is the centerpiece.

Today Nahuel Huapi is one of the oldest and most popular national parks in South America. It has something for everyone, and is to Argentines as Banff National Park is to Canadians: a honeymoon destination that also offers summer music festivals, winter ski races, regional museums, and elegant Old World hotels and restaurants, all

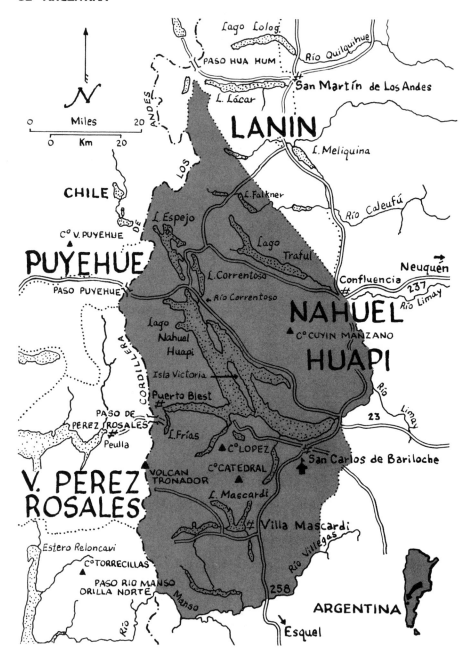

set against a backdrop of breathtaking mountain scenery.

Nahuel Huapi's rugged mountains, alpine glaciers, and well-established trails attract hordes of high country backpackers every austral summer. Serious anglers from around the world come to fish in the park's plentiful streams and clear, cold lakes, hoping to catch trout and salmon. Nahuel Huapi's dense, silent forests beckon those who seek respite from the frenetic business world of Buenos Aires. And Bariloche, a sophisticated resort community, attracts those who seek to be seen in fashionable places.

The park encompasses a variety of landforms and vegetative communities because it extends from the highest peaks of the continental divide to the beginnings of the parched plains of Patagonia—a revealing cross-section through temperate South American ecosystems.

The highest peak in the park is Tronador (Thunderer), an extinct volcano 11,722 feet high. The name refers to the frequent rumbles caused by ice falling from the face of several glaciers (*ventisqueros*) that cling to the mountain's three peaks. According to an ancient Mapuche legend, the rumbling is a warning sent by pygmy-like creatures who are the mountain's custodians, and who will slay with tiny arrows those who venture too close to Tronador.

One of Tronador's glaciers, Ventisquero Negro, is readily accessible by road. Car rentals or tours can be arranged in Bariloche for the 50-mile (80 kilometers) drive to the glacier. The drive is exceptionally scenic, for the road parallels the entire length of Gutierrez and Mascardi lakes, and follows the north fork of the Río Manso to its source. The road is paved from Bariloche to Villa Mascardi, a hamlet on the shores of the lake, but thereafter it becomes a steep dirt road, only one car wide in many places. Traffic is carefully controlled on this road; vehicles must drive toward the mountain during prescribed hours, and away during other hours. Check with the police in Bariloche before departing to avoid long delays.

The road ends at the bottom of a magnificent cirque ringed with a score of waterfalls, many of which are whipped into the sky by winds that roar through the peaks above. The resulting humidity has created true hanging gardens on the terraced walls of the cirque. Yellow fairy slippers, daisies, chickweed, red and yellow monkeyflowers, red fuchsias, and wild strawberries are among the species that North Americans will recognize in these gardens. A campsite, and a small, simple restaurant are tucked into the trees near the road's end.

Cerro Catedral (Cathedral Hill) is a conspicuous turreted ridge that lies southwest of Bariloche. It is accessible by means of a cable car that transports skiers in winter and sightseers in summer. The 7,000-foot ridge top affords stunning views of surrounding lakes and mountains, and is a jumping-off point for several popular alpine trails, described below. Cerro López and Cerro Otto, somewhat lower mountains, also offer excellent views. Both peaks can be reached by road or trail, and both are ski areas in winter. Cerro Otto is of particular interest to naturalists, for you can see (but not collect) fossils of marine bivalves on the northwest shoulder of the peak, and fossils of plants in roadcuts between kilometer posts 2 and 7 on the way to the top.

Most of the summits are above timberline, and are typical alpine vegetative zones. Sedges, mosses, and grasses predominate, and shrubs and herbaceous plants are characteristically stunted. Wildlife is scarce on these popular mountaintops, but a fortunate sightseer may spot one of the many condors (*Vultur gryphus*) that frequent the area. They resemble eagles at a distance, but are readily distinguishable by the creamy neck ruff.

The park contains six large lakes and dozens of smaller ones, but immense Lago Nahuel Huapi dominates the entire region, and even moderates Bariloche's weather. Sixty miles long, with more than 200 square miles of surface, the lake has several major arms (*brazos*), and boats regularly cross it between Argentina and Chile. In fact, Lago Nahuel Huapi is the final link in one of the most unusual short journeys in South America: travelers can cross the Andes by taking a series of ferry trips across alpine lakes and bus trips over mountain passes. (See "Location and Access" in this chapter.)

Isla Victoria and the Quetrihué Península are two popular destinations. They are in the famous arrayán forests, the only places in the world where visitors can see the arrayán (*Myrceugenella apiculata*), a rare myrtle-like tree, in large numbers. In fact, 3,500 acres of the Quetrihué Península have been set aside as a tiny park in its own right, Los Arrayanes National Park.

Pure stands of arrayán exist only on the northern tip of Isla Victoria and the southern tip of the Quetrihué Península (*Quetrihué* means "place of myrtles" in the Mapuche dialect). These pure stands are not very large—40 acres or so—but they are truly unique, and have been given extraordinary protection by the Argentine government. The groves are set aside as "Inviolate Natural Monuments," and visitors are warned to keep to nature trails that wind through these forests and not to wander off on their own.

The bark of the arrayán is pale orange, and it curls into parchment-like scrolls on older trees. The tree produces a profusion of pure white flowers in January and February, and shortly thereafter bears tiny blue-black, edible fruits. Individual trees are not particularly striking, but their rarity invests them with a peculiar appeal. The charm of the arrayanes reveals itself in the pure stands, for the trunks of mature trees are severely contorted, and with little strain of the imagination visitors can imagine themselves wandering through groves of van Gogh's twisted cypresses.

Isla Victoria has other attractions. Shortly after disembarking from one of the comfortable boats that dock daily, a visitor may see here a tree that looks like a ponderosa pine, and there one that resembles a sequoia. The trees are indeed what they appear to be, and so are the Douglas fir, Jeffrey pine, metasequoia, Monterey cypress, and other trees from the world over. The trees have been introduced, of course, making the island into a silviculturist's delight.

Exotic animals have also been introduced to the island. Three species of deer, introduced before ecological relationships were well understood, have brought about serious alterations of the island's biological equilibrium. The ecology lesson was not wasted, however, for the island was the site of South America's first park ranger school, and study of the risks associated with introduction of exotic species is part of the curriculum. Between fifty to 100 students attend the school—now in Bariloche—each year before taking up assignments in other parks. The school is international, with students from Chile, Paraguay, Venezuela, and other Latin American countries.

Take a walk to the steep cliffs on the west side of the island to visit the cormorant rookeries. These birds were once thought to be blue-eyed cormorants (*Phalacrocorax atriceps*), a marine species that somehow found itself at home on a freshwater lake. This curious situation stirred up considerable debate among ornithologists, and the controversy rages on, but the presently accepted view is that the birds belong to a subspecies that has adapted to fresh water and abandoned the sea. This subspecies has been given the elegant name *Phalacrocorax atriceps lacustris*, the lake cormorant.

The forests of Nahuel Huapi are representative of the Andean-Patagonian ecosystem. Four zones, including the alpine zone described above, are readily distinguishable.

Bizarre formations of wind-sculpted limestone are common near Nahuel Huapi National Park, Argentina, as in the Valle Encantado (Enchanted Valley) and in the nearby valley of the Río Traful.

The western zone is the region between the Chilean border and the western margins of *lagos* Traful, Mascardi, and Gutierrez. It extends approximately to the arrayán forests on Isla Victoria. Annual rainfall is high in this zone: 120 to 160 inches per year. Vegetation is lush and dense. The park's forests are primarily beech, of the genus *Nothofagus*. The coihue (*Nothofagus dombeyi*), an evergreen beech that sometimes exceeds 100 feet, predominates at lower levels; "The Grandfather," located on the road between Laguna Frías and Puerto Blest, is over 650 years old. The ñire (*Nothofagus antarctica*), or antarctic beech, is a common smaller tree, often associated with the coihue. Winter's bark (*Drimys winteri*) and the cedar-like alerce (*Fitzroya cupressoides*) are also common. The dominant tree at higher elevations is the lenga (*Nothofagus pumilio*), a deciduous beech whose leaves turn the park's mountainsides red-orange in autumn.

The central zone extends to the eastern edges of *lagos* Traful and Nahuel Huapi. The principal trees in this less humid zone are the radal (*Lomatia hirsuta*), valued for its attractive grain, and the ciprés (*Austrocedrus chilensis*), a coniferous member of the cypress family.

Xerophytic shrubs predominate in the dry eastern zone, although groves of ciprés and radal flourish in areas where moisture persists. Valle Encantado (Enchanted Valley) lies within this zone. The valley extends for 25 miles along the Río Limay (Crystal River, in Mapuche), the powerful river that drains Lago Nahuel Huapi. Tertiary limestone formations loom over ciprés groves along this valley, transformed by wind and rain into bizarre shapes given such names as Castillo (Castle), Dedo (Finger), Dedo de Dios (Finger of God), Cangalla Chilena (Chilean Packsaddle), and so on.

A wide variety of wildlife is found in the park, but few of the animals are easily observed except on Isla Victoria, where deer are common. Five species of deer are found in the park, of which two—the pudú and the huemul—are native to South America. Both are endangered species.

The pudú (*Pudu pudu*) is a fairy-tale creature, a spaniel-sized deer that seldom exceeds 15 inches at the shoulder. It inhabits the park's humid forests, but is extremely shy and rarely seen in the wild.

The huemul, or Andean deer (*Hippocamelus bisulcus*), was once the king of the southern forests, but was hunted nearly to extinction during the last century. Today the huemul is still rare in the park.

The three non-native species of deer are red deer (*Cervus elaphus*), dama deer (*Dama dama*), and axis deer (*Axis axis*). The red deer, which closely resembles the elk common in America, and the smaller dama deer are European deer, but the axis deer evolved on the Indian subcontinent. Biologists and other park authorities acknowledge that the introduction of these species was a serious mistake, and transplanting exotic species is no longer encouraged.

Mountain lions and mountain cats, foxes, weasels, river otters, and other mammals are found in the park, but are rarely encountered by tourists.

Birds are not as abundant in these southern mountains as on the Pampas or in rain forests, but are more readily observed than other animals. Among the more interesting of the twenty or so species bird watchers might sight in Nahuel Huapi are condors, Magellanic woodpeckers, and torrent ducks.

Woodpeckers are called carpinteros (carpenters) by South Americans, and one of the more spectacular is the Magellanic woodpecker (*Campephilus magellanicus*), called carpintero grande (big carpenter). They are large birds, up to 17 inches long, and are black with white wing bars. Males, with a bright scarlet head and crest, are unmistakable. Like the ivory-billed woodpecker, they require snags and older trees for food and nesting sites, so look for them in stands of the oldest, largest beeches you can find. Try tapping on trees to attract their attention, and listen for their calls, which are rather raspy squawks.

Fishermen are most likely to encounter torrent ducks (*Merganetta armata*). Since these small ducks feed almost exclusively on stonefly larvae, they are found only in

Views of Ventrisquero Frías (Frías Glacier) and a ring of waterfalls reward those who take the bus and launch trip to Puerto Frías and hike the 7-mile Laguna Frías trail.

habitat appropriate for stoneflies and attractive to fishermen: clear, rocky, swift-flowing streams. They are shy birds, usually seen in pairs, always in the midst of whitewater cascades or swift boulder-studded runs, which they negotiate with ease. They are difficult to stalk with a camera, for they swim underwater, upstream or down, as quickly as fish, and once they dive may not reappear again within a hundred feet or more.

Visitor Facilities

The tourist is king in Nahuel Huapi, and accommodations for tourists are among the best in South America. People come to Bariloche to ski, hike, climb, sunbathe, sail, swim, gamble, sightsee, flirt, shop, dance, get married, and simply to be seen. They wear mating plumage, preen at sidewalk cafes, and crowd the sidewalks, coffee-houses, shops, discos, restaurants, and the single seedy casino. The town is an international tourist center, busy night and day, with dozens of hotels, including plenty for those who wish to avoid the boisterous streets. Several small, comfortable inns are located on the shores of Lago Nahuel Huapi some distance from town; most of the other lakes in the park have at least one waterfront hotel.

Over a dozen organized campgrounds are scattered throughout the park; undeveloped campsites alongside lakes or rivers are common outside of town.

A pleasant restaurant graces Isla Victoria; overnight camping is permitted there.

Information for tourists is exceptionally well organized. At Bariloche's tourist office on the Central Plaza, tourists can obtain excellent maps as well as brochures printed in several languages that describe tours, hotels, campsites, restaurants, and park attractions. The Automóvil Club Argentino or Argentine Automobile Club (ACA) in Bariloche (785 Avenida 12 de Octubre) is another good source of useful maps and brochures at reasonable prices.

Recreation

Nahuel Huapi is appropriate both for adventurous travelers who like to strike out on their own and for those who prefer the efficiency of organized tours.

FISHING. Trout and salmon were introduced into the waters of Nahuel Huapi just after the turn of the century. They flourished, and the fishing in Nahuel Huapi and its neighboring park, Lanín, is now world renowned. Virtually every lake and stream in the park contain brown, rainbow, or brook trout, and several contain landlocked salmon. Trolling is the preferred method of fishing in the larger lakes, but fly-fishing is effective in the smaller lakes and in the streams. A few exceptionally productive rivers, such as the Traful, Manso, and Machico, are restricted to fly-fishing only.

Fish are abundant, and occasionally awesome. Brown trout here can reach 35 pounds, and rainbows 20.

Ruca Malen, at the northern end of Lago Correntoso; Río Manso; Lago Hess; Río Correntoso; and, for landlocked Atlantic salmon, Río Traful, are especially recommended for fly-fishermen.

Fishing season extends from mid-November to mid-April. A license is required, and may be purchased for fifteen days, one month, or for the season.

Licenses, information, and regulations may be obtained at the park office (*intendencia*) in Bariloche, or from regional offices in other parts of the park.

HIKING, CAMPING, AND BACKPACKING. Nahuel Huapi is one of the few national parks in South America with a well-developed network of good trails and alpine refuges. The principal hiking areas are Puerto Blest, Tronador, Cerro Catedral, and Cerro López.

Laguna Frías Area. To reach this area, hikers first travel by scheduled boat to Puerto Blest, then take a short bus ride to Laguna Frías, then another boat to Puerto Frías. Several trips can be made from Puerto Frías:

1. Refugio Rudi Roth, sometimes called Ruyi Riyi. A hike of approximately 8 miles (13 kilometers) to the top of a ridge on Mount Vichadero affords view of Tronador, Lago Nahuel Huapi, and several Chilean volcanos. An excellent day hike. **Caution:** Enquire about the condition of the refuge if you plan to use it for overnight shelter.

2. Puerto Frías to Puerto Blest via Laguna Los Clavos. A 12-mile (19 kilometers), infrequently used trail. Many blowdowns litter this path through dense, pristine forests.
3. Ventisquero Frías. A 7-mile hike along the Río Frías through dense woods and groves of bamboo and ferns brings hikers to the steep glacier that is the river's source. Many blowdowns also block this trail. This is an area of very heavy rainfall, so wear appropriate clothing.
4. Paso Las Nubes to Pampa Linda. Approximately 8 miles (13 kilometers) long, a continuation of the trail to Ventisquero Frías. There is a good campsite at the top of the pass. The trail passes through several vegetative communities and crosses several streams before reaching the road to Tronador, near Pampa Linda.

Tronador Area. The popular Refugio Otto Meiling lies about 4 hours from the end of the road to Ventisquero Frías, near Pampa Linda, southeast of Mount Tronador. Training in mountaineering is regularly conducted in the area by the Club Andino Bariloche (Bariloche Alpine Club).

Cerro Catedral Area. A number of loop trips to three refuges begin at the upper terminal of the Villa Catedral cable car. Well above timberline for most of their length, these trails enter the heart of Nahuel Huapi's high country. Meals and beds are available at Refugio Frey and Refugio San Martín for those hikers wishing to travel light.

Cerro López Area. Refugio Cerro López may be reached by road or by a 4-hour hike from Colonia Suiza on the outskirts of Bariloche. The nearby ridgetop offers spectacular panoramas of the area. Refugio Sigre, on the shores of Laguna Negra, can also be reached by a 4-hour hike from Colonia Suiza, and is linked by trail to the trails and refuges of the Cerro Catedral area.

Many maps distributed in the park are not up to date. Trails (*picadas* or *senderos*) indicated on maps may no longer be maintained, and new trails not shown. Since most refuges in the park are operated by the Club Andino Bariloche (Avenida Elflein near Calle Morales), backpackers should go directly to the club for current information on trails and refuges.

MOUNTAINEERING. Climbers must register their plans with park authorities; climbers should also contact the Club Andino Bariloche prior to ascents. Weather can be a critical factor in climbs in the park, and the club is the only source of trained mountain-rescue teams.

Historical and Cultural Aspects

On November 6, 1903, Francisco P. "Perito" Moreno, a well-to-do engineer-explorer, decided to donate approximately 75,000 acres of land he owned in the vicinity of Laguna Frías to the government of Argentina. He made his offer contingent upon a single condition, but that condition changed Argentine history and firmly established Perito Moreno as the father of his country's park system. He insisted that the land be set aside for the enjoyment of all Argentines.

Such a notion was unknown in those days, and the government took several months to think it over. Eventually, the offer was accepted, and in 1904 the first national park in South America, and the third national park in the western hemisphere, somewhat larger than Yellowstone, was born.

Climate and Weather

The climate is temperate. Summers are not too hot, nor are winters too cold. December to April are the best months to visit; May and June are rainy. Even during summer, however, good raingear is a must, for rainfall is heavy year-round in the western edge of the park.

Location and Access

Nahuel Huapi is situated in the Andean Region of Neuquén and Río Negro provinces, well into northern Patagonia. Although the park is a thousand miles southwest of Buenos Aires, it is decidedly not off the beaten track, for it is readily accessible not only from within Argentina, but also from Chile. It should not, however, be avoided for this reason, because most of the park itself is accessible by road, boat, and trail in a manner uncharacteristic of most South American parks.

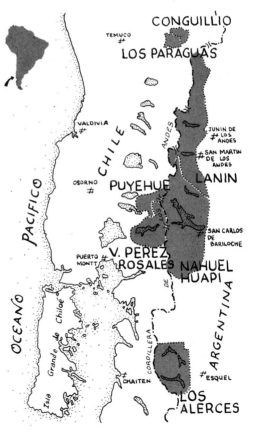

Direct flights to Buenos Aires and other provincial capitals are frequent. Bus and taxi services transport passengers to and from the airport, 8 miles (13 kilometers) from town.

Comfortable trains from Buenos Aires to Bariloche are operated by General Roca Railway; pullman service, diners, and private compartments are available.

Bus lines connect Buenos Aires to Bariloche through national routes 3, 22, and 237. Those driving their own vehicles may reach Bariloche by direct routes from almost any point in Argentina. One may also drive or take a bus from Osorno, Chile, through Puyehue and across Puyehue Pass, entering the park near the northern tip of Nahuel Huapi Lake, or from Villarica, Chile, through Pucón and across Tromen Pass, further north. Both passes are closed during austral winter.

One of the most pleasant ways to reach or depart the park is to cross the Andes from Chile via the glacial lakes. This trip is possible only during summer. Visitors who make this trip usually travel to the Chilean city of Osorno, from which they travel by bus to Parque Nacional Vicente Pérez Rosales. The passengers are delivered to Lago Todos los Santos, where they board a ferry that takes them to the eastern end of the lake. Another bus then transports them first to Chilean customs, and then on winding mountain roads across the border into Argentina. The road drops steeply to the shores of Laguna Frías, where passengers complete Argentine customs formalities and board yet another boat that ferries them to the opposite end of the lake. A 2-mile (3 kilometers) bus ride brings visitors to Puerto Blest, on the shore of Lago Nahuel Huapi. A final boat ride brings passengers to Puerto Pañuelo, directly across from the broad green lawns of the defunct Hotel Llao-Llao. Built in the massive style of the hotels in Yellowstone, Glacier, and the Canadian Rockies, its name derives from the Mapuche word for an edible fungus called Indian bread (*pan del Indio*) that parasitizes the coihue. The trip is remarkably comfortable, a journey for lovers and dreamers.

Glossary

altura	altitude, high place
bosque	forest
caña	rod, usually fly rod; also sugarcane
cerro	hill, mountain
cormorán	cormorant
cumbre	peak, summit
lago, laguna	lake
mirador	observation point
mosca	fishing fly, as well as the insect
pescar	to fish
salmón encerrado	landlocked salmon; the species is *Salmo salar sebago*, the Atlantic salmon
trucha	trout
trucha arco-iris	rainbow trout (*Salmo gairdneri*); *arco-iris* means rainbow
trucha de arroyo	brook trout (*Salvelinus fontinalis*); introduced from the U.S. in 1904. Also called *trucha fontanilis* or *cabeza de acero* (steelhead)
trucha marrón	brown trout (*Salmo fario*), introduced from Europe in 1906
venado	deer

LANIN:
In the Shadow of the Volcano

Just as Nahuel Huapi is dominated by an immense lake, Parque Nacional Lanín is dominated by an immense volcano. Lanín Volcano is perpetually snowcapped, and has the classical symmetry of Fujiyama. The Indians of the area avoided Lanín, believing it to be the abode of a powerful evil spirit, but modern travelers seek out the volcano and its striking surroundings.

While Lanín resembles neighboring Nahuel Huapi, important differences lend each park a special character. Lanín, for example, is not uniformly covered with dense forests. Although the terrain is mountainous, the park impresses the visitor as spacious, open country. There are no towns or villages in the park, and few developed facilities for tourists. As a result, the park is never crowded, and although ranching is permitted in some areas, the park has an unmistakably pristine character. Lanín also has several natural features that Nahuel Huapi lacks, including hot springs and monkey puzzle trees. Finally, although fishermen the world over have heard of the fishing near Bariloche, the true fishing meccas are the streams born in the lakes of Lanín.

Lanín is a good park for campers. Over two dozen campsites at various levels of development are established in the park, but undeveloped campsites are abundant on virtually all of the lakes and streams.

The park can be conveniently divided into six distinct ecological regions, each associated with at least one major lake. From north to south, they are:

LAGOS ÑORQUINCO, RUCACHOROI, AND QUILLEN. Many trees common in Nahuel Huapi are also found in this region: ciprés, lenga, coihue, and ñire. But a different beech, the raulí (*Nothofagus nervosa*), and a tree of striking aspect and ancient history, the pehuén (*Araucaria araucana*), make their appearance in this zone.

The raulí is easily distinguished from other beeches by enormous leaves, some 4 to 5 inches long. A deciduous beech, the raulí may reach 50 feet in good circumstances, and is often found near coihue. *Coihue* means "place near water" in the Mapuche dialect, reflecting the fact that coihue—and raulí—are often found on lakeshores and along streams. The raulí is valued highly for its wood, and has suffered seriously from commercial exploitation. As a result, measures for protection of the species have been introduced. Several large stands of raulí have been declared *areas intangibles,* in which the trees are protected.

North Americans know the tall pehuén by the name monkey puzzle tree, or araucaria. The English common name derives from the stiff, spiny leaves that encircle its twigs and branches. These branches arch upward, and their concentration near the top of older trees lends the trees the appearance of giant parasols. The pehuén is a primitive conifer, little changed from the forms that have been identified from fossil remains elsewhere. The thumb-sized seeds, rich in carbohydrates, were once a basic food of the Araucana Indians. The tree is rare, and, as a living relic, is completely protected within the park. Several pure stands (*pehuenales*) are found in the northern region, especially in the vicinity of Lago Ñorquinco and Lago Rucachoroi.

A small colony of Mapuche Indians lives in the vicinity of Lago Rucachoroi. They now raise cattle and sheep, but still gather the seeds of the pehuén as a foodstuff.

Excellent campsites lie alongside all of the lakes in this region. Lago Quillen is especially recommended because of the spectacular profusion of fuchsias (*Fuchsia magellanica*) along its shores, and because of the large numbers of raucous austral parakeets (*Enicognathus ferrugineus*) and austral blackbirds (*Curaeus curaeus*) that live in the shoreside thickets.

The Río Quillen is an excellent fishing stream, but somewhat overpopulated, and the trout tend to be small. The lower Río Aluminé, bordered by Argentine Ruta 23, is a highly recommended fly-fishing stream.

LAGO TROMEN. Lanín Volcano dominates this region. The volcano is accessible to tourists, for a dirt road that becomes a major route between Argentina and Chile in the summer passes within a few miles of the mountain at Paso Tromen (Tromen Pass). Eastward from the pass, the road passes rapidly through the transition zone from forest to dry steppes. The higher slopes of the volcano are covered with pehuén, and for several miles the road passes through stands in which these rare trees predominate, with lenga or ñire growing in shrub form as the understory. As travelers move east, more clearings appear. Several good campsites lie along this road. The road then drops to the drier lowlands, passing through fields of volcanic rock and ash. For several miles, the road follows the valley of the Río Malleo, which has cut through several layers of columnar basalt—remains of old lava flows.

Lago Tromen is typical of most of the lakes in Lanín: large and clear, set in steeply rising, forested mountains.

Take advantage of the relatively easy access to climb Lanín Volcano, a live volcano 12,615 feet high. Since the peak is on the Argentine/Chilean border, it may be

For obvious reasons, South Americans sometimes call the pehuén the parasol, *or* umbrella tree. *Lanín National Park, Argentina*

necessary to obtain permission from military authorities in Junín de los Andes. Inquire at the *intendencia* (and stock up on supplies) in Junín before departing. The easiest way to get to Lanín is to take the bus that goes from Junín de los Andes to Temuco, Chile, across Paso Tromen. Hitchhiking is slow, but possible. The starting point is the Argentine border station at Tromen, where courteous staff will point out the trailhead. Plan on taking one day to reach a hut at about 8,300 feet, and a second day to reach the summit and return to Tromen. Since the peak is snowcapped, you will need crampons and an ice ax.

Evidence of the volcanic origin of the park is evident in this region. Many mountaintops, mesa-like, are capped with resistant layers of black basalt laid down by old lava flows. Outcrops of volcanic rock are common.

LAGOS CURRUHUE AND HUECHULAFQUEN. Huechulafquen is the largest lake in the park; it also supports some of the largest trout in the world. The lake's outlet (*desembocadura,* called *boca* for short) is a famous fishing site for brown trout, which can reach 20 to 30 pounds. A daily fee is charged for the privilege of fishing in this spot.

The *boca* becomes the Río Chimehuin, another stream noted for its excellent fishing. The Chimehuin is a large stream, but is braided into several easily waded channels for much of its length. The neotropic cormorant (*Phalocrocorax olivaceus*) is often seen on this and other rivers of the park. This sleek bird is glossy black, and may be distinguished from other cormorants by the tuft of white feathers at each side of its head.

The crested caracara (*Polyborus plancus*), a carrion hawk, is relatively common in the dry valley of the Chimehuin. These birds are agile fliers, with narrow, pointed, falcon-like wings, and are often spotted hovering with rapid wing-beats as they look for the carrion or small animals on which they feed.

The road on the north shore of Lago Huechulafquen passes through diverse countryside—dense thickets of bamboo, forest, and open meadows. The vistas of the lake and mountains are splendid; near the end of the road, massive Lanín Volcano heaves into view and soon dominates the northern horizon. Campsites are plentiful, and a first-class hotel is located near the narrow strait that connects Lago Paimún with Lago Huechulafquen. Rental boats are available on this lake, as on most of the other lakes in the park.

In a deep valley a few miles from Lago Epulafquen are Termas Lahuen-Co (the Lahuen-Co Hot Springs). Water from the springs (about 160 degrees Fahrenheit) is piped to five large tubs in a scrupulously clean bathhouse. The baths are considered to be highly therapeutic. An attendant supplies towels and ensures privacy. Several comfortable campsites are available in which visitors may stay free of charge for up to ten days. The facilities are open from December to April. Limited provisions are available. The hot springs are in a very isolated wilderness location, and visitors should inquire at the park offices in San Martín before their visit. The popularity of the hot springs is regional, so visitors are unlikely to encounter other foreigners. The spot is well off the beaten tourist path—a delightful hidden gem.

To the west of Termas Lahuen-Co, the road passes near the Escorial, a dramatic zone of solidified rivers of intensely black lava, many of which are so recent that even simple plants have not yet begun the process of recolonization. The road then winds through dense forests of coihue, raulí, and pehuén along the south shore of long, narrow lakes Curruhue and Little Curruhue, both of which have excellent campsites, before entering the next region of the park.

LAGO LOLOG. This wild region is almost totally uninhabited. The scenery is a combination of large wilderness lakes set in high mountains that is typical of Lanín, and the road passes through the transition zone from dense, humid forests of beech to dry lowland plains. The region's outstanding feature is the overabundant population of red deer. Because they have seriously degraded the vegetation and threaten the native species, hunting of red deer is permitted within Lanín. Careful observers will note the hedged brush that is characteristic of vegetation in areas where the number of browsing animals has exceeded carrying capacity.

LAGO LACAR. Lago Lácar is a long, narrow lake popular for recreation. Large tour boats ply its waters, hauling passengers from San Martín to the westernmost end of the lake. Passengers who wish to can overnight at the simple hostel in Hua-Hum. A road links Hua-Hum to another hot spring near Lago Queñí; several hiking trails are maintained in the area. Hikers should inquire about the current condition of trails at the *intendencia* in San Martín.

San Martín de los Andes is a modern, prosperous town set among the dense stands of ciprés trees that cover the valley bottom at the end of Lago Lácar. Although the town relies on tourists, it is not nearly as boisterous as Bariloche. Hotels for every budget and several excellent restaurants are found along its quiet, tree-lined streets.

LAGO MELIQUINA. A zone of varied forests, this region encompasses the southernmost stands of two of Lanín's most interesting trees, the raulí and the pehuén.

Two excellent fishing streams, the Río Caleufu (Running River) and the short, spirited Río Filo Hua Hum (Snake's Belly River) flow through the region. Club Norysur, on the shores of Lago Meliquina, is an internationally known fishing club, and one of the few places south of Bariloche to obtain well-tied fishing flies.

Visitor Facilities

Although there are not as many facilities for tourists in Lanín as in Nahuel Huapi, visitors will have few problems finding bed and board nearby. There are hotels and restaurants in San Martín, Junín, Rahué, and Aluminé, and nearly every major lake has accommodations for visitors. Because of the current pace of inflation in Argentina, it is futile to quote prices, but rates for meals and lodging range from moderate to expensive.

Recreation

With one exception, Lanín offers rather conventional sightseeing and camping activities in an alpine environment. The exceptional activity, of course, is the extraordinary fishing. A comprehensive description of the opportunities for superb trout fishing in this park is beyond the scope of this book, but there are hundreds of miles of top-caliber streams and enough lakes to explore in a lifetime. The best place to obtain accurate information about fishing is in sleepy Junín de los Andes, the jumping-off point for the major lakes as well as the fabled waters of the Collon Cura (Stone Mask), Chimehuin, Aluminé, Malleo, Curruhue, Quilquihue, and Caleufu rivers. Fishing guides are available, but visitors can also obtain vehicles and explore several rivers at their convenience, either camping out or staying in hotels. Argentine road maps—available at the Auto Club in San Martín—are among the best in the world, and considerably cheaper than a guide.

A wise first stop for the visitor is the park headquarters in San Martín. Park service personnel are courteous, make every attempt to answer the questions of non-Spanish-speaking visitors, and distribute brochures when available.

Climate and Weather

The climate in Lanín is moderate and temperate, requiring no special considerations. Snow sometimes begins in May, and can continue well into October. Summer lasts from about mid-November to mid-April. Fishermen should delay visits until after mid-January, in order to avoid the possible effects of a late spring runoff; streams are generally in prime condition in February and March. Skiers attracted by the new ski facilities just outside San Martín will find the best conditions in July and August.

Location and Access

Immediately north of Nahuel Huapi, Lanín is accessible by road from Bariloche, Neuquén, or from Chile via Paso Tromen (summer only). Frequent bus service is available on all of these routes.

Trains from Buenos Aires pass through Zapala, from which visitors may reach San Martín or Junín by bus. Frequent scheduled flights from Buenos Aires serve Chapelco Airport, which lies halfway between San Martín and Junín.

Glossary

evite incendios	avoid fires; i.e., prevent forest fires, a common sign
nieve	snow
proveeduría	grocery store, place for provisions
termas, termales	hot springs
volcán	volcano

⊡ LOS ALERCES:
The Sequoias of the Southern Hemisphere

At about the time Greek masons first set chisels to the stones they would fashion into the Parthenon, a gust of wind swept through an Andean glade, freed a tiny seed from its cone, and spun it to the forest floor. The seed lodged in a warm, moist spot, and soon sprouted and began to grow. Gautama Buddha was born and died while the tree grew. Alexander the Great marched to India, Julius Caesar was assassinated, and Christ was born; the tree grew on. The Crusaders tramped to Jerusalem, Pizarro invaded Peru, men learned to fly, and still the tree grew.

The tree grows today in Parque Nacional Los Alerces, and is one of the oldest living things on the face of the earth. Argentines call this ancient species of tree "alerce" (ah-LEHR-say); botanists call it *Fitzroya cupressoides*. A sign in the park expresses the attitude of the park service toward alerces: *Un arbol es un ser viviente. No lo hiera, ni rompa sus ramas ni arranque su follaje.* "A tree is a living being. Do it no harm; neither break its branches nor tear its foliage."

Alerces are the sequoias of South America, ancient and massive. They are conifers that may exceed 150 feet in height, with trunks more than 12 feet in diameter. The largest of these dignified giants are located in remote sections of the park, but a well-developed system of transportation by boat and trail, described below, has made them accessible to all visitors who wish to see them.

Like Nahuel Huapi and Lanín, Los Alerces is situated in the Andes, in a setting of extremely rugged snowcapped mountains, large lakes, and nearly pristine forests. Small glaciers are commonplace, and wildflowers are profuse. The park supports a rich admixture of forests; almost all of the trees found in the more northern parks of the temperate Andes are present in Los Alerces, concentrated into dense stands at all canopy levels.

Los Alerces is very nearly an ideal national park. The scenery is magnificent, accommodations are attractive as well as comfortable, museums and nature trails assist the traveler in interpreting the park's natural features, and crowds seldom offend the pensive visitor.

The best starting point for a visit to Los Alerces is the village of Villa Futalaufquen, at the southern tip of the lake of the same name (*futa* means "large," *laufquen* means "lake"). Several buildings of wood and hewn granite on immaculately groomed grounds house administrative offices and visitor facilities. Many of the trees on the grounds are identified by small signs at the base of their trunks. The visitor center (*centro de interpretación*) contains a small but well-designed natural history museum that illustrates features of regional forests, insects, paleozoology, and paleobotany, as well as exhibits of Indian artifacts, small mammals, and an especially good display of the region's bird life. The museum even maintains a small aquarium, and features a slide show on the park. In the vicinity of a nearby small chapel, a short, self-guiding nature trail winds through the dense woods. Trees, common shrubs, and vines are identified for the visitor.

After a visit to Villa Futalaufquen, the visitor should take the boat tour that enters the heart of the park, ultimately reaching the silent, hidden world of the alerces. The tour is long, some 10 hours, but it seldom grows tedious, as many such trips do, and is an indispensable part of a visit to Los Alerces. The trip begins at Puerto Limonao, a tiny port 3 miles (5 kilometers) from Villa Futalaufquen, where smartly attired crews welcome visitors aboard one of three park-owned passenger launches.

These spotless 50-foot launches carry up to forty-five passengers, and are extremely comfortable. Spectacular sightseeing begins the moment the launch pulls away from the dock and brings the Andes into full view. The forests to the east of the launch show signs of exploitation, but the dense forests to the west are untouched by human activities. As the launch rounds rocky Punta Brava, Cerro Químico, an imposing mountain that drops abruptly into the lake, comes into view. In the distance, the series of granite peaks called *Cordón Pirámides* can now be seen. Most of the sharp spires of this chain of peaks are flanked by alpine glaciers. The chop on the lake increases dramatically as the launch clears Punta Brava and heads into the prevailing winds that howl toward the steppes from the mountains.

Soon after Punta Brava, the launch pulls up to a primitive dock at Playa Deseado, where passengers may disembark for an excellent lunch in a building of burnished knotty pine set in a dense grove of lengas and ciprés. Several colorfully decorated tables overlook the gravel beach, and across the lake looms Cerro Químico.

From Playa Deseado, the launch continues northward to the narrow strait that separates Lago Futalaufquen from Lago Verde. The 2-mile strait, called Río Arrayanes, is one of the more exciting stages of the trip, for the captain must avoid rocks and snags and weave through shallows to stay in the channel. The strait has no rapids, but the current is fast, and the launch is often forced to pass so close to shore that passengers can pluck leaves from overhanging branches. In some years the strait's water level is too low to permit boats to safely pass through. The larger launch draws 44 inches, and frequently crosses sand bars with only inches to spare.

The strait takes its name from the stands of arrayán that line both of its banks. The arrayanes bloom in late February and early March, transforming the strait into a colonnade lined with creamy-white blossoms.

After clearing the strait, the launch enters small Lago Verde, actually more blue than green. Steep cliffs border its northern and southern shores, and thick stands of bulrushes occupy the shallows. To the east of the lake is a low stretch of wooded land—a terminal moraine—beyond which lies Lago Menéndez, hidden from sight. The launch heads toward the moraine and shortly pulls up to a dock at Puerto Lago Verde.

Passengers disembark here, and walk along a gentle 0.5-mile (1 kilometer) path to Lago Menéndez. Near the end of this 15-minute walk, the trail enters a dark grove of large beeches, turns sharply, and dips to a covered boathouse at Puerto Chucao. The boathouse, situated in a shallow, well-sheltered cove, holds three launches identical to the one from which passengers just disembarked. Just outside the cove, whitecaps break where the water is exposed to the full 12-mile fetch of Lago Menéndez.

Passengers settle into a new launch, and as soon as it leaves the cove, Cerro Torrecillas, the park's centerpiece peak, looms into full view. The mountain is an upthrust massif, whose broad south-facing wall is covered with ice and snow. The ice splits into two glaciers that grind their way down opposite sides of the mountain's weathered face. The launch travels along the west shore of the lake, then crosses it and passes through a narrow channel south of Isla Grande, a series of maneuvers that give passengers the best possible views of Torrecillas and its glaciers. As the launch nears Torrecillas, passengers get a view down the length of Brazo Norte (North Arm) to the distant snowy peaks that mark the continental divide and the border with

The grounds of park headquarters at Los Alerces National Park are formal and immaculate, yet in perfect keeping with their surroundings.

Chile. The launch continues northward under the brow of Torrecillas until it reaches the dock at El Sagrario (Repository of Sacred Objects).

This remote dock is the starting point for perhaps the finest nature trail in temperate South America. In just over 1 mile (1.6 kilometers), the trail passes through cool green tunnels of bamboo (*chusquea*), dips under enormous windfallen logs, passes immediately alongside roaring waterfalls and cataracts, overlooks hidden lakes, and winds through groves of ancient alerces. The trail is dirt, of course, but sturdy wooden bridges and steps are provided at appropriate points.

A variety of flora is identified for the visitor on this trail: ferns (*helechos*), several species of common shrubs, including the Magellanic fuchsia, and such familiar trees as the coihue, arrayán, and winter's bark are placarded. The star of this show, of course, is the enormous alerce, named *árbol milenario* (the thousand-year tree) or *el abuelo* (the grandfather), near the end of the loop.

Botanists agree that alerce (*lahuán* in Mapuche) is a species in decline. The tree is well adapted to the cooler, moister climate that once prevailed in the southern Andes, but unable to flourish successfully under the ecological conditions of the present temperate climate. The alerce is a vanishing species. Park authorities indicate that the individual featured on this trail is neither the largest nor the oldest alerce, but it is nevertheless impressive: nearly 200 feet tall, and over 7 feet in diameter at its base. Through the use of carbon-14 dating techniques, the tree has been determined to be 2,600 years old!

Look closely for the fungi called Indian bread (*pan del Indio* or *Llao-Llao*) along this trail. These fungi, ascomycetes of the genus *Cyttaria*, are rounded growths on the trunks of the trees they parasitize. Different types of fungi attack different species of beech. The orangish *Cyttaria darwinii*, which may reach 3 feet in diameter, attacks only the coihue, while a smaller, grayish cyttaria only attacks the lenga.

Park launches stop at the trail for just over an hour, so visitors cannot dawdle for long on the trail. Backpackers or overnight campers can be dropped off at the trail, and be picked up by a later boat, but only with written authorization from the Intendencia in Villa Futa. In order to return passengers to Puerto Limonao before darkness falls, the launches leave El Sagrario *promptly* at the announced time. Do not be late. The return journey is not a repitition of the morning's trip, although the launch plies the same waters, for the shadows have changed, and hues of sunset now tint the mountains and lake.

Visitor Facilities

Several inns, from simple to elegant, are located in the park. The biggest one can accommodate up to forty guests. Most of the others are situated on the eastern shore of Lago Futalaufquen, and cater primarily to fishermen. The inn on Lago Verde is recommended for those interested in a quiet corner of the park from which to walk to Lago Menéndez, Río Arrayanes, or other nearby rivers—all of which support trout. Several organized campgrounds, some with hot showers, are also within the park. Backcountry camping is permitted, but prior permission from park authorities is required. Two small stores near the Intendencia stock supplies for campers.

Hotels and restaurants for every budget are also available in nearby Esquel, a small, picturesque town established by Welsh immigrants. Several travel agencies in Esquel offer tours of the park; check at the friendly and efficient tourist office in the bus terminal for information.

Recreation

The most efficient means to see the park, and a thoroughly enjoyable experience, is via the boat that takes visitors to lagos Futalaufquen, Verde, and Menéndez.

Los Alerces is primarily a sightseeing park. Because of the dense forests, hiking is restricted to a few trails. Backpackers, however, can visit areas very rarely visited by others by being dropped off at the final stops of the boat tours. Only a handful of backpackers take this opportunity each season, and it is a guaranteed method of finding solitude in areas that are seldom disturbed by man.

Los Alerces is well known to trout fishermen as a park whose lakes produce enormous fish. All of the major lakes in the northern half of the park—Futalaufquen, Menéndez, Verde, and Rivadavia—are linked by streams large enough to permit easy passage of fish from one lake to another. The largest fish are consistently caught in Lago Menéndez, from which, in a single memorable day several years ago, three rainbows weighing 23, 24, and 27 pounds were caught.

The trout were introduced, of course, but have flourished. Another introduced animal that has flourished in Los Alerces is the European hare (*liebre*); countless hares scamper about in the thickets and glades of the park. The wild boar (*Sus scrofa*) was also introduced from Europe, but is very seldom observed.

As in all of the Argentine parks of the Patagonian Andes, fishing season runs from mid-November to mid-April. A license is required. Boats and guides are available through several of the hotels in the park.

Climbing is permitted, but only with written authorization. Horseback rides can be arranged.

Historical Aspects

A significant portion of the southern section of the park has unfortunately been lost to the demands of Argentine industrialization. In 1971, construction was begun on a large dam across the outlet of Lago Situación, in the southeastern corner of the park. The reservoir that formed eventually inundated not only Lago Situación, but a chain of three other lakes that extends nearly to the Chilean border. The reservoir, Presa de Futaleufu, is now the largest body of water in the park, and furnishes hydro-electric power for the aluminum plant in Puerto Madryn on the Atlantic coast, 330 miles to the east.

Climate and Weather

The climate is temperate. No special precautions are required, but visitors are advised to procure good windbreakers and raingear for the boat trip. Summer winds—not cold, but strong—blow out of the west regularly. The park is open year-round, but local transportation can be difficult in winter. The best weather corresponds to fishing season: mid-November to mid-April.

Location and Access

Los Alerces is in the northwest corner of Chubut Province in the Patagonian Andes. It is readily accessible, but lies at the northern edge of the truly remote part of Patagonia. North of Los Alerces visitors are never far from towns; trappings of civilization are relatively commonplace. But to the south begins the real Patagonia: one may travel for hours (and on back roads, for days) without seeing a sign of human habitation or another vehicle. Impressive names on maps turn out to be no more than a windswept crossroads or a lonely gas station and a small country store. It is several hundred miles south to the next real town.

Transportation by air to Esquel is available from Bariloche and Trelew on the coast. Take advantage of the low rates offered by Argentina's military airlines, Lineas Aéreas del Estado (LADE), to reach Esquel. Frequent buses also travel to Esquel from Bariloche and from the coastal towns.

If you are a train buff, and don't mind 51 hours or so on a train (sleeping cars are available), you can reach Esquel from Buenos Aires by rail. From Ingeniero Jacobacci, a dusty desert town east of Bariloche, a steam engine puffs along a narrow-gauge railway to Esquel, the southernmost point on South America's connected rail system. For a full account of this journey, read Paul Theroux's *The Old Patagonian Express* (see "Selected Bibliography").

Glossary

apague su cigarillo	put out your cigarette
cabalgata	horseback ride
cuide al bosque	take care of the forest
goce del paisaje	enjoy the landscape or scenery
no grabe	don't carve on (the trees)
pesca vedada	fishing forbidden
proteja la fauna	take care of the animals

PENINSULA VALDES: Zoo of the South Atlantic

Get out a map of South America and look at the Atlantic coast near the continent's southern tip. About halfway between Buenos Aires and the Strait of Magellan, a small goblet-shaped chunk of land juts from the coast into the South Atlantic and forms the southern boundary of the Gulf of San Matías. The land is the Valdés Peninsula, an unusual geographical feature and one of South America's best wildlife showcases.

Península Valdés barely misses being an island, for it is attached to the mainland by a thread of land so narrow that visitors can easily see ocean on both sides of the road that crosses the isthmus to the peninsula. This bleak peninsula, so tenuously attached to the continent and virtually surrounded by ocean, is the site of the lowest point in South America.

The peninsula itself is treeless, arid, and unattractive. Low scrub covers its rolling, often monotonous terrain. Roads yield clouds of brick-red dust on sunny days and turn to slimy goo in the slightest of rains. But Península Valdés is easy to reach and relatively easy to explore. It and nearby points are *the* places to go to see penguins, sea lions, seals, elephant seals, whales, dolphins, guanacos, rheas, maras, tinamous, and a variety of seabirds.

The key to seeing this wildlife undisturbed is to avoid the routine sightseeing circuits. Not that local tours are without value: visitors will generally see plenty of wildlife on tours of the area conducted by travel agencies in nearby towns. But visitors will see more wildlife under less hectic circumstances if they rent a car and set out on their own to explore some of the many roads that skirt deserted beaches and reach isolated coves and headlands.

The three primary areas to explore in the region are Península Valdés itself, Punta Tombo, and Cabo Dos Bahías (Two Bays Cape).

The seaside town of Puerto Madryn is the gateway community for Península Valdés. The town's economic mainstay is a huge aluminum smelter that poses a considerable pollution threat to the gulf on which it lies, but tourism has grown rapidly as the wildlife values of nearby areas have become more widely recognized. Plenty of accommodations are available, and most organized tours originate here.

The entrance to Península Valdés lies near the narrowest point of the isthmus, 50 miles (80 kilometers) north of Puerto Madryn on Ruta 2, and the first noteworthy feature lies not far from the entrance. A short side road near the entrance building leads to the shore of Golfo San José and the Reserva Isla de los Pájaros (Bird Island Reserve). The reserve comprises a 6-acre island, accessible by foot at low tide. It was once the nesting site of over a dozen species of birds, among them gulls, cormorants, oystercatchers, herons, egrets, and ducks. Thousands of birds crowded the island during the austral spring, but the disturbances created by wandering visitors caused many birds to abandon their nests, and finally to abandon the island altogether. By the time protection was established, only seven species were nesting on the island, but the protection has paid off and bird populations are once again increasing. Visitors are no longer allowed on the island, but huge binoculars installed at a government-built observation point permit visitors to see the nesting birds. Use the binoculars to study the flamingos that frequent the tidal flats in spring and summer, and to search for signs of the huge southern right whale, *Eubalaena australis*, which breeds in the waters of the Golfo San José. In the southwest corner of Golfo San José, 5 miles (8 kilometers) west of the *isla*, is the Riacho San José. A *riacho* is an estuary, and what makes this estuary unique is the extreme tidal range, which can reach 88 feet. Beachcomb in this area with great care.

The next stop should be the *lobería* at Punta Pirámides. A *lobería* is a seal or sea lion rookery, and during the breeding season, more than a thousand southern sea lions (*Otaria flavescens*) crowd the sandstone shelves at Punta Pirámides. Sea lions and fur seals are so-called "eared" seals. Members of the family have small external ears and can turn their hind flippers forward so as to walk—after a fashion—on land.

Males, up to five times the size of the females, and 9 feet long, arrive first at the rookeries, usually in November or December. They select a section of rock as their territory, and defend it vigorously from other males (bulls) as the females begin to arrive. Most of the defensive fighting is mere posturing accompanied by loud bellowing, but deep scars and bloody froth indicate that some of the battles are in deadly earnest. As summer progresses, the bulls gather about them as large a harem of females as they can hold together. The young, conceived the previous summer, are born in January. Dark and extremely playful, they cavort in groups in shallow water, usually under the watchful eye of a female babysitter. As at all sea lion rookeries, bedlam prevails, and the din is terrific.

From Punta Pirámides, Ruta 2 heads toward Punta Delgada, the easternmost point of the peninsula. About 18 miles (29 kilometers) from Punta Pirámides, a salt flat shimmering white under the sun comes into view to the north of the road. This glistening wasteland, Salina Grande, is several miles in diameter and lies 138 feet below sea level, the lowest point on the South American continent.

Ruta 2 continues through low scrub and occasional patches of green meadows near sheep *estancias*. Besides the ubiquitous sheep, visitors will see family groups of guanacos, lesser rheas, tinamous, and maras.

Tinamous are the brown, roadrunner-like birds that scamper into the brush as cars pass by. About fifty species of tinamous inhabit South America, but most of the birds seen on Península Valdés are elegant-crested tinamous (*Eudromia elegans*). These

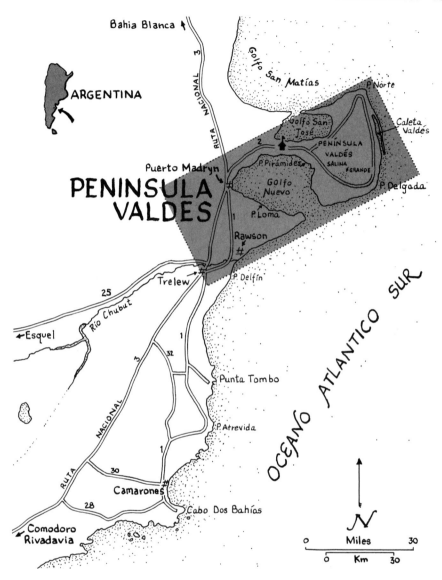

are the largest of the tinamous, nearly 18 inches long, and like other members of the family they have flute-like voices, and rarely fly. The males of this ground-nesting species incubate the eggs, noted for their glossy, porcelain-like surface and pastel coloration. Tinamous are quite tasty, a characteristic that led to relentless hunting, but since the establishment of protection measures populations are rebounding rapidly, and tinamous are now extremely abundant on the peninsula.

One of the more humorous roadside sights is the mara, or Patagonian hare or cavy. Maras (*Dolichotis patagonum*) are Patagonia's ecological answer to jackrabbits. They have long ears, though not so long as hares, enormous hind legs on which they bound off through the brush, and the faintly bewildered look of jackrabbits. They are not related to rabbits, however, but belong to the family caviidae, which includes capybaras, agoutis, and guinea pigs. Adult maras are 2 feet long and, like capybaras, have bizarre squared-off snouts. Shy animals, they do not sit still for photographs, but at night their curiosity often gets the best of them, and the ring of glowing eyes around a campfire usually belongs to maras.

At Punta Delgada, Ruta 2 swings north to parallel the outer coast of the peninsula. Punta Delgada itself is a military zone and casual visitors are not welcomed with enthusiasm, but the beaches north of the zone are prime places to get off the beaten track. For about 12 miles (19 kilometers), Ruta 2 traverses a flat, mesa-like plain some 200 feet above the sea. The roadbed is frequently only a few yards from the lip of a sheer cliff overlooking the beach. Stop at nearly any point along this stretch of road, grab your binoculars, walk to the edge of the cliff, and look over; you will see what appear to be short, sun-bleached logs rolled up onto the beach. Occasionally one of the "logs" will move, and if you look more closely you will see that they are elephant seals (*Mirounga leonina*). Dozens may be viewed from a single observation point, and if you settle down for a nice long lunch high above the sea, you may also see whales, dolphins, sea lions, fur seals, and a few penguins. These animals are virtually undisturbed because few visitors put forth the effort (and risk) to make their way to the beach from the cliffs. The road nears the beach at only one or two spots in this area, but in a few places it is possible to get down the cliffs and reward yourself with some of the finest beach wildlife hiking on the face of the earth.

Caution: The cliffs are very dangerous, not to be trifled with. Inspect your route of descent carefully, and be certain that you can get all the way to the beach before setting out. Also, do not approach wildlife closely. The wildlife itself is not dangerous, but if animals are unduly disturbed they may be forced to leave the area, and may abandon their young or be forced into the sea and into the waiting jaws of predators.

One need not negotiate cliffs, however, to see elephant seals at close range. One of the best places on the peninsula to see them, and to camp, is at the mouth of Caleta Valdés, about 21 miles (34 kilometers) north of Punta Delgada. A *caleta* is an inlet, and Caleta Valdés, nearly 20 miles (32 kilometers) long, makes up over a third of the peninsula's east coast. Most of the *caleta* is extremely narrow, separated from the open sea only by barren heaps of surf-polished stones. Elephant seals tend to concentrate on the cobble beaches in the vicinity of the mouth of the caleta; access to the beaches is easy along its entire length.

Sea lions and seals belong to the family pinnipedia. The family is divided into "eared" forms, which include sea lions and fur seals, and the so-called hair seals. The hair seals lack external ears and cannot turn their hind flippers forward, and so must wriggle about awkwardly on land. The docile elephant seals that lie on the beaches of Península Valdés during the austral spring and summer are the largest of the pinnipeds. Their common name derives in part from their size (males attain lengths of more than 20 feet, and can weigh over 3.5 tons), and in part from the elongated snout of the male, which swells even more during the breeding season.

Small numbers of elephant seals are found in North America along the coast of California, but most of the world's populations live in southern seas, coming ashore only on the coasts of Antarctic islands and the Valdés Peninsula. Fortunately for visitors, an estimated 4000 to 5000 elephant seals now frequent over a hundred miles of

Family groups of guanacos are common sights on Península Valdéz, at Punta Tombo, and at Cabo Dos Bahías.

the peninsula's beaches, from Punta Delgada all the way to Punta Buenos Aires, at the northern edge of Golfo San José.

Elephant seals are among those rare animals that have few predators. Those few predators, however, are formidable—killer whales and man. Whenever you look for wildlife on the beaches, do not ignore the open sea. Several species of whales, including killer whales, ply these waters, and they are easy to miss if you are not looking for them. Authoritative accounts document instances in which killer whales have beached themselves trying to reach resting elephant seals. The most destructive predators, as usual, have been men, who in their quest for blubber and oil (a single individual yields upwards of 80 gallons of oil) nearly exterminated the seals by the turn of the century. Although elephant seals have been commercially exploited in recent years on the South Georgia Islands, they are protected elsewhere, and populations are increasing.

Elephant seals spend most of the winter at sea, come ashore to breed in spring, return to sea for about two months, then return to the coasts in fall to molt. On arrival for breeding season, they establish a territory on the beach, and defend it vigorously (and loudly) from the incursion of other males. They almost never leave the beach during breeding season, living entirely on fat reserves stored in thick layers of blubber. They seek to establish a harem of seven to ten females, which, like sea lions, arrive pregnant and breed almost immediately after bearing their young.

Elephant seals lay torpid in the sun for most of the time they are ashore; do not expect acrobatics from them. They may cough or scratch themselves with a flipper only once during several hours. Indeed, some observers liken them to logs in activity as well as appearance. But if you are patient (and lucky), you might observe a dispute between males, and if you get up early or stay up late during a brightly moonlit night, you will see them move about, for they are most active at dawn, dusk, and at night. They are graceful in water, but ashore their mode of locomotion is almost painful to watch. They are so immense that their front flippers barely touch the ground, and since they cannot use their hind flippers to push themselves, they can move only by dorsoventral undulations of their muscles, somewhat like immense caterpillars or huge, rubbery maggots. At full speed, they achieve the pace of a man walking. Near the mouth of the *caleta*, the mounds of cobbles are lined with the shiny trails of elephant seals that have made their way from the outer beach over the narrow peninsula to the waters of the inlet. Look carefully in the lagoon-like waters of the *caleta* for them, for they like to float under the surface with only their nostrils and eyes exposed.

Ruta 2 parallels the *caleta* north from its mouth toward Punta Norte. At its northern end, the *caleta* becomes wide and contains several brushy islands. Look on these islands and the peninsula across the *caleta* for groups of guanacos, and check along both shores for small groups of penguins.

Punta Norte lies about 12 miles (19 kilometers) from the northern end of the *caleta*, another stretch of road that parallels beaches that are barely out of sight, yet seldom visited by tourists. Punta Norte is the site of the second-largest sea lion rookery on the peninsula. This reserve was created in 1967 primarily for the protection of the southern sea lion as well as the southern sea elephant. Visitors are separated from the seals by a fence, but several trails lead to adequate viewpoints. Although the sea lion colony at Punta Pirámides is larger, Punta Norte is the preferable site, for visitors can get closer to the animals and see sea elephants as well as sea lions.

From Punta Norte, Ruta 3 returns to Punta Pirámides, a 40-mile (64 kilometers) trip that completes a loop around the peninsula. A glance at a map indicates that many of the peninsula's beaches are difficult to reach, and therefore seldom visited, yet on this loop you will have seen most of the wildlife that inhabits the Patagonian coast.

One other animal remains, but it is so interesting that it warrants a long side trip.

You might see a few penguins on the Peruvian coast, on the shores of Tierra del Fuego, or along the beaches of Caleta Valdés, but if you are not going to Antarctica and you wish to truly experience these wonderful birds, you need to go to one of the two major penguin rookeries (*pingüineras*) near Península Valdés: Punta Tombo or Cabo Dos Bahías.

The primary attraction of both reserves is penguins, but each is distinct enough to warrant a visit. They lie at some distance from towns; Punta Tombo is 130 miles (209 kilometers) south of Puerto Madryn, and Cabo Dos Bahías lies 115 miles (185 kilometers) farther south. It takes time to reach them, but as you weigh your options, remember that they are well off the beaten path, unique in the western hemisphere, and that there is a great deal to see along the way.

Punta Tombo, the reserve nearest to Península Valdés, may be reached via Ruta

1, a good dirt road that heads south from Rawson, or via side roads that branch east from paved Ruta 3, 50 miles (80 kilometers) south of Trelew. Junctions are uncharacteristically well marked by Patagonian standards, making it hard to get lost. Roads are generally good, but some cattle guards have missing rails. Slow down if you see sticks or piles of rocks on the roadside or at the edge of cattle guards.

A small fee is charged at the entrance to the reserve, 1 mile (1.6 kilometers) or so from the pingüinera. Tarry awhile at the entrance; a pleasant snack shop has been constructed, and the park rangers are knowledgeable, helpful, and interested in meeting fellow wildlife enthusiasts. Then head down the winding road to the beach, and the penguins. The road ends at a parking area a few yards from the ocean, and visitors suddenly find themselves in an ocean of penguins. As far as the eye can see, from horizon to horizon—penguins.

The visitors' area is fenced, but a number of trails extend away from the road. Visitors need not fear being unable to see and photograph the birds at close range, for the fences are for people, not penguins. The birds pay no attention whatsoever to fences, and nest anywhere they can find space, including the parking lot, so drive carefully. The parking lot and trails are surrounded by nests, and a constant stream of penguins going back and forth between nests and the sea crosses the areas set aside for visitors.

The vast majority of these birds are Magellanic penguins (*Spheniscus magellanicus*), but their more common name is jackass penguin, as you will have discovered from at least 0.5 mile (1 kilometer) away. The birds' cry is remarkably similar in pitch, timbre, and duration to the hoarse braying of a donkey, and the combined volume of up to a million *pairs* of penguins braying away for all they are worth is a most unbirdlike sound not soon forgotten. A great deal of the fun of a visit to a *pingüinera* is the noise, which picks up considerably in the evenings. A reasonable guess is that the constant braying is necessary to guide individuals to their mate's nest, but groups of birds often bray in chorus, penguin glee club behavior a bit more difficult to explain.

The male excavates a shallow burrow in the earth, often beneath a low shrub, in which the eggs are laid. The eggs are then incubated alternately by male and female. In December, some birds will still be sitting on eggs, while others will be guarding one or two roly-poly gray chicks. Penguins are incredibly brave parents, and do not abandon their nests as visitors pass by a few inches away. Visitors, in fact, should be cautious when near the birds; their beaks can inflict nasty cuts. When an intruder approaches too closely, penguins point their beaks at the interloper, rotate their heads from side to side, and hiss. If they are hissing at you, you are too close, and about to get bitten.

The penguins' chief worries are the ever-present gulls, which swoop in on unguarded eggs, and great skuas (*Catharacta skua*), 2-foot-long predatory gulls with hooked bills that can carry off a chick. The occasional shriveled corpses of skuas with pierced skulls indicate, however, that predators do not always win the contests.

Humans have a peculiar fascination with penguins, probably due to their somewhat human appearance. Some of us find them to be hilarious creatures, and cannot watch them for long without breaking into laughter. Others find them smelly, noisy, and monotonous in their great numbers. Yet others consider penguins to be unlikely creatures trapped in an evolutionary limbo; well adapted for water, they must never-

Magellanic penguins guard their chicks from attacks by skuas and other predators at the nesting grounds at Punta Tombo.

theless spend some time on land, where they are absurd. Some people can watch penguins for days on end; for others, an hour or two will suffice. Part of the experience of going to a *pingüinera* is to find out what effect penguins have on you. But remember, almost everyone shoots more than enough pictures of penguins to bore their friends half to death.

Penguins and seabirds are not the only wildlife at Punta Tombo. Groups of guanacos are common on the hillsides near the reserve, and rheas often wander about among the penguin nests, apparently oblivious to the din.

Punta Tombo is a colorful reserve, primarily because of scarlet strata exposed by the sea. In bright sunlight, the visual landscape comprises these red rocks, brilliant green brush (in spring), blue sea and sky, and the puffy white cumulus clouds characteristic of Patagonia, a striking combination of colors.

Another place to go for wildlife in this area is Cabo Dos Bahías, near Camarones, a tiny seaside village. It is the most remote reserve in the area, and in many respects the most interesting. To reach it from Punta Tombo, return to Ruta 1, travel south 82 miles (132 kilometers) to Camarones, and then an additional 19 miles (31 kilometers) past Camarones to the reserve. It is a long journey over dirt roads, but through fascinating country loaded with wildlife. Halfway to Camarones, Ruta 1 nears the sea at Cabo Raso, a wild, starkly beautiful coastline. A few lonely buildings are scattered about, some in disrepair, some under repair. Miles and miles of deserted shingle beaches extend in both directions. The land is moor-like and austere, precisely the spot for anyone seeking a spectacular, empty coast far from the madding crowd. A cabin at Cabo Raso would be a get-away-from-it-all location of the first order.

The *pingüinera* at Punta Tombo has a far better reputation than the one at Cabo Dos Bahías, but it is perhaps not quite merited. Punta Tombo has quantity, but Cabo Dos Bahías has quality. Most travelers who have visited both places prefer Dos Bahías for scenery and wildlife. It has a little bit of everything: penguins, rabbits, flamingos, maras, two species of sea lions, fur seals, guanacos, rheas, foxes, and seabirds in abundance. It also lacks two features despised by campers: biting flies and cactus.

A further advantage of Dos Bahías is that camping is permitted, unlike Punta Tombo, and hotel accommodations are available in nearby Camarones. A bonus for visitors to Dos Bahías is the presence of arrowheads. Worked chips of both chert and obsidian lie everywhere. Ask the ranger where and how to look for them, and ask to see his extensive personal collection. Both reserves merit a visit, but if circumstances permit a visit to only one, the wiser choise is Cabo Dos Bahías.

Visitor Facilities

Puerto Madryn is the nearest town to Península Valdés, and is loaded with hotels, restaurants, and services for tourists. A pleasant place to camp near town is the Argentine Auto Club campsite on Playa del Pozo at Punta Loma, site of yet another sea lion rookery. The reserve lies 7 miles (11 kilometers) east of town. On day hikes from this beach, visitors can expect to see armadillos, rheas, foxes, guanacos, skunks, and maras. Glistening sheets of white or clear quartz cover many outcrops, and lie sprinkled over the ground like broken glass. Fossilized oyster-like bivalves are common, many with shells that have been replaced by this crystalline substance.

The only public accommodations on the entire peninsula are at Puerto Pirámides: an ACA motel and a small, comfortable hostería. Food and gasoline are available. Camping is permitted at several designated sites on the peninsula, but not in the immediate vicinity of rookeries. Campers are advised to bring plenty of their own water.

Punta Tombo has no accommodations for visitors, and camping is prohibited in the vicinity of the *pingüinera*. Twenty miles (32 kilometers) toward Trelew from the Punta Tombo road, however, a side road from Ruta 1 leads 5 miles (8 kilometers) to a secluded free campsite on a lovely beach. The sign Isla Escondida (Hidden Island) indicates the turnoff to the beach.

Camping is permitted at Cabo Dos Bahías, and a small, friendly hotel with good food is situated in nearby Camarones.

Recreation

Wildlife observation is the primary reason to visit this area, but it is also a good place for fossil hunters, arrowhead hunters (not, however, on the reserves), and inveterate beachcombers. Surf fishing is a popular pastime, and Puerto Madryn is becoming a center for skin diving and scuba diving. Equipment may be rented at dive shops in town. Divers with experience in warmer waters will find the marine life here relatively uninteresting.

Climate and Weather

Spring and summer (October through April) are the best times to visit the area. Days are warm and nights are cool, with protection necessary from the heat of the day and the chill of evening. Rain falls occasionally, but very occasionally. Rainstorms here are like desert rainstorms: clouds grow black and ominous, great sheets of rain fall from them, but most of it doesn't reach the ground. A far more important consideration is timing. All of the animals (except whales, which breed in September and October) can be seen during the warm seasons of the year, and it is important to time a visit accordingly. To appreciate the spectacle of the *pingüinera* at Punta Tombo, try to visit when the population is high. The best months are October and November, and February and early March. During December and January, parents are herding the chicks to water and should not be disturbed. Visitations may be prohibited after March, when the birds are returning to sea. During the rest of the year, the rookery is virtually deserted. Elephant seals breed in early August, a poor time to visit, and then leave, but they return in November and stay until about March. Late spring and early summer months, November to February, are the best times to see most birds.

Location and Access

Península Valdés, Punta Tombo, and Cabo Dos Bahías are all located in Chubut Province on the Patagonian coast. The nearest large city is Trelew, reached by daily flights from Buenos Aires and other northern cities. Puerto Madryn is a 1-hour bus ride from Trelew. Both cities have hotels and restaurants suited for all budgets, and a number of travel and tour agencies can arrange trips by excursion bus or van to all three reserves. Puerto Madryn is the logical city from which to arrange transportation to Península Valdés, although companies in Trelew also tour the peninsula. Hitchhiking on the peninsula is possible during summer, although competition is intense on weekends and traffic is light on weekdays. It is also possible to hitchhike to Punta Tombo and Cabo Dos Bahías, but be prepared for long delays, for traffic is sparse. No public transportation serves Punta Tombo, but a weekly bus leaves Trelew for Camarones. From there, taxis continue to the sea lion and penguin rookeries. Check at the tourist office at the bus station in Trelew for schedules.

The best way to see the reserves is to rent a car, following your own pace and your own whims. Exchange rates fluctuate too rapidly in Argentina to provide for accurate predictions of costs, but in 1988 it was possible to rent a car in Trelew for $17 per day plus 22 cents a mile (U.S.), not an unreasonable price if split among several passengers.

Glossary

lobería	sea lion colony
lobo marino	sea lion
pingüinera	penguin colony
pingüino	penguin

BOSQUES PETRIFICADOS AND CUEVA DE LAS MANOS: Glimpses into the Past

BOSQUES PETRIFICADOS (PETRIFIED FORESTS). Some travelers to Patagonia complain about the monotonous character of the treeless steppes that lie between the Andes and the chilly waters of the South Atlantic. Sparsely covered with small, tough shrubs and scattered spikes of sere bunchgrass, populated by tarantulas, lizards, snakes, armadillos, and almost no people, Patagonia indeed presents a forbidding aspect to strangers. It was not always that way.

During the Jurassic Period, about 140 million years ago, Patagonia was covered from the Pacific coast to the Atlantic coast by a dense temperate forest. Araucaria, sequoia, cypress, even palm trees flourished in moisture-bearing breezes that drifted from the Pacific across the narrow southern wedge of the continent. The incessant westerly winds so characteristic of Patagonia were humid in those days, because the Andes, youngest of the world's mountain ranges, had not yet been born.

Then, at the beginning of the Cretaceous Period, the earth shuddered deep below the west coast of the continent, and titanic convulsions began to form the Andes. Volcanos sprouted like weeds, and the mountains began to arise. Instead of life-sustaining water, the westerly winds brought lethal volcanic ash to the area. Some forests were literally buried in the ash, and those that survived the ash succumbed for lack of water, for the winds now had to rise above a mountain range, where they dropped their moisture. By the time they reached the plain, they had become the dessicating winds of present-day Patagonia.

For millions of years Patagonia dried out. All traces of the huge forests vanished. Although the region's new climate was dry, each summer brought a few thunderstorms to the steppes. Rainstorms were rare, but torrential. Slowly, the wind and rain together shaped the landscape, and began to release the ancient forests from their tombs of ash. But the trees uncovered by the winds were now made of stone.

Although petrified wood is a commonplace mineral, petrified forests—in which entire trees, some still standing, are fossilized—are relatively rare. Argentina has three; all are in Patagonia, and one is significant enough to merit protection as a natural monument.

These forests lie in moonscapes of eroded cliffs, gullies, cones, and the fields of cobbles and gravel that cover so much of Patagonia. A tremendous variety of colors are imparted to the landscape by eroded strata: red, orange, black, pink, buff, white, moss green. Scattered over this polychrome terrain is petrified wood, from giant stumps and huge logs to piles of tiny wood-like chips of stone that tinkle like wind chimes at the touch of a visitor's foot.

Time a visit to a fossil forest at dawn or late evening, for the sky plays an important role in the scenic character of these forests. Patagonia is noted for its skyscapes—day and night—and they lend a unique quality to what would otherwise be somber desert landscapes. Sunrises and sunsets tend to the spectacular, and even daytime formations of puffy cumulus clouds, classic thunderheads, sheets of rain, lightning, and rainbows are dramatic. At night these pollution-free skies lend a strobe-like intensity to starlight.

Most of the trees are araucarias, not quite the same as trees that now grow in the Andes, but their ancestors, proaraucarias (*Proaraucarites mirabilis*). Some trees in these stone forests are huge; many trunks exceed 6 feet in diameter and 90 feet in length. Not only logs, which are usually hollow, but stumps, roots, branches, and occasionally cones have been petrified. The remarkably wood-like appearance of the stone is enhanced by living lichens that eke out a precarious existence on its surface. Cellular structure is readily discernible, and bark and cambium layers easily distinguished from heartwood. Some of the wood has the buff, chalky appearance of ordinary petrified wood, but other portions have been silicified or agatized into richly colored, translucent stone.

The stone is beautiful, and, until recently, visitors from the world over carted off as much petrified wood as they could carry. Large logs were frequently loaded onto ships bound for foreign ports at the nearby port of Comodoro Rivadavia. Recognizing that the forests were being hauled away faster than they were being uncovered, government authorities finally took steps to protect them. The most extensive petrified forest, in north-central Santa Cruz Province, was set aside by the federal government in 1954: Monumento Natural Bosques Petrificados (Petrified Forests Natural Monument). Two smaller forests were set aside by the government of Chubut Province as geologic reserves in 1971: Bosque Petrificado José Ormachéa and Bosque Petrificado Victor Szlapelis.

The Monumento Natural is the largest of the three preserves, 25,000 acres, but is also the most difficult to reach. It lies 27 miles (43 kilometers) east of the main highway through Patagonia, Argentine Ruta 3. The turnoff to the monument is 53 miles (85 kilometers) south of the village of Fitzroy. The nearest coastal towns are Puerto Deseado (150 miles; 241 kilometers) and the much larger oil town, Comodoro Rivadavia (170 miles; 274 kilometers), both served by public transportation. Inquire in the tourist office in Comodoro Rivadavia about arranging transportation.

The Monumento Natural is almost literally in the middle of nowhere, on a plain composed largely of basalt and small basaltic mesas left over from ancient lava flows. The wind is incessant, and gusts have been clocked at 90 miles per hour. Dust devils

Some petrified araucaria trees in Argentina's Bosques Petrificados exceed 6 feet in diameter and 90 feet in length.

swirl over the plains; occasionally several are in view at once. Lenticular mirages shimmer on the horizon. More than 200 petrified tree trunks are scattered over 40 square miles.

The provincial reserves are not as large as the Monumento Natural, but are much easier to reach. Both lie south of Sarmiento, a small farming community notable for long lines of Lombardy poplars that divide the fields and orchards around the town, a sharp contrast to the surrounding desert. The Ormachéa Reserva lies 31 miles (50 kilometers) from Sarmiento off Argentine Ruta 26, and the Szlapelis Reserva lies 18 miles (30 kilometers) further down the same road. In summer, bus tours frequently go to the reserves from Sarmiento, and taxis are affordable for small groups. Ask for information in the hotels. Hitchhiking is also possible (summer only).

At all of the reserves, rangers take groups on short loop trips, but you will see better examples of petrified wood, other fossils, and even artifacts if you are willing to hike farther than most visitors. In order to prevent pilfering, unescorted hikes are not permitted, but most rangers are more than willing to take longer hikes than usual to show you special sites off the regular tourist loops. Ask the rangers at the Ormachéa Reserva to show you the location of the fossil leaves.

Sarmiento has plenty of accommodations for visitors, although in summer hotels may fill up early in the day. Overnight camping is permitted in the forests only in the immediate vicinity of ranger stations. Do not attempt to camp elsewhere for the sake of solitude, for you may be suspected of planning to carry off souvenirs. Potable water and restrooms are available. Snacks and cold drinks are available at the Ormachéa Reserva.

An afternoon at the reserves or a full day at the Monumento Natural is sufficient to see most of what is there. Wear clothing appropriate for steady sun and steady wind. To put what you are seeing into some sort of perspective, remember that these petrified logs are older than the Andes themselves.

CUEVA DE LOS MANOS (CAVE OF THE HANDS). During the winter of 1520, Ferdinand Magellan and his crew camped at the present site of San Julian in Santa Cruz Province. One morning they were surprised and alarmed by the discovery of enormous footprints not far from camp. They decamped without incident, but the discovery was later described to a mapmaker in Spain, who named the land on which they had camped Tierra de los Patagones (Land of the Bigfeet). We now know that the early inhabitants of Patagonia wore clothes fashioned from guanaco skins, and their huge furry moccasins probably accounted for the footprints, but little else is known about the people for whom Patagonia was named. We know that these Indians, most commonly called Tehuelches, were a tall race, good tool-makers who lived on guanacos, rheas, armadillos, geese, wild fruits, and berries. They were occasionally hostile to early white explorers and settlers, but quickly fell prey to liquor and diseases brought to Patagonia by these invaders, and are today virtually extinct.

But the Tehuelches were also artists, and some of their handiwork has survived. Although evidence of early habitation has been found throughout Patagonia, most discoveries were made in the foothills of the Andes. Artifacts from excavations in Neuquén Province, near Lanín and Nahuel Huapi national parks, have been dated to between 8000 B.C. and 9000 B.C. Later, about 1000 B.C., a form of primitive artistry developed among the Tehuelches, and they began to paint figures in caves and other protected areas. Cave paintings are relatively abundant in the precordillera; however, among the finest are those found in the Cueva de las Manos (Cave of the Hands), not far from the town of Perito Moreno.

Like Perito Moreno and Los Glaciares national parks, the caves are in a remote corner of a remote region, but travelers who made it this far can easily get to the caves. The best place to seek transportation is the nearest town, Perito Moreno. Check at hotels or the tourist office in town for taxis that will take visitors to the caves. Seek to split the fare among a group. It may be possible to hitchhike, but *only* during summer, for traffic is practically nonexistent in winter. Bring a swimsuit.

Thirty-five miles (56 kilometers) south of Perito Moreno (the town, not the park) on Argentine Ruta 40, a side road turns east. Four miles (6 kilometers) down this side road lies an *estancia* at which you should ask permission to travel to the caves (permission will be granted; it is a matter of courtesy to the landowner). At the *estancia*, you will find the first of three gates you must pass through to reach the caves. Leave the gates as you find them, open or closed.

Early Patagonian artists left these eerie outlines of hands at sacred sites throughout Patagonia. Cueva de las Manos, Argentina

The rock formations along the access road are brilliantly colored; nearly every color of the rainbow is represented among the outcrops and eroded strata, a refreshing contrast to the drab countryside south of Perito Moreno. About 17 miles (27 kilometers) from Ruta 40 is a parking area at the edge of a 1500-foot-deep canyon. Descend two sets of cliffs and cross the canyon to reach the caves, which lie on the opposite side. Trails are not well marked, but to find the trail from the parking area, face the canyon, and walk left for about 50 feet to a trail that descends a steep gulch that cuts through the first set of cliffs. Once through the gulch, the trail cuts diagonally across the side of the canyon, and leads to the river. A shorter trail, steeper but safe, leads through a second gulch, at the head of which a 10-foot-tall white pole is buried. Wade the river—it is calf-deep in the summer, but has a few deep pools for a refreshing dip.

The trails that lead up the other side of the canyon to the caves are easy to find.

Two principal sites lie at the bottom of 500-foot cliffs of red sandstone: one is a shallow cave; the other, 100 yards north, is a shelter beneath a long overhang. These two sites contain the largest number of drawings, and both should be explored.

An unmistakably surreal quality pervades the artwork that greets the eye at the top of the trail. Hands, hands everywhere, fingers spread, some superimposed on others, in colors surprisingly bright considering their age and the natural substances from which the dyes were manufactured. Hands of red (dark, rusty, brick red), black, white, and rich yellow; white hands against a painted red background, yellow hands framed against brown or red backgrounds.

At several sites in Patagonia are figures of hands obviously fashioned by an artist who flattened his palm, fingers spread, against a stone surface, then blew dye through a hollow reed around his hand, creating in effect a silhouette of his own hand. Hands of this type exist at the Cueva de las Manos, but here also are hands that are painted in, rather than outlined.

In addition, there are figures of guanacos, lizards, spiders, fish, and stylized symbols such as zig zags, circles, hands reaching for objects like oxen yokes, and so on. The aesthetic quality of the artwork is as much a result of the juxtaposition of groups of figures as of the figures themselves and their colors.

Unfortunately, a few paintings have been defaced and several modern vandals have added their names and signatures to the walls, but most of the work is intact.

Depending upon which trail you take, allow from 45 to 90 minutes to reach the caves from the parking area, 1 to 2 hours to contemplate the paintings, an hour for a dip in the river (highly recommended), and another 45 to 90 minutes to return to the car. Try to arrive in early morning, when the colors of the canyon and surrounding hills will be highlighted. Visitors should try to reach the caves by midday, when the light will be good for viewing the paintings.

Take something to ward off the sun, good footwear for the trails, and long pants to protect against the many spiny shrubs, nettles, and thistles.

It is sad indeed that we know so little about the Tehuelches, and the art that survived them. No one who sees these paintings and roams about the region, however, will doubt that the Tehuelches knew something about magic, for enchantment pervades this silent, remote canyon.

Glossary

bosque	forest
fósil	fossil
hoja	leaf
madera	wood
petrificado	petrified
raíz	root
tronco	trunk

🔲 PERITO MORENO:
Park of the Founder

The character of Patagonia changes quickly as the traveler journeys southward from Esquel. Paved highways give way to dusty roads, distances between towns grow immense, and the towns acquire a roughshod, frontier appearance. Signs of human habitation diminish, and the traveler finds himself in the eerie, empty landscapes we usually associate with Patagonia.

This wild country is the setting for Parque Nacional Perito Moreno. The park has several features in common with the Andean parks hundreds of miles to the north: it lies alongside the spine of the Andes, encompasses a network of large lakes, and bears unmistakable signs of glacial origin. But there the resemblance ends. No elegant hotels, no glistening launches, no buses of gawking tourists greet the eye. A vast silence pervades this park, broken only by the wind and occasional cries of birds. A single weathered sign beside a dusty road informs the traveler that he has finally reached one of Argentina's most remote and unspoiled national parks.

Francisco P. Moreno was an Argentine naturalist and geographer fascinated by the astonishing scenery characteristic of the Patagonian Andes. A tireless traveler, he explored these mountainous regions in the late 1800s, naming such well-known Patagonian features as Lago Argentino, Lago San Martín, and Cerro Fitzroy. Moreno was wisely selected as the Argentine expert or "ace" (*perito*) on the team determining the demarcation of the border with Chile, and in return for his services was rewarded with grants of lands in the regions he explored. In 1903, he donated a portion of his lands to the republic, lands which formed the nucleus of what eventually became Parque Nacional Nahuel Huapi. Perito Moreno worked throughout his life on behalf of national parks, and is today honored as the founder of the Argentine national park system. His namesake park is an appropriate memorial, for it is the most pristine of the Andean parks, and has changed little in the century that has passed since he explored these wild landscapes.

The park is shaped like an immense amphitheater ringed with snowcapped mountains. In the "amphitheater" lie the park's most striking features, a series of eight large

interconnected lakes and dozens of small, colorful, kettle-like ponds. The park actually straddles South America's continental divide, for the waters of seven of the lakes drain into the Pacific Ocean, and the eighth drains into the Atlantic. Intrepid travelers can hike along the streams *downhill* through the Andes into Chile, and on to the Pacific Ocean. Such a hike would be a fine adventure, but more of an expedition than a simple backpack trip, for the point at which the waters finally reach the sea is itself the uninhabited heart of one of the most desolate regions of southern Chile.

Cerro San Lorenzo, at 12,160 feet the highest peak in Patagonia, lies just outside the park, but dominates the northern horizon. In the northeast corner of the park are the peaks of the Sierra Colorada (Colored Range), an array of mountains streaked with red, purple, buff, and gray strata of limestone and sandstone. South of San Lorenzo is Cerro Pirámide (Pyramid Peak, 7,218 feet), and west of Lago Mogote lie the triple peaks of Los Tres Hermanos (The Three Brothers). Cerro Arido (Dry Peak, 6,414 feet) is literally surrounded by lakes: to the northeast, Lago Volcán; to the northwest, Lago Península; to the west, Lago Mogote; to the south, Lago Escondido (Hidden Lake); and to the southeast and east, the largest of the lakes, Lago Belgrano. Cerro Miel (Honey Peak), also 6,414 feet, lies between Belgrano and Lago Burmeister.

The relatively high elevation of the park lends observers the impression that they are above timberline, for most of the lakes are surrounded by low, krummholz-like trees and shrubs. Only the somewhat lower watersheds of Nansen and Azara lakes support extensive groves of lengas, the high beech, and smaller numbers of coihue, the evergreen beech.

Because of the high elevation of these mountains at this southerly latitude, they are permanently capped with snow and ice. The combination of perpetual erosion of multicolored strata and the differing sizes and depths of the lakes has given the lakes the colors of the rainbow. These vary somewhat with the season, but are usually as follows: lakes Mogote, Península, and Volcán range from nearly white to pearly gray, Belgrano is turquoise, Azara is lime green, Escondido sky blue, Nansen turquoise blue, and Burmeister from slate gray to green. Even the small ponds scattered across the park share this paint-pot attribute, ranging from milky white to acid green, and occasionally tomato red. A brilliant sight indeed is a flock of pink flamingos strutting slowly through the shallows of a pea-green pond.

Streams here are typical high-energy glacial waters—milky, braided, and ice cold. The seven lakes on the western side of the continental divide are connected in such fashion as to create a ring of lakes, beginning with Lago Mogote and ending with Y-shaped Lago Nansen, from which the Río Cabrera begins its winding way toward the Chilean border and, finally, the Pacific Ocean. Lago Burmeister is the only lake that drains to the Atlantic, by way of Río Chico.

The waters of Perito Moreno are considered priceless by Argentine environmentalists because they are pristine in the biological sense. In the decades prior to World War II, several species of trout and salmon from Europe and North America were introduced to rivers and lakes throughout temperate Argentina. The trout flourished, making their way into virtually every suitable watershed on the eastern side of the Andes, and today provide outstanding sportfishing in almost every Andean park in Argentina. Unfortunately, the native fish, which could not successfully compete with the more efficient and aggressive trout, have nearly become extinct. In the prewar rush to introduce trout to Argentine waters, however, the watersheds of Perito Moreno were somehow overlooked, and the trout have not been able to reach the park by their own means. As a result, the principal fish native to these waters, the peladilla (*Haplochiton taenitus*), has survived.

Surprisingly, the peladilla strongly resembles trout in shape and habits; it even has the characteristic well-developed adipose fin. Silvery to coffee-brown in color, it seldom exceeds 10 inches in length, a likely reason for its inability to compete with the trout, which grow massive in Patagonian waters. It spawns in midwinter, a curious adaptation, and is also found in Australia and New Zealand, further evidence that these three land masses were once joined. Although scorned by fishermen, the

Lago Belgrano, largest of the lakes of Perito Moreno National Park, Argentina

peladilla will take a fly. It is best left undisturbed, though, for it is a living relic, much admired by biologists who consider it to be an innocent victim of unwitting ecological mismanagement.

In general, wildlife is not abundant here, probably because of the austere climate. Still, guanacos are common along the road to the park and on the enormous peninsula that juts into Lago Belgrano. European hares and armadillos are among the most commonly sighted animals. Park literature indicates that the huemul (*Hippocamelus bisulcus*), the medium-sized deer of the southern Andes, is common in the park, but local ranchers insist that none have been seen in over thirty years.

Most of the birds common in Patagonia will be seen in Perito Moreno: buff-necked ibis, southern lapwings, sheldgeese, flamingos, condors, and rheas.

The two best ways to experience Perito Moreno are to stop by local *estancias* for information and to climb some mountains.

Because the park receives few visitors, the Argentine Park Service does not maintain a staff of rangers. Visitors are not thrown completely upon their own resources, however, for the managers and staff of four sheep *estancias* along the eastern margins of the park are hospitable, proud of the park, have excellent maps, and gladly orient visitors to its most notable features. The *estancias* are La Rincón, La Oriental, Lago Belgrano, and Río Roble.

From Estancia La Oriental, try climbing Cerro León. An easy, 2-hour climb gives visitors spectacular views of the northern end of the park and its technicolor lakes and ponds. The fossil-loaded Sierra Colorada are visible from Cerro León. Dress for strong, cold winds.

To hike into the interior of the park, go to Estancia La Rincón, and ask about the condition of the wooden footbridge that crosses the long west arm of Lago Belgrano.

At Estancia Lago Belgrano, ask for directions to Lago Burmeister (you will pass a road that leads to the lake about 3 miles (5 kilometers) *before* you reach the *estancia*, but it would be wise to inquire about the condition of the road). South of the *estancia*, along the north shore of the southeast arm of Lago Belgrano, are small dry *arroyos* that contain small weathered rocks, some of which enclose snail-like fossil ammonites.

A comfortable campsite lies in a grove of lengas at the eastern end of Lago Burmeister, 10 miles (16 kilometers) from the road to Estancia Lago Belgrano. A climb up Cerro Miel, on the north side of Lago Burmeister, is recommended for broad vistas of the central portion of the park. A trail on the south side of Lago Burmeister leads to Lago Nansen—about a 10-hour hike.

A few miles northeast of Lago Burmeister, the road parallels shallow Río Roble. Across the river to the south lies a low, reddish hill—almost a rounded outcrop—that merges with the flat steppes. In the northern face of this hill, a series of caves and deep recesses are visible. Park across the river from this hill and wade over, for there is much to see. Many of the caves and recesses contain pictographs, including sharply detailed drawings of red-and-white guanacos, stylized zigzags and concentric circles, and eerie outlines of hands. Along the hillside and the shore of Lago Burmeister, keep an eye out for spots at which shiny black chips of obsidian are strewn about on the ground. These mark *picaderos*, Indian tool-making sites at which you may find parts of arrowheads, spear points, scrapers, awls, and other tools.

Fossils can be found in almost any part of the park. While they are not as common as spring flowers in a meadow, any persistent fossil hunter will find a variety of them in a day's hike. Among the more interesting fossils are ammonites, small octopus-like creatures that lived in snail-like shells during the Cretaceous Period, when dinosaurs ruled the earth. When the dinosaurs vanished sixty-five million years ago, so did the ammonites. Their polished black fossilized shells, up to a foot in diameter, can still be found in certain places, and this park is one of those places. Crinoids, tubular coral-like creatures that fossilize in the form of dark cylinders up to an inch in diameter; imprints of leaves; petrified wood, including whole tree trunks; and corals and bivalves are also in the area.

Indians and early settlers of Patagonia hunted rheas and guanacos with a sling-like weapon called a *boleador*, made of three leather thongs, each with a round stone about the size of a handball tied at one end, and tied together at the other ends. The device was whirled overhead and then flung at the legs of a fleeing animal. If thrown correctly, the thongs wrapped themselves about the legs, and brought the animal down. The stones, called *bolas*, usually had a groove cut around them into which the thong was fitted. They were sometimes lost, however, and in addition to primitive tools, sharp-eyed hikers may come across *bolas*. Be advised that zillions of handball-sized round rocks are scattered about in Perito Moreno, but only a few of them have the characteristic groove of a bola.

Note: By all means look for fossils and artifacts, for they are one of the great treasures of this park, but please leave them behind for other curious wanderers.

Reminders of the past found in Perito Moreno National Park: on the left, a bola, a round, grooved rock once part of a weapon used by early inhabitants to bring down rheas and guanacos; on the right, a fossil ammonite, several hundred million years old.

Visitor Facilities

There are virtually none. You must camp (and provide your own provisions), but you can camp anywhere. In this park, the lack of facilities seems more appropriate than unfortunate. It is difficult to get to this park and difficult to see once you've arrived, but this very difficulty accounts for the pristine character of the park, and transforms a visit into an adventure.

Recreation

Perito Moreno is a park for leisurely hikes, fossil and artifact hunting, and scrambling up mountainsides for views from the top.

Climate and Weather

The best time to visit Perito Moreno is from December to March, and indeed, it is likely to be inaccessible at other times of the year. Perito Moreno has a more rigorous climate than any other park of the southern Andes. Summer temperatures rarely exceed 55 degrees Fahrenheit, and winter temperatures often dip to well below zero. Snow can fall on mountaintops at any time of year.

Cold westerly winds blow almost all day, all night, all year, and have been clocked at over 65 miles per hour. Lengas are dramatically wind-sculpted at exposed sites, especially at the east ends of the lakes. Little rain falls in summer, but enough snow falls in winter to close many of the roads. *Caution:* Summer rainstorms can render some roads temporarily impassable because of mud or deep fords.

Location and Access

Perito Moreno lies against the Chilean border in a remote corner of Argentina, more than 100 miles (160 kilometers) from the nearest small town, and even farther from the nearest railroad station or airfield. No scheduled public transportation reaches the park. As a result, only a handful of resourceful visitors see the park each year.

The nearest town is Gobernador Gregores, 130 miles (209 kilometers) east of the park. Calafate, a town accustomed to providing tourist services, lies 300 miles (483 kilometers) south, and the nearest coast town, Puerto San Julián, is 260 miles (418 kilometers) east. A weekly bus from San Julián passes through Gobernador Gregores to reach Hotel Las Orquetas, the nearest public accommodation to the park, but even Las Orquetas lies 56 miles (90 kilometers) from the park, and no public transportation will get you any closer. It *might* be possible to hire transport to and from the park at the hotel, but such transportation is not guaranteed.

The most certain way to reach the park is to rent a car or, if you can round up a large enough group and arrange logistics, split the cost of a taxi. The town (not park) of Perito Moreno (population 2,000) is situated 200 miles (322 kilometers) north of the park, and is served by LADE airlines from Comodoro Rivadavia. Check at the tourist office for information on renting a car or car with driver in order to visit the park.

Glossary

picadero	Indian tool-making site
viento	wind

LOS GLACIARES:
Glaciers and Tetons

At the southern latitude equivalent to that of Vancouver, B.C., Paris, and Munich, a vast sheet of ice covers much of the Andes. Over 200 miles long and from 25 to 40 miles wide, the ice covers 5,500 square miles of mountainous terrain, an area the size of Connecticut. No fewer than forty-seven major glaciers flow from this massive ice field. Most flow toward the Pacific, but thirteen flow eastward into Patagonia. The part of Argentina into which these glaciers descend is remote, nearly at the tip of the continent, but those who make the trip are well rewarded, for it is one of the great glacial regions of the world, and since 1937 has been a national park—Parque Nacional Los Glaciares.

Los Glaciares means "Glaciers," and the park's three major natural features are majestic mountains, immense lakes, and, of course, the glaciers themselves.

Two thirds the size of Yellowstone, Los Glaciares (2,300 square miles), can be conveniently divided into two distinct parts: north and south. The attributes of the northern part of the park are mountains, particularly Cerro (Mount) Fitzroy and adjacent peaks. This part of the park is better suited for hikers and climbers; accommodations are more rustic, fewer are available, and the area is somewhat more difficult to reach.

The principal attractions of the southern half are glaciers and lakes, though its mountains are not insignificant. The south is particularly well suited for sightseeing, for access is easy from the nearby town of Calafate, and boat tours into remote sections of the park are available.

LOS GLACIARES NORTH: ALPINIST'S LODESTONE.

LOS GLACIARES NORTH: ALPINIST'S LODESTONE. Enormous Lago Viedma and its stunning backdrop, the Cerro Fitzroy chain of peaks, dominate the northern half of the park.

Lago Viedma is so large that it lies within several biotic regimes. Nearly 50 miles long and about 10 miles wide, the lake covers over 400 square miles of Patagonia. The eastern portion of the lake lies in arid Patagonian steppes. Along the dusty road that leads toward the Fitzroy area, visitors are likely to see wildlife more characteristic of steppes than mountains: guanacos, rheas, armadillos, and rabbits. Before long, however, Cerro Fitzroy looms into view, and Viedma Glacier, which spills into the eastern end of the lake, appears. The road passes through an abrupt transition zone between plains and mountains, and on crossing the Río de las Vueltas (Twisting River) the visitor has unmistakably crossed back into the mountains and their beech forests.

The scenic quality of the Fitzroy complex of peaks is matched perhaps only by Wyoming's Grand Tetons. Like the Tetons, these peaks are suddenly and sharply thrust up from flatlands lacking significant foothills. Broad pink streaks are visible in the expanse of gray granite that makes up the peaks, and the immediate visual impact is stunning. Also like the Tetons, a flat plain stretches eastward from them, so that they are struck directly by the first rays of morning sun that breach the horizon, and they are high enough to be backlit by the setting sun. As a result, the peaks undergo kaleidoscopic variations of alpenglow from dawn to dusk. An entire day can be well spent at a single vantage point, watching the peaks cycle through these vivid transformations.

The highest and most imposing peak is Cerro Fitzroy (11,073 feet). Neither Fitzroy nor its neighbors are lofty in Himalayan terms, but because Lago Viedma is only 800 feet above sea level, Fitzroy leaps nearly 2 miles into the sky in, so to speak, a single bound.

In part because several climbers have died attempting to climb Fitzroy and associated peaks, the region has a compelling mystique, especially for Argentine climbers, though the peaks are considered special by climbers of all nations. The first ascent of Fitzroy was achieved in 1953 by a French team, the second in 1965 by an Argentine team. Since then, Fitzroy has been climbed several times by teams from the world over. The names assigned to various routes of ascent attest to its international reputation: French, Argentine, Californian, British, Italian, and so on.

Of nearly equal interest to the world's climbers are several neighboring peaks (*torres* and *agujas*; i.e., towers and needles), which, while not as high as Fitzroy, are striking, and appear to be impossible to climb.

Above: *The dominant landform in Lanin National Park is brooding Lanin Volcano, and the dominant tree on its flanks, a striking living fossil, the monkey-puzzle tree, pehuén or araucaria.* **Right:** *These views of the laguna and the* Torres del Catedral *(Cathedral Towers) await those who hike to Frey Refuge in the mountains behind Bariloche.*

Above: *Glacier-tinted Lago Cisnes is near the sanctum of South America's largest trees, Los Alerces National Park, Argentina.* **Left:** *Early artists left eerie outlines of hands at sacred Patagonian sites, Cueva de las Manos, Argentina.* **Opposite, upper left:** *The author walks among penguins at Punta Tombo, Argentina.* **Upper right:** *The most common Patagonian sheldgeese are ashy-headed geese (Chloephaga poliocephala), cauquén or kaikén.* **Bottom:** *Contests between sea elephant bulls involve elaborate posturing and loud bellowing. These bulls on the beach at Peninsula Valdés are likely in a dispute over females that surround them.*

Above: *A portion of the 3-mile face of Perito Moreno Glacier; in spring, the abundant notro bushes are in brilliant bloom, Los Glaciares National Park, Argentina.* **Left:** *A flying banana, the giant toucan (Ramphastos toco) is common in Iguazú National Park, Brazil.* **Opposite:** *The Cristo Redentor, on Corcovado.*

Left: Few places in South America offer as good an opportunity to penetrate the steamy gloom of a tropical rainforest as Iguazú National Park, Brazil. **Below:** On sunny days, rainbows arch over the cataracts of Iguazú Falls. **Opposite, top:** The blue and yellow macaw (Ara araurana), one of the common macaws of Amazonia National Park, Brazil. **Center:** Giant anteaters (Myrmecophaga tridactyla) and piggy-back young are common in Das Emas National Park. **Bottom:** Brick-red cupinzeiros (termite nests) dot the campos limpos (grasslands) of Das Emas National Park, Brazil.

Above: *Frescos in the church in Parinacota, the tiny Aymara village in Lauca National Park, were executed in 1699.* **Left:** *Spring in the desert surrounding Fray Jorge National Park, Chile*

The most dramatic of these is Cerro Torre, a slender needle of granite usually topped by a treacherous cap of ice known to climbers as the "mushroom." Cerro Torre has claimed several lives, and has been climbed only a few times. Controversy swirls about the first ascents, made in 1959 and 1971 with the aid of mechanically drilled holds and anchors, and some alpinists consider the first ascent to be the one made in 1974, without these aids. Immediately north of Cerro Torre lies Torre Egger, named for an Austrian climber killed during a descent in 1959. North of Torre Egger lies Aguja Standhardt, named for a local rancher. Two other peaks in the Fitzroy chain are named for climbers and adventurers: Cerro St. Exupery, in honor of the French pilot and writer, and Aguja Poincenot, named after a French climber who drowned in the Río Fitzroy.

Because of the popularity of these peaks among climbers, the human aspect of a visit to this part of the park is interesting, even fascinating. At any time, climbers from Germany, Austria, France, South Africa, Argentina, Italy, the U.S., or elsewhere may be camped near the ranger station—affable, cheerful sorts constantly shouting and hurrying to and fro, comparing equipment, climbing stories, and know-how.

One need not be a climber to enjoy this part of the park, however. The relatively open terrain is admirable for both day hikes and overnight backpacks, and trails are better developed than in many other parks. Especially good for views of the main peak is the trail to Base Camp Fitzroy. The trail starts up the west side of the Río de las Vueltas and proceeds up the drainage of the Río Blanco. Atop the broad ridge south of the Río Blanco, several small lakes, including Lago Caprí, provide campsites at which visitors are likely to be absolutely undisturbed, and from which it may be possible—with a spotting scope—to watch the progress of climbing teams on the Torre chain of peaks.

Visitors must register climbing plans and obtain permission from the *intendencia* in Calafate or the ranger station at Río de las Vueltas well prior to undertaking technical ascents within the park.

LOS GLACIARES SOUTH: ICEBERGS IN THE ANDES. By South American standards, Viedma is a giant lake, but Lago Argentino, covering 600 square miles, is larger yet: four times the size of Lago Nahuel Huapi. Unlike Lago Viedma, which is more or less oblong, Lago Argentino has at its western end a series of iceberg-strewn arms (*brazos*) that penetrate deeply into the Andes and provide access by water to the glaciers that lie in deep recesses of the mountains. The lake was not discovered by Europeans until 1873, and was given its name four years later by that indefatigible explorer of Patagonia, Francisco P. Moreno. Because of the number of glaciers that either directly enter Lago Argentino or discharge runoff streams into the lake, rock flour renders the lake chalky green to turquoise, depending on location and the quality of sunlight. The lake was formed by successive advances and retreats of a single gigantic glacier that extended 60 miles farther east than the present easternmost shore of the lake.

Upsala is the largest glacier in the park. Formed by several secondary glaciers, Upsala is 30 miles long, and enters the northern arm (*Brazo Norte*) of Lago Argentino. The northern arm is also called Boca del Diablo (Devil's Mouth) because of its stark scenery and the fierce winds that quickly kick up combers in the channel. Because it is so large and its ice so old, Upsala discharges the biggest and bluest icebergs into the lake. Upsala Glacier is remote, but may be reached and viewed by means of an 8-hour launch trip from Punta Bandera, also the point of departure for other launch trips on the lake. Visitors who wish to spend more time exploring this area afoot may arrange to be dropped off at a refuge near the mouth of Bahía Onelli, (Onelli Bay), or at a campground near the head of the bay, from which a 1-mile (1.6 kilometers) trail af-

The face of Perito Moreno Glacier, Los Glaciares National Park, Argentina

fording excellent views of Bolado and Onelli glaciers leads to Canal Onelli, into which spills steep Glacier Agassiz.

Several other glaciers enter various western arms of Lago Argentino, but, with one notable exception, most are difficult to reach except by launch.

The exception is Glacier Moreno, the best known in the park and one of the more interesting glaciers in the world. In this epoch, only a few of the world's glaciers are advancing, and Moreno is one of them; it is the only glacier in the park not in regression. Further, it is one of the most accessible glaciers of its size. With caution, it is possible to walk to its looming face and chip a few cubes of ice several hundred years old into your beverage. Finally, every few years Moreno faithfully brings about a cataclysm that endangers no one, yet is one of the great recurring natural spectacles of South America.

Fed by several subsidiary glaciers, Moreno grinds its way 22 miles eastward down the Cordillera, directly toward an arm of Lago Argentino known as Canal de los Témpanos (Iceberg Channel). By the time the glacier reaches the lake, it is nearly 3 miles wide, and the top of its face nearly 200 feet above the water. Across the lake another mountain, Cerro Buenos Aires, forms Península Magellanes. In about 1944, the irresistible force met the immovable object, and Glacier Moreno crossed the lake, and slowly crashed into and up the side of Cerro Buenos Aires, mowing down several hundred acres of beech forest in the process.

The glacier had now cut off two more long arms of Lago Argentino—Brazo Rico and Brazo Sur. Water continued to flow into these arms from several sources, however, until the water level in these amputated arms was about 100 feet higher than in the rest of the lake, just on the other side of the glacier dam. In 1947, the water forced its way through cracks in the glacier where it butted up against the peninsula, and formed a tunnel through the ice. Finally, in classic *Gotterdammerung* fashion, with the air full of ear-splitting cracks and the thunder of enormous icebergs breaking away and plunging into the roaring water, the tunnel collapsed in a matter of minutes. For several hours, the excess water in the southern arms thundered through this new channel until the water levels equalized, and calm once again returned to Lago Argentino.

Glacier Moreno, however, continued its inexorable advance.

The channel was soon squeezed shut, and the cycle began anew. Since 1947, the collapse of the tunnel that brings about the reunion of Lago Argentino with its arms has repeated itself with increasing regularity, lowering the level of the dammed-up *brazos* from 60 to 120 feet. In recent years, the event has recurred every third austral summer. The most recent collapse was on February 18, 1988. Try to be there for the next one.

Even during off years, Glacier Moreno is well worth a visit. It is easy to reach, for a good road leads directly to the face of the glacier. Visitors are not likely to have many other opportunities to stare, from a few feet away, at the face of a glacier advancing over the terrain on which they stand. The forest being bulldozed by the glacier is relatively lush, and fuchsias are as common in the understory as weeds. The contrast of this foliage with the stark blue-white ice of Moreno's face against a backdrop of turquoise lakes and black-and-white mountain peaks is a sight not soon forgotten.

Note: *Be very cautious* when approaching the glacier. Though many tourists customarily ignore them, it is wise to respect the signs that warn against approaching the glacier. Several deaths and injuries have been caused by ice falling from the face of Glacier Moreno.

The southernmost portion of the park is visited but rarely, making it a fine place for those who seek solitude, inspiring views of the mountains and glaciers, or fresh trout for supper. An excellent place to accomplish all three objectives is the campground that lies in a grove of lengas on the southern shore of Lago Roca, 34 miles (55 kilometers) southwest of Calafata on Argentine Ruta 0. The distance between the campground and the edge of Lago Roca depends upon how recently the Moreno Tunnel has collapsed. When the water is high, the lake looks normal in every respect and is continuous with Brazo Rico and Brazo Sur, but when the level is low the lake resembles the dewatered reservoirs of hydroelectric projects, and is ringed with broad flats of mud or gravel. Low water does not inhibit the quality of fishing in the lake, and may even enhance it. In spring and summer, birdlife is extensive along the lake. Look for sheldgeese, teros, and caracaras in the extensive grassy flats, for austral parakeets and Magellanic woodpeckers in the woods, for torrent ducks in the streams, and black eagles and condors overhead.

The buff-necked ibis (*Theristicus caudatas*), called bandurria, nests along the margins of the lake. Because of its size, appearance, and raucous calls, the bandurria is one of the most common and conspicuous birds of southern Patagonia. Found from the savannas of Venezuela, Colombia, and Brazil to the *puna* of Ecuador, Peru, and Bolivia, it is seen in greatest numbers in spring and summer in and around the marshes of Patagonia. Adults stand nearly 3 feet high, have a gray-to-black body, males have white wing coverts, and both sexes have the distinctive rufous-orange head and neck that gives them their name. Look also for their long, black decurved bills. Bandurrias travel in flocks, and their metallic honking is one of those unforgettable sounds that forever invokes memories of a certain region.

The road continues for 6 miles (10 kilometers) past the campground, to end on the shore of Brazo Sur. A trail continues from this point along the east shore of the arm that leads to Lago Frías and continues along the west shore of the arm to a refuge across Brazo Sur from Lago Roca. This trail crosses several small streams, and footbridges may be in disrepair, so check on the condition of the trail and the refuge at the *intendencia* in Calafate before proceeding.

Visitor Facilities

The center of activities near the park is Calafate, a small community on the south shore of Lago Argentino, and one of the few true towns in inland Patagonia. The town is named for a large shrub abundant near town, on the shores of the lake, and in many other parks on the Argentine side of the Andes. This spiny shrub bears fragrant yellow flowers that in fall transform into sweet, rather seedy berries. We call the calafate the box-leafed barberry (*Berberis heterophylla*), and its importance to visitors is not so much its beauty (the red-flowered notro and Magellanic fuchsia are far more attractive) as its power. Tradition holds that whoever eats the berries of the calafate is fated to return to Patagonia. Try some, but be advised that the berries temporarily stain lips and mouth a rather deep blue.

Calafate has several small hotels, a campground with hot showers, grocery stores, and several travel agencies that can arrange tours to all parts of the park. Obtain maps and information at the *intendencia* (corner of Libertador Avenue and Calle Bustillo) or at the small tourist office in town. Ask for directions to the colorful Indian pictographs at Punta Gualicho on the shore of the lake, 5 miles (8 kilometers) northeast of town.

The southern part of the park, including Perito Moreno Glacier, lies west of Calafate on Ruta 1505. Punta Bandera, embarkation point for launch trips on Lago Argentino, is 30 miles (48 kilometers) from Calafate. Twelve miles (19 kilometers) west of town, on the way to Punta Banderas, look for a series of eroded stone formations south of the road that look remarkably like a herd of elephants. Watch also for the abundant shorebirds and waterfowl in the chain of small lakes near Punta Banderas.

There are two designated campgrounds on the road to the glacier, one 30 miles (48 kilometers) from town and a second 50 miles (80 kilometers) from town. The Automóvil Club Argentino (ACA) maintains a small hotel and restaurant near the glacier. You do not have to be a member to stay at the facility, but it is often full in summer. Another campground on the shore of Lago Roca is reached via Ruta 0.

Cerro Fitzroy and the western reaches of Lago Viedma in the northern portion of the park are 145 miles (233 kilometers) from Calafate. The nearest lodging to Fitzroy is the *hostería* Refugio Autocamping Lago Viedma, which has a small restaurant and grocery store. If you are not camping, be certain that accommodations are available before leaving Calafate. Pleasant lodging is also available at a hostel on the northern shore of the lake, which has a restaurant and provides guides and horseback rides.

Climate and Weather

Los Glaciares is a summer park. Although tourist season is considered to be from November to April, the best time to visit is from December to March. The average summer temperature is 60 degrees Fahrenheit, but evenings can be chilly. Sunny afternoons may be warm enough for shirtsleeves and the temperature can climb high enough (90 degrees) for skinny-dipping in the smaller remote lakes (Viedma and Argentino are ice-cold year-round). Weather, as usual in the Andes, is highly variable, so visitors must be prepared for anything. Annual rainfall varies from 15 to 35 inches, with the heaviest rain in the mountains. Most of the rain falls from March to May.

Location and Access

Los Glaciares lies in the southwest corner of Santa Cruz Province. Both of Argentina's commercial airlines make frequent flights to Río Gallegos, the nearest Patagonian coastal town; from Río Gallegos, visitors take a connecting flight on LADE airlines to Calafate.

The park lies 1,900 miles (3,060 kilometers) from Buenos Aires by road—a *long* bus ride. The 6-hour bus ride between Río Gallegos and Calafate is worthwhile for the animals you may see along the way (ñandús, guanacos, maras), but buses are usually crowded. It is possible to hitchhike (*viajar en dedo*) to the park from Río Gallegos (or other coastal towns), but hitchhikers *must* be prepared for long delays. Lucky souls can make it in a day; others have been stuck at crossroads for as long as five days.

Glossary

andinismo	climbing
andinista, escalador	climber
brazo	arm, including arm of a body of water
glaciar, ventisquero	glacier
montañeros	mountaineers
picada	trail
témpano	iceberg

A view across Beagle Canal from the slopes of Guanaco Peak, Tierra del Fuego National Park: the snowcapped peaks on the horizon are the Darwin Range, the body of water at right is Lago Roca.

𝗘 TIERRA DEL FUEGO:
The Uttermost Park

Look carefully at a map of South America, and you will note that the sharp east-ward hook the Andes make at the southern tip of South America is comprised mainly of a large, irregular island separated from the mainland by a twisting channel, the Strait of Magellan. The channel existed on maps drawn as early as 1428, but was finally named for the man credited by history with its discovery in 1520, Ferdinand Magellan. On observing numerous plumes of smoke on the island from fires now presumed to have been set by Indians signaling his arrival, Magellan named the island Tierra del Fuego—land of fire—and the name has stuck for nearly five centuries.

Remote, barren, nearly unpopulated, but in a strategic location of global significance, Tierra del Fuego captured the imagination of explorers, adventurers, missionaries, and settlers of every stripe early in its post-discovery history. Titles of various books written about the area give a clue to the nature of this wild region: *Windswept Land of the South; The Fatal Lodestone; The Blind Horn's Hate; Hope Deferred, Not Lost;*

Missionary Martyr; Uttermost Part of the Earth. In more recent years, Patagonia has attracted the attention of sheepmen, oil drillers, tourists, and workers and entrepreneurs seeking the high wages offered to those willing to endure its grim climate, but it still attracts a disproportionate share of adventurers, and a few of its most remote corners have still not been thoroughly explored. In this distant and fabled land lies the southernmost park on earth: Parque Nacional Tierra del Fuego.

Shared by Chile and Argentina, the island of Tierra del Fuego is a faithful extension of the mainland. Its western portion is mountainous—a continuation of the Andean Cordillera, glaciated but lower in elevation—while the eastern part is a continuation of the flat Patagonian steppes, treeless in the drier north, but becoming increasingly forested southward.

The park is remote because Tierra del Fuego is remote—about 2,250 road miles (1,500 air miles) from Buenos Aires, 6,500 miles from New York—and has some sections so isolated as to be nearly inaccessible. Yet the park itself can be reached easily by air, road, and occasionally by sea. Located in the extreme southwest section of Argentine Tierra del Fuego, the park's western border coincides with the border with Chile.

Western Tierra del Fuego bears a striking resemblance to the Alaska panhandle, which lies at the same northern latitude (about 55 degrees), and in many respects is its mirror image: weather—tempestuous, rainy, and foggy for most of the year—is appalling in both places, but has created dense, temperate rain forests that grow to the edge of the sea; the timberline is low; glaciers are common and evidence of Pleistocene glaciation commonplace; fjords are deep, long, and spectacular; streams and rivers flow year-round in every drainage; rugged mountains jut up several thousand feet directly from the sea; lichens, ferns, and mosses are common groundcover plants; sphagnum moss bogs develop in poorly drained lowlands; and the adjacent sea is rich in marine resources.

The resemblance carries over into the population: wages are high, as are prices of goods and services, and the residents (the islanders call themselves Fuegians) are exceptionally friendly, tend to be rugged individualists who scorn the easy life, and consider themselves pioneers on their country's last frontier.

The gateway to the park is itself the southernmost city in the world, Ushuaia (oo-shoo-WYE-uh). The town overlooks the Canal de Beagle (Beagle Channel), named for the ship that carried Charles Darwin on his voyage of discovery in 1831–36; it has a rather dilapidated, frontierish look to it. In recent years, Ushuaia has responded to the influx of international tourists who are anxious to add Tierra del Fuego to their itineraries or are on their way to Antarctica. Accommodations are plentiful and expensive.

Parque Nacional Tierra del Fuego is not huge by South American standards, but is still large enough in which to get thoroughly lost—240 square miles of very rugged country. Since the Andes curve to the east in this region, the park comprises portions of four parallel mountain ranges separated by deep valleys oriented northeast to southwest.

In the isolated northern section of the park, one valley is occupied by Lago Fagnano, a 70-mile-long glacier-carved lake that extends into Chile and empties into an arm of the Strait of Magellan. A 5-mile section of the lake and adjacent mountains lies within park boundaries, and except for the Argentine and Chilean border stations, the area is pristine. It can be reached only by a long boat ride or a long and difficult hike over the mountains from the southern part of the park. It is possible to cross into Chilean territory via Lago Fagnano, but only with current and proper documentation from authorities of both countries, usually obtainable in Ushuaia. Adventurous kayakers have made the trip, continuing on to explore the remote fjords and glaciers that descend north from the Darwin Range, the highest and least explored mountains of Tierra del Fuego.

Note: Because Lago Fagnano lies parallel to prevailing storm tracks, and because sheltered bays and anchorages are scarce on many parts of the lake, self-guided trips on this lake should be undertaken only by experienced boaters.

The southern portion of the park is readily accessible; its entrance lies 8 miles (13 kilometers) west of Ushuaia. The park has only 11 miles (18 kilometers) of road, so a tour of the park by car could be completed in a short afternoon, but the park's attributes warrant a more leisurely visit.

The southern part of the park contains rivers large and small, another large glacial lake, the shore of the Beagle Channel, and several self-guided interpretive trails. These trails are the best way to encounter the biological surprises of the park.

SENDERO LAGUNA NEGRA (Black Lagoon Trail). A prominent sign marks the head of this 0.25-mile loop trail that leads to a small lake well advanced in the process of becoming a sphagnum moss bog (*turbal* or *pántano*). A number of signs identify trees and shrubs, illustrate successional stages in beech forests and the development of bogs, and describe damage caused by the hordes of European rabbits that hop about practically underfoot along this trail.

Rabbits are not native to Tierra del Fuego. Introduced to the northern part of the island in the 1930s and in the vicinity of Ushuaia in the 1950s, they quickly became a plague, since few natural predators remained to keep populations in check. Sheepmen have tried with little success to reduce their numbers with poison gas and a disease specific to rabbits, myxomitosis.

Laguna Negra is typical of Fuegian sphagnum moss bogs. Composed of thick, dome-shaped mats of sphagnum mosses, lichens, liverworts, ferns, and a few hardy reeds, and elevated as much as 6 feet above surrounding land, they can range in color from gold to bright green to scarlet. They deal effectively with competition from other plants by choking out seedlings, and are usually surrounded by a ring of bleached, dead beech trees. *Caution:* The moss bogs are soft and spongy underfoot, and may overlie dangerously deep layers of mud and organic material, so take care while exploring them.

Bogs often support a few spectacular wildflowers, including gentians and orchids. Look closely along the mossy margins of Laguna Negra and you will see sunlight glinting from droplets of clear liquid suspended on the end of filaments on small, racquet-shaped red leaves. These droplets identify *Drosera uniflora*, a tiny insectivorous plant related to our own sundews. Insects become trapped in the gummy fluid and are digested by the plant. The plants are minute, some less than an inch across; visitors must look very closely to find them.

SENDERO DE LOS CASTORES (Trail of the Beavers). Just down the main road, west from the Laguna Negra trailhead, the 0.5-mile (1 kilometer) Beaver Trail leads south to Lapataia (lah-pah-TYE-uh) Bay. This is a wet trail; wear good boots. Perhaps because they are not native, beavers (*Castor canadensis*) are of great interest to most South Americans. They were introduced, along with muskrats, in the 1940s, and have flourished in many of Tierra del Fuego's streams. Sheepmen, however, heartily dislike them. The trail leads visitors past a series of beaver ponds and through a beech forest, a portion of which is being drowned by the incursion of the ponds. The trail continues to an overlook of Lapataia Bay and the Beagle Channel, and drops to intersect a dirt road at the head of the bay. Abandoned ranch buildings lie at the end of the road, Argentine Ruta 3, the southern end of the Panamerican Highway. If you have been driving through South America, this *is* the end of the road.

LAPATAIA TRAIL. From the end of the road at the head of Bahía Lapataia it is possible to walk to Chile in about 2 hours, provided one has obtained documentation from Argentine and Chilean authorities in Ushuaia. The trail follows a forested valley between Cerro Recalada to the south and the Pyramid Range to the north, and reaches the sea again at broad Bahía Yendegaia in Chilean Tierra del Fuego. Check in at the Chilean *carabinero* post—very friendly folks—before returning.

BAHIA ENSENADA TRAILS. A short side road from Ruta 3 leads south to Bahía Ensenada, a pleasant cove with excellent views of the channel and the Chilean islands to the south. Camping is permitted at this site, and trails lead along the coast in both directions from the turnaround. The trail to the west passes an abandoned sawmill, and eventually reaches the shore of Bahía Lapataia. At coves along this trail, you will find middens—heaps of oyster, mussel, and clam shells left by Indians near favored foraging sites. The east trail leads to an abandoned copper mine on the slopes of Mount Susana. Because these are popular trails, marine mammals are scarce in the waters near the trailheads. Seals, sea lions, and otters were once abundant, but the only mammal you are likely to see in these waters is the southern sea lion (*Otaria byronia*).

The abundance of seabirds, however, to some extent makes up for the absence of marine animals. Both of the world's largest flying birds—the condor and the albatross—live in the region. Condors are most commonly sighted in the mountains, but occasionally patrol beaches in search of carrion. Albatrosses spend most of their time at sea, and are most easily seen on the boat tours offered by several firms in Usuhaia, but they have been sighted from shore in the park. The marine birds you are most likely to see include the great grebe (*Podiceps major*), giant fulmar (*Macronectes giganteus*), several cormorant species (*Phalacrocorax* sp.), black-necked swan (*Cygnus melancoryphus*), and many species of terns and gulls. Among the shorebirds, two noisy species of oystercatcher are common on the beaches, the Magellanic oystercatcher (*Haematopus leucopodus*), black and white with a bizarre orange bill, and the larger black oystercatcher (*Haematopus ater*).

Argentina has three different types of flightless birds. Penguins are one, rheas another, and the third is the flightless steamer duck (*Tachyeres pteneres*), so named because of its comical method of locomotion. It can't fly, but when it is in a hurry it runs across the water and madly flaps its wings in circular fashion, whipping up a great deal of foam and spray when underway and resembling nothing so much as an old-fashioned paddle-wheeled steamer. These big ducks (up to 14 pounds) can move faster than a man can run by this means, and dive very well. A related species, the flying steamer duck (*Tachyeres patachonicus*) can fly (poorly), but prefers to steam about like its waterbound cousin, and sometimes makes use of freshwater lakes in Patagonia and Tierra del Fuego.

Sheldgeese or upland geese are collective terms for five species of South American birds that resemble geese but are more closely related to ducks. Four species spend some part of their lives in the extreme south of the continent. Called cauquén or kaikén by Argentines, they are one of the unforgettable wildlife sights of Patagonia and Tierra del Fuego. One species, the kelp goose, is exclusively marine, but the rest are land birds that occasionally make use of the sea. The land birds are incredibly abundant; flocks may contain hundreds of birds, and it is not uncommon to see thousands during the course of a day's drive in Patagonia or Tierra del Fuego. They are found on the island from November through May, feeding in every meadow in sight, and raising their families on nearby watercourses. The most common is the Magellan goose (*Chloephaga picta*), with white head and rump, and the rest of its plumage barred black and white. The rarest—and most beautiful—is the colorful ashy-headed goose (*Chloephaga poliocephala*), the only species of sheldgeese with a distinctly gray head. The ruddy-headed goose (*Chloephaga rubidiceps*) is the smallest of the sheldgeese, and is native to Tierra del Fuego.

The birds have managed to survive despite the organized efforts of sheepmen to reduce their numbers. In a classic example of ecological mismanagement, Patagonian and Fuegian sheepmen drastically reduced the numbers of the geese's principal predators, the Patagonian and Fuegian foxes, at the same time clearing land to encourage growth of the short grasses of the steppelands, the geese's primary food source. Lacking predators and with plenty of food, the population of sheldgeese soared, of course, and they became the principal competitors of the sheep for the grass. Appalled, the sheepmen, claiming that from two to eight geese ate as much grass as one sheep, had the geese declared a national plague in 1972, and instituted a campaign to eliminate them. Hunters were paid 5 cents for each egg, gosling, or pair of legs brought in, and in the early years of the program hundreds of thousands of birds were killed in this manner.

One species escaped this misguided depredation, presumably because it does not eat grass—the kelp goose (*Chloephaga hybrida*). Though often found near kelp beds, the birds do not eat kelp, but rather the green sea lettuce, ulva. Usually in pairs, and always near shore, they are easy to recognize because the male is entirely white and his mate is nearly all black.

OTHER TRAILS. (1) Two miles (3 kilometers) inside the park entrance, a steep 0.5-mile (1 kilometer) trail leads north from Ruta 2 up the flank of Cerro Pampa Alta (High Meadow Peak) to an overlook providing a fine view of the Beagle Channel, Ushuaia Bay, and Chilean islands and waters to the south and west. (2) The first road to the right past the park entrance leads to Río Pipo Falls, an indifferent cascade but a pleasant campsite, and trailhead for the Lago Fagnano trail. This 20-mile (32 kilometers) trail follows the Río Pipo to its headwaters, crosses the Martial Mountains, and descends past a large glacial tarn to Lago Fagnano. The trail passes through splendid glaciated mountains rarely seen by visitors, but unless you can arrange a return trip by boat on Lago Fagnano, the only way to return is the way you came.

Visitors to Parque Nacional Tierra del Fuego are in the midst of southern temperate rain forests. They are called southern beech forests to distinguish them from our own beech forests, and Magellanic forests to distinguish them from identical beech forests in New Zealand and from the similar forests of Patagonia. No one who has hiked through one will have any doubt that the forests of this park are rain forests. They are almost tropical in appearance and lushness, primarily because of the prolifer-

A family of ashy-headed geese (Chleophaga poliocephala) *on the waters of Lapataia Bay, Tierra del Fuego National Park; sheldgeese* (cauquenes) *are common sights on fresh and salt waters of Tierra del Fuego and Patagonia.*

ation at low elevations of an incredible variety of bamboos, ferns, mosses, and epiphytes. It is because of the density of these fast-growing understory species that visitors must make standard procedure of checking with park authorities before making any long-distance backpack trips in any forested parks in southern South America.

The Magellanic forest is less complicated than it sounds, for only five species of trees grow in Argentine Tierra del Fuego, and of these three are beeches.

One of the more interesting trees is the canelo, or Winter's bark (*Drimys winteri*), whose name derives from historical events. Thirty-three-year-old Francis Drake entered the strait in 1578, a period when scurvy customarily decimated the ranks of all sailors on long voyages and often led to disaster. Upon learning that Patagonian Indians used canelo (also called cinnamon tree) for medicinal purposes, Drake's captain, John Winter, insisted that his crew use the bark of the tree in their food and to make tea, in an effort to stave off the ravages of scurvy. The effort paid off for both men, for Drake went down in history as the second man to circumnavigate the globe, and Winter's name will forever be attached to this tree. The best place to find the tree in the park is along the edge of the road to Bahía Ensenada. Look under the beeches for shorter trees with 3- to 4-inch-long lance-shaped evergreen leaves, white flowers with six petals, and spicy bark and seeds.

Leña dura, or pickwood (*Maytenus magellanica*), is more a tall shrub than a tree, seldom exceeding 10 feet in height, and is of little interest except as a highly sought-after firewood.

The dominant trees in Magellanic forests and in the park are the coihue Magellanes, or evergreen beech (*Nothofagus betuloides*), and the lenga, or high beech (*Nothofagus pumilio*). Coihue Magellanes is the largest beech in Tierra del Fuego, and the only evergreen. It differs from the coihue of the more northern parks of Patagonia only in flower and leaf structure, and is usually found in groups amid the more numerous lengas.

The lenga favors the relatively warm temperatures and abundant rain brought by maritime winds, and is usually found on valley floors and near lakes and the coast. Its deciduous cousin, the ñire, or Antarctic beech (*Nothofagus antarctica*), creeps highest up the mountainsides, and brings the brilliant red, yellow, and brown tones of fall to Tierra del Fuego from March to May. More water-tolerant than other beeches, they are often found near marshes, bogs, and other areas subject to flood. They are usually the trees that have been transformed into bizarre wind-shaped krummholz at the upper limits of timberline on the mountainsides, and are the first trees to turn color in the fall. All three types of beeches are parasitized, but it is the poor ñire that seems to carry the heaviest burden of hangers-on. Many ñires near the beaver ponds and Laguna Negra are almost completely shrouded with mistletoe-like myzodendron, which possesses chlorophyll but lacks roots, and uses the tree to obtain its basic nutrients. As if myzodendron were not enough, many ñire are also draped with dense curtains of the gray-green lichen usnea, which we call Spanish moss. Finally, along the less heavily traveled parts of the trails, are ñires that have been parasitized by all manner of fungi, among them the pan del Indio, Indian bread or Darwin's fungus (*Cyttaria* sp.). Cyttaria forms round white or yellow balls on the trunks and branches of beeches, but was actually only one of the "breads" used by the Indians, who ate virtually all of the many kinds of fungi that grow on the trees of this forest.

The accessible beech forests of Tierra del Fuego have been exploited for scores of years, and signs of that exploitation are particularly evident near the park, Ushuaia, and eastern Lago Fagnano. Much of the logging between Lapataia and Ushuaia was carried out by the inmates of a military prison that was in operation from 1902 to 1911. (The old prison still stands, a red-roofed building south of Ruta 3 about 3 miles (5 kilometers) west of Ushuaia.) What appears to be a gigantic clear-cut on the slopes of Martial Mountain directly behind Ushuaia, however, is the result of a 1918 forest fire rather than logging.

Visitor Facilities

Facilities and services for tourists abound in Ushuaia. Every first-class hotel and any of a half-dozen or so travel agencies offer trips by bus, boat, or private vehicle to just about anywhere in Tierra del Fuego, including Cape Horn and villages on the Chilean Islands to the south. Trips can even be arranged to Antarctica from Ushuaia, although under ordinary circumstances they are very costly. Because of its remote location, prices of all goods and services are significantly higher in Tierra del Fuego than elswhere in Argentina (or Chile), and hotels fill up quickly during the short summer season. Check at the tourist office (Avenue San Martín 524), a friendly and helpful place, for a list of accommodations, and names and addresses of families who will take in and feed lodgers for modest fees.

Some of the excursions that can be arranged from Ushuaia are: to the park (3 hours); to Lago Fagnano, a scenic trip that crosses Garibaldi Pass, north of Ushuaia (4 hours, 60 miles [97 kilometers] round trip); to Río Grande, the only other town on Tierra del Fuego (all day, 300 miles, 483 kilometers); to Isla de los Lobos (Sea Lion Island) by launch (3 hours); scenic flights over the Beagle Channel (30 minutes); and to Martial Glacier—on Martial Mountain, behind Ushuaia—on foot (5 hours).

In the park itself, the Hostería Alakush ("steamer duck" in the Yahgan tongue) offers accommodations on the shores of the Río Lapataia, and visitors can obtain provisions and meals at the hotel's small *confitería*. Campsites with tables, fire pits, and rest rooms are located near the hostería at Lago Roca. Less developed campsites are situated on the shores of the Río Pipo, at Bahía Ensenada, and at Laguna Verde.

Recreation

As described above, the best way to experience Parque Nacional Tierra del Fuego is to walk around in it. Short and long trails provide for both hiking and backpacking. Opportunities for wildlife observation are limited because of relatively low populations, but bird watching is rewarding in forested sections of the park and along the seacoast. Because of relatively high tidal ranges, opportunities for beachcombing and tide-pool exploring are excellent. Virtually anything growing along the seacoast is edible. Boating is possible on Lago Roca and Lago Fagnano. Finally, trout fishing is good in the lakes and streams.

Historical Aspects

Near the Hostería Alakush is a reconstructed Indian village, designed to give visitors some idea of the life led by the original inhabitants of Tierra del Fuego. Of the four tribes with distinct languages and habits that once populated the island, only one survives.

The Haush were nomadic hunter-gathers who were driven by more aggressive tribes into the extreme eastern tip of Argentine Tierra del Fuego. They did not use boats, but lived by hunting guanacos and gathering food from forest and seashore. No Haush survive.

The Onas were the most war-like of the Fuegian tribes. Like the Haush, they were a nomadic inland people that depended upon the guanaco for their survival. A tall people, with some men over 6 feet, they inhabited the bulk of the island, primarily the treeless steppes of the north and east. The last Ona died in 1969.

The Alacaluf were canoe Indians who lived along the straits and channels of western Tierra del Fuego and the southern coasts of Chile. They seldom ventured inland for fear of the fierce Onas, and survived exclusively on what they could garner

from the sea and seacoasts. Because the lands they occupied were so rugged and iso-
lated, they experienced somewhat less contact with white men than the other tribes.
Perhaps for that reason, more Alacalufs have survived into modern times. About
twenty Alacalufs are known to be alive, most of whom are settled in the vicinity of
Puerto Eden, a tiny village on desolate, rainswept Wellington Island 300 miles up the
Chilean coast.

The Yahgans were also canoe Indians who occupied the southernmost channels
and offshore islands of Tierra del Fuego, and survived on the rich resources of the
coast. They inhabited the coast that is now part of the park, and the old shellfish middens seen along sea trails in the park were most likely created by Yahgan tribesmen.
Four Indians taken back to England by Captain Robert Fitzroy on his voyage of 1830
were Yahgans. These Indians were given the Dickensian names of York Minster,
Jemmy Button, Boat Memory, and Fuegia Basket, and presented to the queen. When
Captain Fitzroy returned the three survivors to Tierra del Fuego three years later (Boat
Memory had died in England), one of the other members of the ship's company was a
young naturalist by the name of Charles Darwin.

Although they were the southernmost inhabitants of the earth, occupying lands
remote in the extreme, the Yahgans had the appalling bad luck to live along the margins of a heavily used ship channel, so their contacts with white men were early, frequent, and often hostile. Fights with settlers, but primarily diseases, quickly reduced
their numbers, and they, too, are now extinct.

Climate and Weather

Fuegians have a number of familiar adages about their weather: "If you don't like
the weather, wait five minutes—it'll change"; "In summer we can have all the seasons
of the year in one day"; "We have two seasons—winter and February"; and so on.
There is a grain of truth in all of them.

The main season for the park is November 15 to March 31, and during any part of
that interval the weather is unpredictable. It can rain at any time and, at higher elevations, snow at any time. The park receives about 40 inches of annual precipitation,
but influences of microclimate and rain shadows are dramatic, so it can be rainy on
one side of a mountain and sunny on the other. Clear skies and sunshine might persist
for ten straight days, followed by ten days of pelting rain. Visitors must therefore be
prepared for rain, and in spring and fall for snow, even though they may experience
neither. Waterproof jackets and boots are a necessity. Median summer temperatures
are about 48 degrees, winter 27 degrees. Even in good weather, winds can be fierce at
high elevations and on unsheltered coasts, so sweaters and good windbreakers are
needed, summer or winter.

Location and Access

As remote as it is, Tierra del Fuego is but a few hours from Buenos Aires by jet.
Daily connecting flights may be boarded in almost any other city in Argentine
Patagonia. Night flights are significantly cheaper on the country's two major airlines
(Aerolineas Argentinas and Austral). All visitors to Tierra del Fuego (or Patagonia)

should seek, however, to book flights with Lineas Aéreas del Estado (LADE), Argentina's military airline, whose prices can be as little as one-third of the price of commercial flights. These flights fill up quickly, of course, but cancellations are common, so it is often worth a trip to the airport to seek a standby seat.

The buses that leave Ushuaia several times weekly for northern points in Argentina and to Chile provide comfortable rides over rough roads, and give visitors a chance to see the forests, steppes, and seascapes of Tierra del Fuego, plus an opportunity to enter Chile and cross the windswept Straits of Magellan. It is relatively easy to reach Chile's Torres del Paine by bus from Ushuaia, either via Río Gallegos and Río Turbio in Argentina, or via Punta Arenas and Puerto Natales in Chile.

Hitchhiking is possible in Tierra del Fuego, but traffic is often light and competition fierce during summer months; hitchhikers must be prepared to deal with delays.

Glossary

bahía	bay
confitería	roughly, snack bar
fogón	fire ring or barbecue pit
helechos	ferns
hongos	fungi, mushrooms
lengal	grove of lenga trees
musgos	mosses
picada, sendero, tramo	trail

View from Corcovado: Copacabana Beach, yacht-filled Botafogo Bay, and Sugar Loaf; right, Ipanema and Leblon beaches. Tijuca National Park, Brazil

4
▓▓ BRAZIL

Brazil has twenty-five national parks and twelve biological reserves that range in size from a thousand to nearly six million acres. They vary from tiny offshore islands to highland retreats for the wealthy to vast tracts of steamy Amazon rain forest. To reach a few, transportation is as easy as stepping onto a city bus and getting off at the end of the line; for others, one must mount a full-fledged expedition. It is nearly impossible to see Brazil's parks in a week or two, however, for Brazil is the fifth-largest country in the world, and occupies almost half of South America.

Brazil is a relative latecomer to the national park movement. Its first park, Itatiaia, was established in 1937. But once the idea took hold, Brazil set out to establish a significant system, and today over twenty-seven million acres (42,470 square miles, an area slightly larger than Ohio) has been given over to parks and reserves— 1.3 percent of this immense country. Nearly a quarter of this land was set aside in only four years, from 1979 to 1982, and government management plans call for even more land to be obtained for parks and reserves.

The parks were established for the usual reasons: to protect exceptional scenic and natural attributes, including flora, fauna, waters, and geological features, and to provide scientific, educational, recreational, and cultural opportunities for the public. The biological reserves, however, were not established for general public use, but rather are intended primarily for scientific and educational purposes, or to protect species on the verge of extinction. Public use of these reserves is not encouraged, and in some cases is prohibited altogether.

Brazil's parks and reserves are administered by a division of the Ministry of Agriculture called the Instituto Brasileiro de Desenvolvimento Florestal (Brazilian Institute of Forest Development), or IBDF. The IBDF has acquired parklands much faster than it has been able to obtain funds for personnel to manage them, and has had to allocate sparse resources in uneven fashion. As in other South American countries, travelers will encounter some parks with well-developed visitor facilities and others with no services at all.

Travelers intending to visit Brazilian parks are encouraged to write or visit the offices of IBDF (IBDF, SAIN, Avenida L-4 Norte, Brasilia, Distrito Federal, Brasil) for information, maps, and current publications. Published information is in Portuguese, of course, but many staff speak English and Spanish.

Nearly every state in Brazil now has either a park or reserve, or is planning for one or more in the near future. Most existing parks lie along Brazil's densely populated southeast coast, among them Itatiaia and, on the outskirts of Rio de Janeiro, Tijuca. One park in the extreme south of Brazil, Aparados da Serra, regularly receives winter snowfalls, while in Parque Nacional Amazonia, in the Amazon Basin, the temperature never drops below 65 degrees Fahrenheit, and hovers about 80 degrees most of the time. Several parks have been established on the temperate highlands of central Brazil; the most interesting is Parque Nacional Das Emas, remote and difficult to reach, but loaded with wildlife. Brazil's best-known park, Iguaçu, is visited by many international travelers. Shared with neighboring Argentina (where it is known as Iguazú), it

is the site of the most famous waterfall in South America, Catarata do Iguaçú (Iguaçú Falls).

From the perspective of foreigners, the factor that contributes most to enjoyment of Brazilian parks is the Brazilians themselves. Brazil sees itself as the United States of South America—a vast, potentially rich melting pot. In general, Brazilians like Americans and make no bones about it. Tremendously curious about the United States and its people, they politely ask visitors endless question about themselves, their family, friends, house, job, dog, car, neighborhood, and so on. Most Americans reciprocate this warmth, and are continually astonished by Brazilians, among the friendliest and most uninhibited people on the face of the earth. No people, rich or poor, are quicker with a smile for strangers than Brazilians. A chance companion on a plane or bus in Brazil may well relate his or her life story to you, and end the story by extending a sincere invitation to meet his or her family, and stay at his or her home for the evening, the weekend, or the week—whether you speak Portuguese or not.

Brazilians are special. You will not soon forget Brazil and its wonderful people.

ᜂ TIJUCA:
Carioca Playground

Rio de Janeiro is often called the most beautiful city in the world. Constructed on both flatlands and steep, green hillsides around a large harbor graced with numerous blue coves and long sandy beaches, the city is justly compared to San Francisco. Glistening white skyscrapers and apartment complexes are built to the edge of the famous beaches along its irregular coastline—Ipanema and Copacabana. Rio is a city created for lofty overlooks, and every year thousands of visitors troop to two of the most famous of them—*Pāo de Açucar* (Sugar Loaf) and Corcovado (Hunchback)—for a bird's-eye view of the city.

Rio is informal; its residents—called *Cariocas*—are famous for their easygoing nature. It is no accident that the best known and most riotous of the many carnivals in Brazil takes place in Rio. Life is far from perfect in Rio; smog obscures the sun on breezeless days, traffic is appalling, street crime is on the rise, and dense slums (*favelas*) of desperately poor city dwellers usually occupy the highest slopes of the hills around the bay. But in other respects, Rio has it all: pleasant climate, rich nightlife, sandy beaches and warm seas, handsome men and gorgeous women. Small wonder that nine million people live there.

In the center of this metropolis, a most unlikely place to encounter a natural area, is Parque Nacional Tijuca. The park is Brazil's second smallest, taking up a mere 8,150 acres, but do not pass it up because of its size, for it is one of the country's loveliest parks, the views from its heights are incomparable, and it is the most accessible of all Brazilian parks.

Tijuca comprises three distinct sectors, separated by busy freeways, each dedicated to different uses. The northwest sector, Serra da Tijuca, is primarily a recreation area with picnic facilities and trails that lead to the nearby peaks Tijuca and Papagaio. The most popular tourist center in this sector of the park is Cascatinha, an area next to a waterfall with a small hotel, restaurant, and picnic sites.

Virtually every traveler who reaches Rio de Janeiro, foreigner or Brazilian, eventually visits the northeast sector, Serra da Carioca. A number of narrow, steep roads in this sector wind through dense subtropical vegetation and connect several viewpoints that overlook the city and ocean. The most famous of these is the top of Corcovado, on which has been constructed the Monumento Cristo Redentor, a 130-foot statue of Christ built on a mountaintop 2,330 feet above the city. The statue can be reached by car, taxi, tour bus (not recommended), or cog railroad (you can get to the railroad station at Rua Cosme Velho by taxi or one of several buses). If you can tolerate heavy and aggressive traffic, an excellent way to see the park is with a rented motor scooter.

The third sector, Pedra Bonita and Pedra Gavea, encircles the peaks of those names, and is basically roadless. Use of this sector is limited to members of Brazilian mountaineering clubs, who practice their skills on the steep granite peaks, and members of hang-gliding clubs, who sail from the summit of Pedra Gavea to the beaches nearly 3,000 feet below.

Almost 45 miles (72 kilometers) of good paved road wind through two sectors of the park, connected to seven entrances that link the park to various city neighborhoods. The park can be seen from the roads in a single day, but there is much to see,

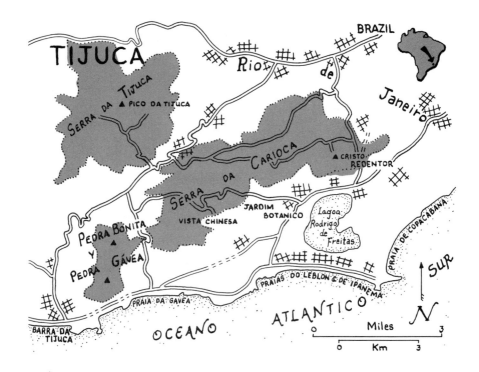

and two days are recommended, three if you wish to hike a trail or two. City buses reach the outskirts of the park, but do not enter. Tour buses do enter the park and stop at many (not all) of the most interesting sites, but because the stops are so short tour buses are not recommended.

Before entering the park, travelers interested in natural history would be wise to visit two other places in Rio. The first is the Quinta da Boa Vista (once a Brazilian emperor's private park), reached by any of several buses from the center of town. A small, but well-stocked natural history museum (Museu de Fauna) on the grounds introduces visitors to Brazilian fauna, and the nearby zoo shelters more animals and a large selection of birds both captive and wild. The second place to visit lies at the foot of the Serra da Carioca sector of the park—the famed Jardím Botánico (Botanical Gardens). Nearly two centuries old, the gardens cover 350 acres and contain 500 species of trees, shrubs, and flowering plants. More than 140 species of birds have been observed in the gardens. Many of the plants are labeled, and an orchidarium brings to easy view many flowers not ordinarily seen in the field because they grow high in the forest canopy.

The museum, zoo, and gardens offer one of the finest opportunities in the world for visitors to familiarize themselves with tropical flora and fauna, and with this introduction travelers can visit Brazil's other parks with an excellent idea of what they can expect to see.

Fecundity rather than biological parsimony is the rule in Tijuca. Every square inch of soil, and most of the branches of the park's trees, support some kind of plant. The roads through the park wind through exceptionally lush forests of scores of different tree species, tree ferns, and palmitos adorned with lianas, philodendrons, and epiphytic orchids and bromeliads. At least five species of epiphytic cacti of a single family, ipsalia, hang precariously from branches and trunks of trees.

Technically, visitors are passing through a humid tropical rain forest, but only the most discerning visitors will notice that the park's forest is not a surviving patch of the virgin forest that once covered this part of Brazil, but is, rather, a secondary forest in its entirety. A few clues stand out here and there, such as the presence of exotic species, breadfruit among others, but it takes an expert to detect them. (More on this later.)

When the primary forest disappeared centuries ago, its animal inhabitants also disappeared, so visitors cannot expect to see a full spectrum of animals usually associated with a tropical rain forest. IBDF staff have for many years operated a program of faunal reintroduction, however, and are justly proud of their progress to date. As elsewhere, animals are sparse near the roads, but along the hiking trails one might glimpse squirrels, coatimundis (*Nasua rufa*), common marmosets, and the three-toed sloth (*Bradypus tridactylus*). Look for monkeys feeding on breadfruit in the trees near the Macaco (Monkey) entrance to the park.

Plenty of bugs and a few venomous snakes have repopulated the park, but the most successful colonizers are the birds. A head-spinning variety of tropical birds inhabit or pass through Tijuca. A description of these birds is far beyond the scope of this book, for Tijuca is for those bird-watchers skilled enough to recognize such esoteric species as the white-barred piculet, white-eyed foliage-gleaner, grey-headed tody-flycatcher, rufous-browed peppershrike, violaceous euphonia, wedge-tailed grassfinch, and scores of other birds few of us have ever heard of.

Since the views from the park are primary attractions, it is essential to visit on days that are clear (to avoid fog and low clouds) and windy (to clear smog from the suburbs). The most impressive view is from the Cristo Redentor statue on Corcovado, but do not pass up the other viewpoints. Among the most outstanding are Bella Vista, Dona Marta, Mesa do Imperador (the Emperor's Table), and especially the Vista Chinese, a Chinese pavilion overlooking the Botanical Gardens, Ipanema and Leblon beaches, and Rio's exclusive Jockey Club suburb. The park is open all night; do not ignore night views.

Scattered through the park are well-tended original and restored remnants of colonial and imperial Brazil in the form of small monuments, classic fountains, quaint stone statues, and porcelain maps that add a pleasant dimension to the park's atmosphere and hint at the complexity of its history.

For views of a different portion of Rio, hike the 2-hour trail to the park's highest point, Pico de Tijuca (3,350 feet), from the end of the road that passes Cascatinha in the Serra da Tijuca sector of the park. The trail climbs about 1,200 feet (366 meters), but has plenty of switchbacks, and the views of the harbor are incomparable.

Recreation

Tijuca is a sightseeing park for foreigners, and a treasure for *Cariocas*. It provides opportunities to drive, walk, pedal, picnic, hike, and try out all manner of death-defying activities without leaving Rio de Janeiro. The park is sufficiently large to cre-

The Cristo Redentor, on Corcovado

ate an atmosphere distinct from the city, in which urbanites can appreciate the sights, sounds, and smells of a forest environment.

Visitors should not expect to ever have much of Tijuca to themselves; over two million people visit the park every year.

Historical Aspects

Hundreds of years ago, Tijuca (a Tupi Indian word for marsh or bog) was, along with the rest of the southeast coast of Brazil, covered with tropical rain forest. The park is in a region first settled by Europeans in 1565. It proved to be a popular area, and the settlement grew apace, increasing demand for wood for construction and charcoal. In a few decades, the forests of Tijuca had disappeared, consumed in order to construct Rio and fuel its cooking fires.

By the late 1600s, the logged-over forests of Tijuca were completely replaced by huge tracts of sugarcane, which was cultivated until about 1765, when coffee attracted the attention of the world. The cane fields were quickly replaced by more profitable coffee-growing plantations (fazendas). These plantations remained in production until about 1818, when Rio's city fathers noted that pure water was no longer available, and that enormous landslides from the slopes of the Tijuca peaks were becoming commonplace. An early lesson in ecosystem management was learned the hard way: complete deforestation and centuries of agricultural misuse had destroyed Rio de Janeiro's principal watershed. It took nearly fifty years for the government to act to correct the problem, but in 1856 the first lands were set aside for the purpose of restoring the watershed.

In 1861, Major Manuel Archer was given the herculean task of restoring the forests of Tijuca and, by so doing, saving Rio de Janeiro. Archer was equal to his task; within a few years he had planted seedlings and cuttings of some 100,000 trees, most but not all native to southeastern Brazil, and the restoration of Tijuca was under way. In subsequent decades, more lands were appropriated by the government, more trees were planted, and Tijuca was designated a national forest. Finally administration of the area was handed to IBDF, and in 1961 Tijuca became Brazil's sixth national park.

Tijuca's present forests are not exactly as they appeared centuries ago, for they are a combination of natural regeneration and the monumental effort of Manuel Archer, but all agree that the restoration has been a resounding success, and park personnel take great pride in the feat. Today 95 percent of the park is covered by forest, and with the assistance of IBDF the fauna is also returning. Rio has a guaranteed supply of fresh water from nearly 150 watercourses that flow into the city from the park, and the Cariocas now place great value on the small tropical rain forest that lies in the midst of their city.

Tijuca is one park in which convenient accommodations are not a problem. The park is literally surrounded by one of the world's most interesting and lively cities. Several restaurants are scattered in strategic locations in the park, and those who prefer to stay within the park confines may do so at the small hotel at Cascatinha or near the Cristo on Pico Corcovado.

Climate and Weather

Tijuca is open the entire year, and may be visited at any season. The park receives about 80 inches of annual rainfall, but less rain falls in "winter" (June through August) than during the rest of the year. Summer rainfalls are usually brief and refreshing. Temperatures are also lowest in winter—about 65 degrees Fahrenheit average, but there is little difference between winter and summer, when the average temperature is about 72 degrees. Shorts and short-sleeved shirts are fine during the day; take a light sweater with you for visits after dark. Spring (September) is announced by a sudden profusion of blooming flowers, but some trees will always be blooming during the other seasons.

Glossary

Note: On speaking Portuguese—a traveler's tale widely told in South America is that if you speak Spanish, you will automatically be able to communicate in Brazil. The tale is not quite true. Most Brazilians will be able to understand your Spanish if you speak slowly and clearly, but you may not be able to understand their reply, unless they also reply in Spanish. Although many Spanish/Portuguese cognates exist, Portuguese is a singsong, nasal language, and not as strictly phonetic as Spanish. The country is so large that there are distinct differences in pronunciation of certain letters and diphthongs from one part of the country to another. In some areas, the words *grande* and *Brasil* are pronounced almost exactly as in Spanish, but in other areas they are pronounced GRAN-jay and bra-SEE-oh, respectively. The city Curitiba is pronounced coo-ree-CHEE-bah by its residents.

It will take your ear a while to grow accustomed to Portuguese, and take your tongue somewhat longer, but an enormous part of the load of struggling with another language is eased by the basic good nature of the Brazilians, who, if they cannot make you understand how to get somewhere or other, will simply take you there.

Glossary

abrigo	not overcoat, as usually used in Spanish, but shelter, refuge
cascatinha	cascade, pronounced cahs-cah-TEEN-yah
fazenda	farm, plantation, or ranch
morro	hill
papagaio	parrot
pedra	rock
pico	peak
piquenique	picnic, pronounced pee-kay-NEE-kay
portão	gate
trilha	trail, pronounced TREE-yah

Eerie weathered striations on the slopes of Agulhas Negras Peak are among the strange geological features of Itatiaia National Park, Brazil.

ITATIAIA:
The Alps of Brazil

Few visitors to Brazil realize that the country has mountains that exceed 9,000 feet in elevation. Some of the highest of these peaks are in the Itatiaia Range, which lies about halfway between Brazil's two largest cities, Rio de Janeiro and São Paulo. No ski resorts cling to the mountainsides, but snow occasionally dusts the range, and in these mountains Brazil established its first national park, Parque Nacional Itatiaia (pronounced ee-tah-T'YIE-yah).

The park is fairly small by Brazilian standards—74,000 acres—but it spans a wider range of elevations than any other Brazilian park. Visitors can wander through a humid rain forest at 2,300 feet, or hike on the Serra da Montiqueira Plateau (7,200 feet), most of which lies above treeline and is dominated by the third-highest peak in Brazil, Pico das Agulhas Negras (Black Needles Peak), a deeply fissured gray prominence that reaches 9,144 feet. This elevational variety gives hikers an opportunity to see a vertical slice through central Brazil, a diversity of habitat that is quite rare in tropical latitudes. This attribute has not escaped the notice of geologists, botanists, zoologists, ecologists, and naturalists, and as a result, Itatiaia is one of the most thoroughly studied parks in South America.

The lower portion of Itatiaia was originally an agricultural colony, and like much of southeast Brazil was nearly deforested in the late 1800s to make room for coffee *fazendas*. The colony was unsuccessful, however, and in about 1920 the area was converted into a government biological research station that achieved far greater success. From 1922 to 1927 many famous ground-breaking studies of tropical flora and fauna were carried out at the research station; as early as 1913 a Brazilian botanist, Alberto Lofgren, suggested to government officials that Itatiaia should be set aside as a national park. Ideas often move slowly through bureaucracies, however, and it was not until 1937 that 37,000 acres of lowlands were devoted to Brazil's first national park. In later years, park administrators began to recognize principles of ecological integrity, and in 1982 the park was doubled by an incorporation of an additional 37,000 acres of high plateau (*planalto*).

Altitudinal zonation is distinct in Itatiaia. Three climatic communities exist in the park: tropical, subtropical, and temperate.

THE TROPICAL ZONE. Below 4,900 feet, visitors are in the tropics. The trees are not as high as in the Amazon forests, but like those of Tijuca they are almost entirely secondary; fifty years ago, pastures covered most of these forested slopes. The slender and graceful palmito palms (*Euterpes edulis*) are one sign of a tropical forest, and palmitos are common in the lower portion of the park. Most of the trees are evergreens, which support other non-deciduous plants in riotous proliferation; cacti, orchids, bromeliads, begonias, philodendrons, lianas, mosses, lichens, and flowering vines cover everything.

It grows cool but never cold in true tropics, and since that suits most Brazilians, the lower part of the park is the more developed. A few vacation homes—inholdings from colonial days—lie along the road, and two old but comfortable hotels, several guest houses, and campgrounds are located just inside the entrance to the lower part of the park.

One of the features near the park headquarters (*sede*) is the *cascatinha da Marombá*, the cascades of a small, rocky stream called the Rio Marombá. The stream plunges into a series of pools, collectively called Lago Azul, that are large enough to swim in, and unbelievably refreshing after a hot afternoon hike. **Caution:** Rio Marombá is subject to flash floods if rain is falling on the *planalto*; bathe with caution, and not alone.

A road lined with picnic areas (and a 1.2-mile [2-kilometer] streamside trail) passes Lago Azul and Véu da Noiva (Bride's Veil Falls), one of the few falls given that name that actually resembles a bride's veil.

But for a few large and loud monkeys that hang about the hotels, and a couple of other exceptions, very little fauna can be seen in the park. One of the exceptions is insects—more than 100,000 species have been identified in the park. The other exception is birdlife, for the park is rich in birds, and international bird-watching tours invariably include Itatiaia in their itineraries. Nearly 250 species have been identified within park boundaries. The largest populations are found in the tropical section of the park, especially toucans, toucanets, flycatchers, parrots, and a dozen tanager species. On the *planalto,* birds are less abundant but more unusual; many species are found

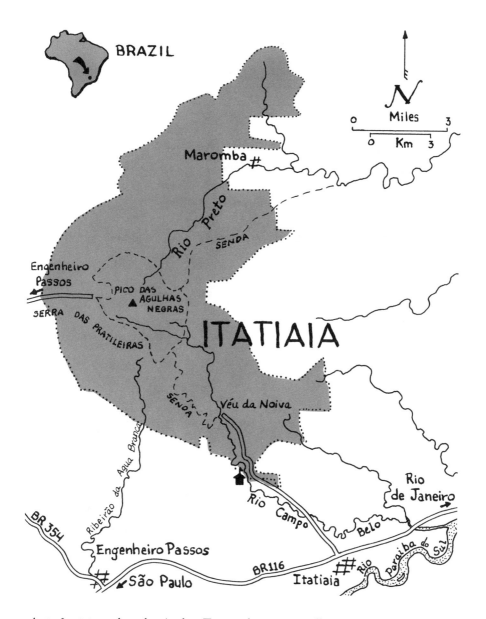

only in Itatiaia and in the Andes. Two trails are especially recommended for birders: from Hotel Simón to Tres Picos (4 hours), and the Barbossa Rodriguez trail downstream from Lago Azul (2 hours).

THE SUBTROPICAL ZONE. Between 4,900 feet and 6,500 feet, the relatively open tropical forest gives way to shorter, thicket-like woods. Stands of bamboo and, on south-facing slopes, scattered survivors of the once broad forest of Paraná pines, a type of araucaria (*Araucaria angustifolia*), cover the slopes. In Itatiaia, the subtropic zone is the most primitive section of the park, a transition zone between the tropics

The Apple (Maçã), a bizarre rock formation in the planalto section of Itatiaia National Park, Brazil

and the high plateau. No roads or other visitor facilities have been developed in this zone, and the only way to see it at close hand is by trail.

THE TEMPERATE ZONE. The portion of the park above 6,500 feet is completely different from the rest of the park and most of Brazil. In the Upper Cretaceous Period, a huge volcanic batholith forced its way up through the earth's crust, creating both the massif now known as the Itatiaia Range and a plateau that averages about 8,000 feet. The rocks of this massif, tipped nearly vertical and exposed to wide temperature extremes and seasons of torrential rains, have weathered into bizarre formations more typical of a lunar landscape than a Brazilian highland. Over 560 square miles of the Itatiaia Range are made up of this strange wilderness of stone, a geological phenomenon known to exist in only one other place in the world, near Kola, Sweden.

It is cool, sometimes freezing, on the plateau. Vegetation consists of small bushes, thick groves of dwarf bamboo, sedges, tall bunchgrass clumps, and here and there a very small tree. Brush can be impenetrable, but it is usually possible to maneuver around thickets.

Most travelers consider the rock formations to be the most spectacular features in the park. The uptilted strata and weathering have created interesting effects, on large and small scale. The most famous of the formations are Maçã (the Apple), Tartaruga (Turtle), and Prateleiras (the Shelves). The first two are huge rounded boulders balanced so precariously on stone pedestals that it appears as if a gentle nudge would tip them into a journey down the mountainside that would only end at the bottom of the Atlantic. The third is a jumble of enormous slabs of rock standing on end and leaning against one another, a pile of giants' building blocks. The parapet-like Prataleiras obstruct the view over the Paraibo Valley far below. To find a viewpoint, visitors must negotiate a maze of tunnels and dark natural passageways through the Prataleiras to reach the side of the rocks that overlook the valley.

Visitor Facilities

The nearest facilities outside the park are in the town of Itatiaia, 6 miles (10 kilometers) from the park entrance, on the highway between Rio and São Paulo.

Facilities in the low section of the park include the park entrance office, administrative offices, a museum that includes displays of park flora and fauna, picnic and camping areas, cabins, hostels, and two hotels. The campgrounds are not well sited with respect to scenery. This section of the park is patently overdeveloped, and park managers have reacted by limiting camping and living facilities. No more than twenty tents are permitted in the campground on any night. As a result, space fills up quickly on Brazilian holidays. Reserve space by writing to the Administracão do Parque Nacional de Itatiaia, Itatiaia 27540, Estado Rio de Janeiro, Brasil. Groceries are not available in the park; bring your own food unless you plan to eat in hotels.

The *planalto* is far more primitive, and therefore less crowded. The only developments there are a park guard post, a campground with water and sanitary facilities in a spectacular mountainous setting, a hostel (*abrigo das rebouças*), and several trails. A rough 15-mile (24 kilometers) trail from the campground links the *planalto* to the lower part of the park via the Véu de Noiva waterfall, and gives hikers the opportunity to see the entire range of elevational zones. From the end of the road to the hostel, trails lead toward the summits of Agulhas Negras and the lower Pico Cristal. A 1-mile (2 kilometers) trail also leads to Maça and Tartaruga from this point. The famous rocks are at the left (north) end of the Prataleiras, the conspicuous granite-like outcroppings to the southeast of the road.

Location and Access

Itatiaia lies within two Brazilian states: in the northwest corner of the state of Rio de Janeiro and the southeast corner of the state of Minas Gerais. It is just off BR 116 (Rodovía Dutra), the freeway (*rodovía*) connecting Rio with São Paulo, 102 miles (164 kilometers) west of Rio, and 160 miles (257 kilometers) east of São Paulo. The entrance to the lower part of the park lies 6 miles (10 kilometers) north of the town of Itatiaia.

A separate road, BR 354, leads to the *planalto* portion of the park. To reach the *planalto*, drive 8 miles (13 kilometers) west of Itatiaia (the town), and turn north on BR 354 toward Caxambú. BR 354 becomes the highest road in Brazil, leading to the pass that divides the two states, Rio de Janeiro and Minas Gerais. At the top of the pass, a sign indicates the road to the *planalto* entrance to the park, 9 miles (15 kilometers) from the turnoff.

Access to the lower part of the park is easy. Daily buses reach the town of Itatiaia from both Rio and São Paulo; visitors can also take the trail from either direction.

Schedules are erratic. Ask for a ticket to the Itatiaia Station. Hotels in the park sometimes arrange bus tours through the lower part of the park, but this is not really necessary. Hitchhiking in this part of the park is easy.

Access to the *planalto* is a different story. Hitchhiking is possible but undependable, for the area is remote, unpopulated, and not heavily visited. Check first at the hotels, which occasionally arrange tours to the *planalto*. Visitors can also try a group rental of a taxi in Itatiaia (the town) and hike back, or, as a last resort, rent a car.

Glossary

abrigo	hostel, shelter
agulhas negras	black needles
cachoeira	small cascading stream, pronounced kah-SHWAY-rah
maça	apple
planalto	high plateau
prateleira	shelf
rodovía	freeway
sede	headquarters
tartaruga	turtle
véu da noiva	bride's veil

⊡ APARADOS DA SERRA:
The Crack in the Shield

During the Permian Period, when fish ruled the earth, a gigantic basin formed in the zone now occupied by southern Brazil and northern Argentina and Uruguay. Through the millenia, the Atlantic Ocean repeatedly flooded the basin, and deep layers of sediments were laid down on the floor of this shallow sea. Over millions of years, as the Atlantic Ocean flooded in and out of the basin, layers of sediment piled atop one another, eventually creating strata up to 2,500 feet thick. These ancient rocks were then lifted to form the highland plateau known as the Brazilian Shield.

Then, toward the end of the tumultuous Triassic Period, about 150 million years ago, one of the most cataclysmic volcanic events in geological history occurred. Huge gouts of lava began to pour onto the surface of the Brazilian Shield, not by means of the sort of explosive eruptions that result in volcanos and ash flows, but rather by slow, constant flows that eventually covered 600,000 square miles of the Shield with as much as 1,500 feet of lava, and put a thick cap of basalt on top of the plateau.

Itaiembezinho—the gorge at Aparados da Serra National Park, Brazil

On the edge of this plateau, not far from the Atlantic coast, gigantic cracks later appeared in the basalt, and the site of the largest of these cracks is Aparados da Serra, Brazil's southernmost national park.

Aparado means cliff or abyss, and *serra* means mountains, so *aparados da serra* translates as "mountain precipices." Part of the term is somewhat misleading, for the terrain in and around the park is high, but not mountainous; it is rather the gently undulating surface of a high plateau. There is no doubt, however, about the term *aparados*. It is a shock to proceed across seemingly endless arid rolling plains and to be stopped short by a dizzying cleft in the earth's crust nearly 2,000 feet deep.

The Tupi-Guarani Indian name for the cleft, Itaimbezinho (roughly, "sharp-cut rock"), is more descriptive of the park's central feature, for what sets this gorge apart from any other 2,000-foot canyon is the abruptness with which it appears. With virtually no warning, the earth falls away from one's feet, and visitors who conquer their vertigo and gingerly approach the edge can peer into an abyss with walls as sheer as an elevator shaft, a slice so sharp through thousands of feet of basalt as to have been made with a cake knife. Nobody knows quite how the gorge was formed. Itaimbezinho and several other smaller but equally sheer canyons in the area are located on fault lines, but the mechanisms that created them have not yet been worked out.

Not surprisingly, two separate climates prevail at Aparados da Serra: a temperate semiarid zone on the plateau and a humid subtropical zone on the floor of the canyon.

Most of the plateau is rolling open grassland, but near the canyon scattered clumps of forest appear. Nearly fifty species of small trees make up these forest clumps, but the most distinctive is the Paraná pine or Pinho de Paraná (*Araucaria angustifolia*). Related to the monkey puzzle tree of the southern Andes, these conifers have an even more parasol-like appearance than their mountain cousins, and have suffered a similar fate—overexploitation. Tall and straight, with trunks up to 3 feet in diameter, Paraná pines are excellent lumber trees that once covered nearly all of the plateaus of Brazil south of Curitiba. Today, nearly all of the Paraná pines left in Brazil are within the boundaries of national parks. Botanists now estimate that 23,000 *square miles* of Paraná pines have simply disappeared into the maws of sawmills.

Although rainfall is fairly low in the park, fog banks rolling in from the sea encourage growth in similar fashion to a cloud forest. Trees of the myrtle family (*Myrtacea*), common in the park, are preferred hosts for epiphytes. It is not uncommon to find a single myrtle supporting an entire community of smaller plants, including bromeliads, orchids, ferns, mosses, lianas, and cacti.

The floor of the canyon is not much higher than sea level, but the fog that brings moisture to the plateau has little effect on the flora far below, a typical profusion of small tree and shrub species adorned with orchids, bromeliads, and pteridophytes. Humidity is kept high on the canyon floor by spray from several waterfalls that plunge into the gorge. Larger falls swell the volume of the Rio das Antas (Tapir River), which flows through a boulder-studded streambed, but small falls never reach the bottom, vanishing into swirls of mist during their 1,500-foot plunge.

The descent from the plateau to the bottom of the gorge is worthwhile, and is recommended for hikers in good condition. A primitive trail begins at the point where the road crosses the head of the canyon. Except for one section where ropes are required to negotiate a 15-foot vertical slab, hikers simply work their way down alongside a small stream. **Caution:** Beware of slick footing near the stream, and of falling rocks throughout the canyon. A rock that has fallen 1,500 feet or so is as dangerous as a cannonball.

Except for a curious absence of birdlife in the stands of Paraná pines, birds are common on the plateau and in the canyon: more than 150 species have been identified in the park. Since the extreme south of Brazil shares a few habitat characteristics with Patagonia, such birds as the buff-headed ibis and southern lapwing live there. Terrestrial fauna are scarce.

Visitor Facilities

A free campground, with picnic tables, water, and sanitary facilities, is maintained at the park, and a small nearby restaurant rents rooms to visitors. Not far away, the Rio das Antas comes to the canyon rim and drops 1,300 feet into a subtropical plunge pool.

Climate and Weather

Aparados da Serra is accessible year-round, but spring (October and November) is the best time to visit to see flowers.

Summer (December through March) is warm, with many sunny days and short but heavy rainfalls. January and February are the warmest months, with maximum temperatures of about 72 degrees Fahrenheit.

Winter is characterized by long spells of light rain and occasional periods of freezing weather and snowfalls. Days are cool, nights cold enough for sweaters. July is the coldest month.

Location and Access

Aparados da Serra is in the extreme southeast corner of Brazil, in the northeast corner of the state of Rio Grande do Sul. The region is populated by families of immigrants of German descent who have farmed the land and created small towns and villages with an unmistakably Bavarian flavor. In many of these towns—Nova Petropolis, Gramada, Canela—scores of small shops and bazaars have sprung up to sell attractive handicrafts of local manufacture.

The park is 112 miles (180 kilometers) from Porto Alegre, capital of Rio Grande do Sul, and 43 miles (69 kilometers) from São Francisco de Paula. Several buses a day link Porto Alegre to São Francisco de Paula and other nearby towns. To reach the park, take a bus from São Francisco de Paula, get off at the park turnoff, and hike or hitchhike the 9 miles (14 kilometers) to the park. Hitchhiking is easy in summer, difficult in winter. On summer weekends, excursions to the park depart from hotels in São Francisco de Paula.

Myrtle trees at Aparados da Serra National Park support entire communities of a wide variety of other plants, including orchids.

Glossary

aparado	precipice, abyss
árvore	tree
beijaflor	hummingbird; literally, flower-kisser
floresta, mata	forest, woods
grama	grass
guarda florestal	park guard
palmero	palm
picapau	woodpecker
pinho, pinheiro	pine, pine tree
trilha, picada	trail, path

⊞ IGUAÇÚ/IGUAZÚ: The Cloud Maker

In the extreme northeast corner of Argentina lies Misiones Province, which occupies a narrow band of territory between Brazil and Paraguay. The northern boundary of the province is formed by the Rio Iguaçú, which separates Argentina from Brazil. Although large, the Rio Iguaçú flows through an area in which large rivers are commonplace. By regional standards the river is undistinguished—but for one remarkable physiographical curiosity: the river abruptly drops off the plateau it drains, and in so doing creates one of the world's great waterfalls, Iguaçú Falls.

Higher than Victoria Falls and twice as wide as Niagara, Iguaçú Falls is a natural phenomenon that reaches out and envelops the senses of visitors. On clear cool mornings, signs of it are visible from a distance—swirling puffs of vapor rising well above the treetops, tinged pink by the rising sun, domed by rainbows. Visitors slowly become aware of a deep hum that gradually swells to a roar. At the river's edge it is possible to feel a faint vibration through the soles of one's shoes.

The falls are the paramount feature of the Iguaçú national parks, not one but two adjoining parks, one in Brazil, the other in Argentina. **Note:** The name for the river, waterfall, and park is spelled Iguaçú in Portuguese and Iguazú in Spanish. Spellings in the text conform to the descriptions of the Brazilian or Argentine sides of this international park. The falls are everything one would expect when an average of 62,000 cubic feet *per second* of water suddenly spills 230 feet over a cliff a mile and a half wide—fascinating, awe-inspiring, even for visitors not particularly attracted to waterfalls. A trip to Iguaçú to see the falls and nothing else is still worthwhile, and well over a million people a year do just that. These parks are by far the most popular in South America, visited by more foreign travelers than any other national parks on the continent.

Visitors depart quite happy to have seen the mighty waterfalls and to have wandered through the multitude of tourist shops in nearby communities. Yet grand as they

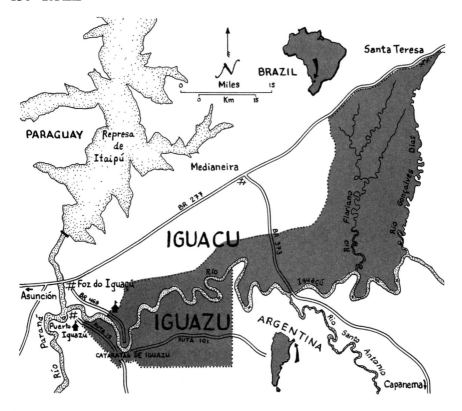

are, the falls overshadow other outstanding attributes of these parks, and most visitors take their leave completely unaware that they have missed one of the finest opportunities in South America to explore and experience a real tropical jungle.

Getting to the edge of a jungle is easy in any of several South American countries; take a plane, bus, or boat to any town in a tropical forest and it's accomplished. But to get *past* the edge, *into* a rain forest is far more difficult than most travelers realize. In most of South America, roads and trails are cut through rain forests in order to develop their resources, to collect or remove a good part of the very flora and fauna that the inquisitive visitor seeks. Roads and trails that connect towns seem to pass through miles of undisturbed jungle, but it is illusory—animals are scarce, the big trees and palmitos are gone, the unusual orchids long ago shipped off to collectors. The real jungle is far off, well beyond the margins of the road.

Yet without roads or trails, the rain forest is usually too dense to enter; the difficulties of moving very far through a tropical rain forest are greater than most of us are willing or able to deal with. The dilemma is resolved at Iguaçú, for access to the rain forest is provided not in order to extract its resources, but to facilitate its maintenance and to protect it. Iguaçú is one of a handful of places in tropical South America where a visitor can wander through a nearly pristine rain forest without having to hack out a path or take the unsettling risk of getting lost. At Iguaçú, it is possible to see a tropical rain forest from the inside out, rather than the outside in.

With respect to crowds, comparison with Yellowstone is apt: visitors who hang around Old Faithful geyser will eventually meet the 2 million other visitors who come to the park every year, but those who take almost any backcountry trail will have large portions of Yellowstone to themselves. Similarly, the falls at Iguaçú are always crowded, but take any of the forest roads or trails, and it is a different world: hot; humid; silent but for dripping water, rustling leaves, and the sounds of birds and insects; almost deserted—the stuff of movies. Go far enough, and you will have the park and its attractions to yourself.

THE FALLS. Iguaçú Falls occur at the point at which the Rio Iguaçú intersects a geological fault in the extensive Jurassic lava flows that formed southeastern Brazil and northern Argentina. The river is 300 miles long and from 1,500 to 3,000 feet wide for much of its length. *I* means water and *guaçu* means "great" in Guaraní, the language of the Indians who originally inhabited the region. The falls are large (at flood stage as many as 450,000 cubic feet of muddy water cross the brink every second), but are not made up of a single massive waterfall. Because the fault line crosses the riverbed in the shape of a large J, the lip of the waterfall is interrupted by several islands and outcrops, and is extremely long—8,860 feet. At its lowest stage, Iguaçú Falls comprises 160 cataracts, but at high water the river forms as many as 260 separate cataracts!

To see the falls properly, visitors should visit both sides of the river. About two-thirds of the lip of the falls belongs to Argentina, and one-third to Brazil. The nations meet in the center of Union Falls, the large cataract that spills into the Garganta del Diablo (Devils' Throat), the boiling, mist-shrouded maelstrom that forms the river's main channel below the falls. Deeper river channels and larger cataracts lie within Brazilian territory, but most of the islands and picturesque individual cataracts are in Argentina. The nature of the riverbed and islands on the Argentine side has permitted construction of a series of elevated catwalks (*pasarelas*) that lead between islands to several observation points with spectacular overlooks. Unfortunately, long sections of some catwalks were destroyed by floodwaters in 1983, but the Argentine Park Service is restoring them as quickly as funds permit. Make sure to explore the *pasarelas*, for it is quite exciting to stroll along a few feet above a river roaring by like an express train.

THE FLORA. Plenty of sunshine, high humidity (close to 90 per cent), warm temperatures, abundant rainfall distributed evenly throughout the year, and soils that rapidly recycle nutrients are the basic ingredients for tropical rain forests of the sort we call jungles. Vegetation is distinctly stratified in such a forest: the upper level is formed by a nearly closed canopy of trees that may exceed 100 feet in height, then an intermediate layer is formed by trees from 10 to 30 feet high; the next layer is composed primarily of shrubs; and finally, on the forest floor, is an herbaceous level.

Among the tallest trees that form the canopy are the lapacho (*Tabebuia ipe*), which reaches 100 feet and sports pink or yellow flowers; the incienso (*Myrocarpus frondosus*), whose greenish-yellow flowers fill the neighboring forest with a rich fragrance; and, tallest of all, the palo rosa (*Aspidosperma polyneuron*), which reaches 130 feet, is often found in association with the slender palmito, and is invariably adorned with scores of epiphytes.

Some species of trees that form the canopy are more abundant than others, but more noteworthy is the extraordinary diversity of the trees. Botanists long ago noted that the diversity of species in a tropical forest is extremely high, while the number of individuals in the species is very low, a sharp contrast to most temperate forests, where a monotonous succession of one or two conifer species might make up a forest thousands of square miles in extent. The forests of Iguaçú are prime examples of this characteristic, for a bewildering assortment of plants greets the eye. One study demonstrated that while an acre of land in Iguaçú might support about 120 trees, the most abundant species might be represented by only six or seven of these trees, which explains why it is possible to hike for a mile or two through a rain forest before seeing the same tree twice.

Visitors who have set out to learn the flora of Iguaçú in a few days have quite a job ahead of them, for more than 2,000 vascular plants have been identified in the park, about 90 of which are large trees, with 150 more small trees and large shrubs.

Tree ferns, and small trees and shrubs that produce numerous fruits and berries, are the most notable members of the intermediate stratum. Yerba mate (*Ilex paraguariensis*) grows at this level of the forest. The leaves of this tree, rich in a caffeine-like alkaloid, are used in the production of *mate,* a tea widely consumed in Brazil, Paraguay, Uruguay, and northern Argentina.

The shrub stratum can be troublesome, and is the principal reason that it can be difficult to move about in some parts of tropical rain forests without a trail. Relatively harmless ferns and bamboos often predominate at this level, but most of the other plants defend themselves with a variety of hooks, spines, thorns, nettle-like stingers, oils that irritate or blister skin, razor-sharp edges, or appalling combinations of these deterrents. Those few bushes that lack obvious weapons of their own seem to harbor and are defended by hordes of stinging or biting insects; some really deadly bushes have both!

The forest floor is an organic mat, littered with fallen leaves, branches, and tree trunks in various stages of decomposition, giving rise to fungi, mosses, lichens, and grasses.

At all strata of the forest above the forest floor grow the epiphytes—mosses, lichens, lianas, bromeliads, philodendrons, begonias, and especially the orchids. The orchid family is the largest in the plant kingdom. Conservative estimates indicate that at least 15,000 species exist throughout the world, from subarctic regions to the tropics, but the rain forests are where they have achieved their greatest success. While virtually every tree in Iguaçú is embellished with orchids in a riotous proliferation of forms, sizes, and stages of development, finding the flowers in bloom is a matter of luck and hard looking. Neither orchids nor other flowering plants here bloom in synchronization with the seasons, since wet and dry or warm and cool seasons are not distinct in Iguaçú.

Two striking epiphytes common in Iguaçú are the güembé (*Philodendron bipinnatifidium*) and the guapoy or strangler fig (*Ficus monckii*). The güembé can germinate in soil and develop a short thick stem, but if it encounters a tree it immediately sends out long branches that climb the trunk to the high, sunny points of the tree, where it

An astonishing variety of epiphytes adorn the trees in the rain forests of Iguaçú National Park.

eventually develops hanging air roots and large leaves. If its seeds fall into cavities or forks in the tree, they germinate where they land, and the new güembés become entirely epiphytic plants, depending upon their host tree for nothing but anchorage and support. The guapoy employs similar tactics, but once well established, its roots begin to thicken and spread until they join and completely encircle the trunk of the host tree. Eventually these roots reach the soil and take a hollow but sturdy trunk-like form that literally strangles the host tree, and supports a more or less ordinary looking tree that started life as an epiphyte, slowly became a normal tree, and then a killer.

The graceful palm that you see around the park, often in the shade of enormous palo rosa trees, is the palmito (*Euterpe edulis*). It is sometimes called the ice cream tree, because oil from its seeds is used in the production of ice cream. Fruit from the tree can be used as a cream substitute for coffee; drop a seed or two into a hot cup of coffee and the heat will extract the oil. Palmitos, however, are all but extinct in Argentina and in much of Brazil, for they are the source of what we call heart-of-palm, the edible core of the upper part of the tree. Because the core includes the tree's meristematic tissue, the tree dies when the heart is removed. As the palmito grows increasingly scarce, the value of heart-of-palm has increased dramatically, and the tree has been subject to relentless thievery even where protected. In 1968 a park guard, Bernabe Mendez, was killed by palmito hunters while on patrol in the park. A school for national park professionals in Argentina's Parque Nacional Nahuel Huapi is named in memory of Señor Mendez. Incredibly, canned heart-of-palm from Brazil can still be obtained in American supermarkets, obviously an egregious purchase.

THE FAUNA. The terrestrial wildlife of tropical South America is notoriously difficult to observe in the wild. As with vegetation, many species can occupy a tract of forest, but their individual numbers are quite low. Many are nocturnal or active only at dawn and dusk. Most are shy by nature, and keep as far from human activities as possible. Adept at hiding themselves in forest shadows, they can take a step or two and vanish from sight into dense tropical foliage if they grow nervous. And because lowland forests frequently flood, many species have evolved arboreal or semiaquatic habits, and live in areas in which it is difficult for would-be wildlife observers to maneuver.

This does not necessarily mean that visitors will not see wildlife. Lucky ones might see a herd of peccaries splash through a stream, or a band of monkeys swing through the forest canopy. But it does mean that those who are determined to see wildlife must give themselves every advantage they can get, even in Iguaçú, where the chances of seeing tropical wildlife are reasonable. First, get up *early*; plan to be on the trail at first light. Also, get away from crowded areas; the more distance you put between yourself and noisy traffic, the more wildlife you will see. Hike silently, in order to listen without calling attention to yourself. Explore the margins of watercourses if possible, and remember to keep an eye on the trees as well as the ground.

The tapir (*Tapirus terrestris*) is the largest jungle animal in South America, reaching nearly 700 pounds. Its body shape is somewhat like a pig, but it has upright ears and a long proboscis-like snout with which it sorts through the foliage and aquatic plants on which it feeds. Never far from water, tapirs spend hours resting in sloughs and backwaters to escape heat and insects. Because tapirs are solitary and sedentary creatures, they are difficult to find, but the tunnel-like trails they make through dense undergrowth are easy to spot. Look for three-toed tracks in these trails. If you startle a tapir in the forest, you will know it even if you don't see the animal, for they do not hide or slink away, but rather crash at full speed right through whatever barrier lies between them and the nearest water—high-speed jungle bulldozers.

Another animal of Iguaçú that crashes noisily through the undergrowth when startled is the peccary or wild pig. These animals are not pigs, but are pig-like in appearance and habits. Two species are found in the park, the collared peccary (*Tayassu tajacu*) and the white-lipped peccary (*Tayassu albirostris*). Collared peccaries, black or dark gray animals that weigh 40 to 50 pounds, move about the forest floor in groups of six to fifteen individuals. Omnivorous, they eat nearly everything in their path— leaves, roots, fruits, insects, reptiles, carrion. A faint band about their chest and shoulders distinguishes them from their slightly larger cousins, the white-lipped peccaries. White-lipped peccaries are more aggressive and forage in much larger bands, consisting of up to 300 animals. As a rule, peccaries flee from humans, but if cornered they do not hesitate to attack predators. Because they travel in such large herds, some authorities consider white-lipped peccaries to be the most dangerous animals of the rain forest.

Both jaguars and mountain lions have been observed in Iguaçú, but if you see more than their tracks, you will be very lucky indeed.

The most common carnivore in the park is the coatimundi (*Nasua nasua*), a brown animal about the size of a housecat, but related to raccoons. Coatimundis have short legs, long noses, and very long tails that are nearly always carried erect. They have mask-like white markings on their faces, but an observer's first sight of the coati is usually its black-and-brown-ringed tail bobbing along above the grass and herbaceous plants on the forest floor. They travel in small bands, are extremely active foragers, and scamper as easily up trees as across the trail.

The most numerous herbivores in Iguaçú are pacas (*Cuniculus paca*) and agoutis (*Dasyprocta azarae*). Pacas are 2-foot-long rodents with short tails and several rows of white spots along their flanks. They can be solitary or in pairs, and eat almost anything green. You are most likely to hear them in very early morning rustling through fallen leaves in search of fruits and nuts. Agoutis, gray and white animals without tails, live in small groups. They have long legs for rodents, enabling them to run very fast, and to squat and handle food with their front paws like squirrels and chipmunks.

Two monkey species are relatively common in the park. The caí or capuchin monkey (*Cebus apella*) has extremely long legs and the long prehensile tail characteristic of New World monkeys. Capuchin means monk, and this small but charming monkey is distinguished by a black skullcap-like mark atop its head. They travel through the canopy in groups of up to 200 and avoid the forest floor as much as possible, obtaining water from epiphytes and carefully searching branches for insects, fruits, and edible leaves. Capuchins are noisy monkeys, and their high-pitched chittering sounds like bird songs.

The howler monkey (*Alouatta caraya*), largest of the New World monkeys, is also noisy, but the noise is completely different in character. Howlers are brownish-black vegetarians that travel in much smaller groups—fifteen to twenty—but have been endowed with tremendous powers of vocalization. The first time travelers hear howlers, they cannot believe that this terrifying sound is being created by a few monkeys rather than a convention of jaguars or a coven of unearthly beasts. The sound, a deep roar of varying timbre and wavering resonance, has a haunted quality guaranteed to raise eyebrows and neck hair. Howlers tend to greet the dawn with their roars—which carry for miles—and among the most unforgettable experiences of South America is listening to the eerie echoes of bands of howler monkeys calling to each other across miles of steamy rain forest as the sun begins to pinken the eastern horizon.

FLYING BANANAS AND BUTTERFLIES. The stability of Iguaçú's climate, abundance of ecological niches, and quantity, variety, and year-round availability of food are factors responsible for the astonishing diversity of birds in the park. This is the park to visit to see trogons, toucans, parrots, hummingbirds, and hundreds of other species of birds.

Trogons are medium-sized birds with long, square tails. Some eat insects, and others fruit. They are not easy to see, for they tend to sit quite still on branches for long periods, darting out occasionally to snare a passing insect and returning quickly to their perch. But look hard, for male trogons are among the most beautiful of birds, metallic green to violet above, with crimson or yellow breasts and stomachs.

Toucans and toucanets usually travel in small groups, and have Technicolor bills nearly as long as the birds they adorn. The giant toucan (*Ramphastos toco*), 18 inches long, has a preposterous yellow bill with a large black oval blotch near its tip. In the air it resembles a flying banana, but its long bill is useful when it's time to crack large fruits and raid the nests of other birds. The smaller red-breasted toucan (*Ramphastos discolorus*) is black, has a red breast, and a gigantic pea-green beak.

Large flocks of raucous parakeets and smaller flocks of parrots patrol the topmost canopies and glide frequently across the river, and hummingbirds zip through the lower levels like bright bullets.

No visitor can miss dusky swifts (*Cypseloides senex*), for they wheel about the falls in hundreds, and appear to dart into and out of the cataracts themselves. The swifts, in fact, nest on the cliffs over which the falls plunge, and some construct their mud nests behind a curtain of falling water.

Another bird easy to spot is the boyero or cacique (*Cacicus haemorrhus*). This blackbird has a crimson rump and back, and is almost always associated with a particular palm tree, the Pindó palm (*Arecastrum romanzoffianum*). The boyero weaves hanging nests at the ends of dangling Pindó fronds, using fibers from other Pindó leaves and cementing the fibers together with a gummy substance from the fruit of a different tree. The hanging nests keep eggs and young safe from almost all predators except the toucan, which can reach the bottom of the nest with its long bill. To counter this threat, boyeros have adopted the habit of nesting close to houses and other centers of human activity, which toucans avoid. Clever blackbird.

Iguaçú is a bird-watcher's paradise, but remember that you should be on the lookout right after daylight and, to a lesser extent, in the evening. Birds have more sense

A young collared peccary (Tayassu tajacu) *roots about in a mud puddle in Iguaçú National Park. Note the faint collar around the front shoulders.*

than many of us, and when it gets hot they rest. But about the time the birds stop to rest, hundreds of butterflies come out: giant iridescent blue morphos; tiny red, blue, and green moths; and hundreds of species with dazzling colors and bizarre forms. Look among the 500 species of butterflies in the park for the ochenta y ocho, a small, common butterfly with white wings on which is printed a conspicuous black 88.

Visitor Facilities

Visitors who dislike being rushed should plan to spend two or three nights in the vicinity of the parks. A good look at the falls requires a full day, and at least one day should be devoted to exploring the rain forest.

To fully experience the falls, travelers need to visit both sides of the river, for the experience is different on each side. On the Brazilian side, a short walkway leads from the hotel to the area below the Garganta del Diablo, and to an observation tower swept by spray from one of the major cataracts. A gift shop and rest rooms are located in the tower, and a bar, restaurant, and picnic area are nearby. The walkway provides a splendid view of the semicircle of cataracts that lie in Argentina. These cataracts, however, are difficult to appreciate from the Argentine side, where visitors get only a partial view from the lower walkway and no view at all from the upper walkway. These walkways are the special attractions on the Argentine side; by island hopping, they take visitors right over the river and to the brink of several cataracts. Refreshment stands are located at strategic points along the walkways. Brazil has no counterparts for these *pasarelas*, for its trails are built into the side of the riverbank. Conversely, until the partially destroyed walkways are completely reconstructed, the best overall view of the falls is from the Brazilian side. In short, both sides have unique features and vistas.

Argentina has constructed several miles of nicely laid out and well marked trails above and below the falls. The lower trail (*circuito inferior*) passes over the base of several smaller falls before reaching the main river; the upper trail (*circuito superior*) follows the brink of the falls and, when reconstructed, will reach an observation point at the edge of Union Falls overlooking the Garganta del Diablo. Climb the tower behind the Argentine hotel for a bird's-eye view of the falls.

Take a light raincoat along on your walks along the falls; the spray can soak through light clothes in an instant, and brief rainstorms are frequent. Take plenty of insect repellent; bugs can be as dense as raindrops, and some bees and wasps are very persistent.

On the Argentine side, take swim gear along on the lower trail; swimming in the pools beneath some of the smaller cataracts is excellent and very refreshing on a hot afternoon. Ask for directions to the bird-watching blind at the marsh (*banado*) and to the Sendero Macuco, a jungle nature trail.

Both countries have constructed luxury hotels (expensive, but nice) on their own sides of the park. The Argentine hotel is more modern, but the Brazilian hotel has a more appropriate tropical motif. Both countries also provide picnic areas in their parks, but overnight camping is prohibited. Campgrounds with hot water, showers, and tables are located not far from the entrances of both parks. Both parks have small natural history museums.

A variety of hotels and restaurants are available in and around the parks' gateway towns, Puerto Iguazú in Argentina and Foz do Iguaçú in Brazil. Buses enter the parks from both towns and cross the border on frequent and regular schedules.

To get off the beaten path and into the rain forest on the Argentine side, drive, hike, or hitchhike down Ruta 101, a road that passes through 25 miles (40 kilometers) of the park, or along the lightly traveled patrol road (*sendero de vigilancia*) that follows the river upstream on the Argentine side. Park guards at stations on these roads will answer questions, and may give permission to camp in this area. On the Brazilian side, hike the narrow 6-mile (10 kilometers) track that leads from behind the park director's house to an upper section of the Rio Iguaçú, an excellent bird and wildlife walk. Obtain permission to stray from the cataracts area at park headquarters, lest you be suspected of poaching.

Park staff have only recently become aware that a significant proportion of visitors are just as interested in Iguaçú's rain forest as in its waterfalls. Staff are very zealous about protecting park resources from poachers and clandestine collectors of birds, plants, butterflies, and so on. For this reason, they are liable to be somewhat suspicious when you ask for permission to enter little-visited areas of the park, and if you do not make the reasons for your request clear, permission may be denied. Explain that you are interested in seeing and photographing the forest and its wildlife, and make a point of mentioning that you do not wish to collect *anything*. (Spanish: *Me interesan la flora y fauna silvestre; para mirar y fotografear, no colecionar.* Portuguese: *Me interesan o flora e fauna selvagem; para olhar e fotografar, não colecionar.*) Staff of both park services, especially biologists, are very enthusiastic about Iguaçú; once they understand your motives and recognize a kindred soul, they will become very cooperative, and may even offer to take you around themselves.

An advantage to stopping first on the Argentine side of the park is that the Argentine Park Service provides much more printed literature on the park and its resources than its Brazilian counterpart.

Before deciding on which country in which to spend the night, check exchange rates and hotel and restaurant prices on both sides of the river. As in any resort area, prices are higher than elsewhere, but it may be possible to significantly offset those costs by seeking accommodations in the cheaper country.

Recreation

Iguaçú is a sightseeing park, a place to explore at close range one of the world's major waterfalls. It is also such a good place to explore a tropical rain forest and its birds and wildlife that it serves as a less adventurous, but reasonable, substitute for the forests of the Amazon Basin.

Historical and Cultural Aspects

Because of an odd historical coincidence, the first European to see Iguaçú Falls made his discovery barely fifty years after Columbus made landfall in the New World. In 1541, the Spanish explorer Alvar Nuñez Cabeza de Vaca and 280 men set out to bring military assistance to the besieged settlers of newly founded Asunción, Paraguay. Instead of traveling up the Paraná River toward Asunción, Cabeza de Vaca headed west through the forest from what is now the coast of Santa Catarina state in southern Brazil. During the course of what became an epic jungle trek, he and his men suffered greatly, and many died, but their journey took them past Iguaçú Falls. Cabeza de Vaca gave the falls the name Saltos de Santa Maria, but the name fell into disuse and the original Indian name stuck. Settlement of the region continued, Argentina and Brazil were created, and nearly four centuries later the two countries began to realize that the waterfall and its surroundings were indeed unique and worthy of protection.

In 1928, the government of Argentina acquired land near the falls with the intention of creating a park at the site. The objective was realized in 1934 with passage of a law that created Argentina's park service as well as Parque Nacional Iguazú. In the early 1970s, additional land was obtained and either incorporated into the park or into an adjacent national reserve to bring the total areas of park and reserve to 137,000 acres.

Brazil created its park somewhat later (1939), but set aside over three times as much land—420,000 acres. The Brazilian park is divided into three zones: a small recreation and development zone near the cataracts; a somewhat larger recuperation zone along the river east of the falls, directly across the river from the Argentine park; and the largest zone, the entire watershed of the Rio Floriano, a major tributary of the Rio Iguaçú. The recuperation zone is tangible proof of the Brazilian government's commitment to the national park concept, for over 400 settlers illegally occupying and cultivating 30,000 acres of parkland were successfully relocated elsewhere, permitting park managers of both nations to enhance and maintain the ecological integrity of the entire park.

Maintenance of ecological integrity is vitally important at Iguaçú. From any direction, visitors to the park pass through thousands of square miles of intensely developed and cultivated land. Iguaçú is an island of rain forest in a sea of land that was once also rain forest, but which was completely deforested for timber, and then cultivated to produce coffee, sugar, cattle, soybeans, and other products. That does not sound like misuse of land, especially when clearing the forest exposed fertile, brick-red soils up to 10 feet deep, but evidence is mounting that the soils in this part of South America cannot long sustain intensive agricultural production without immense infusions of fertilizer and dangerous levels of pesticide. A day will come when these lands will no longer be suitable for intensive exploitation, when it may be necessary to restore the rain forest in order to hasten their recuperation. When that day arrives, land managers of the future will look to the 870 square miles of the two national parks for the plants and animals they will need to reintroduce a rain forest to lands unwittingly overworked. As long as protection is effective, the parks will be nurseries for those future rain forests. The parks are fascinating, but not merely fascinating; they are repositories of the flora and fauna of future generations, and warrant all the protection they can get.

Climate and Weather

Temperatures at the parks generally fluctuate between hot and hotter, although exceptions do occur—on May 17, 1975, snow fell here, the only day in recorded history it has happened. The normal average annual temperature, about 68 degrees Fahrenheit, does not change significantly through the year. In winter months (June and July), the thermometer dips to an average of about 60 degrees. The average temperature in summer (January and February) reaches about 77 degrees, but the heat can be oppressive during the day. The rigors of summer heat are usually compensated for by cool, shirtsleeve evenings, when temperatures may drop by over 20 degrees. Diurnal temperature variations are in fact usually greater than seasonal variations.

Humid winds from the Atlantic bring abundant rainfall that reaches about 80 inches yearly, and is more or less evenly distributed through the year. Clouds and ground fogs are common during winter months. Photographers should note that afternoons are often sunnier than mornings.

The most comfortable time of year to visit the park is June through August, a period with relatively cool days and slightly less rainfall than other months. Be aware, however, that the river is usually highest—and the falls more spectacular—in February or March.

Location and Access

Parque Nacional Iguaçú is located in the southwest corner of the state of Paraná, in the southwest corner of Brazil. The Brazilian gateway city to the park is Foz do Iguaçú, often simply called Foz (river mouth). The nearest large Brazilian cities are Curitiba (12 hours by bus), São Paulo (18 hours), and Porto Alegre (17 hours). Asunción, Paraguay, is a 7-hour bus trip from Foz. Buses between these cities and Foz are fast, comfortable, and frequent. Foz has an airport (19 miles—30 kilometers—from the park), and frequent flights link the town to most major Brazilian cities, Asunción, and, for that matter, Miami and New York City. Local buses travel between Foz and the park several times a day. Several travel agencies and hotels in Foz operate organized tours of both sides of the park; these tours are generally better and cheaper than taxi tours. Hitchhiking is difficult in the vicinity of the park.

The Argentine park is in the northwest corner of Misiones Province in the extreme northeast corner of Argentina. The Argentine gateway city is Puerto Iguazú, 12 miles (19 kilometers) from the park entrance. The nearest large Argentine cities are Posadas (5 hours by bus), Corrientes, and Rosario. Express buses from Buenos Aires take 22 hours (Expreso Tigre-Iguazú; offices on Plaza Once). It is also possible to take an interesting train ride to Posadas from Buenos Aires, and continue on to the park by bus; the train has sleeping and dining accommodations. Several flights a day arrive at Puerto Iguazú's airport from Buenos Aires. The park can also be reached by air from Corrientes, Rosario, or Posadas on less frequent flights.

No matter in which country you intend to stay, if you fly to the park, be sure not to cross a border; that is, do not fly from Río to Puerto Iguazú or from Buenos Aires to Foz do Iguaçú, because international flights are more expensive, and hardly worth the paperwork. Taxis will even go into the jungle. Those who insist on renting a car will need an international driver's license and a great deal of nerve. Driving in Argentina or Brazil is not for the fainthearted.

Glossary

SPANISH	PORTUGUESE	
aguti	cotia	agouti
balcón, mirador	mirante	viewpoint
camino	estrada	road, highway
coati	coati	coatimundi
Garganta del Diablo	Garganta do Diabo	Devil's Throat
mono	macaco	monkey
mono aullador	bugio ou guariba	howler monkey
mono caí	macaco-prego	capuchin monkey
museo	museu	museum
paca	paca	paca
pasarela		raised walkway
paseo	passeio	walk, stroll
pecarí	caitetu	peccary
perdido		intermittent cataract
puma, león	sucuarana	mountain lion
salto	catarata	falls, cataract
sede, intendencia	sede	headquarters
sendero, picada	trilha, caminho	trail
tapir, danta	anta	tapir
tigre	jaguar ou onça	jaguar
vencejo	andorinha	swift, swallow

In October, tall, gangly *seriemas* (Cariama cristata) *nest in the short trees of the* campos sujos *of Das Emas National Park, Brazil.*

🔲 DAS EMAS:
Zoo without Bars

Six hundred miles north of Iguaçú Falls, in the remote heart of the highlands of southern Brazil, lies a little-known park called Das Emas (The Rheas). Das Emas is not easy to reach. Visitors require authorization from the Brazilian Park Service (Departmento de Parques Nacionais) to visit the park, then must make their way from Brasilia over 300 miles (483 kilometers) of nearly deserted roads to arrive finally at a park that they may be required to leave at sunset.

The effort is worthwhile only for visitors in serious search of wildlife, but for those visitors Das Emas is a jackpot; the park is the best place in South America to see many of the continent's typical animals—giant and lesser anteaters, rheas, pampas deer, armadillos, capybaras, tapirs, monkeys, peccaries, raccoons, skunks, coatimundis, toucans, parrots, and many others.

The reason that Das Emas is such a good park for wildlife observation is that animals are abundant and protected, the park has a diversity of habitats, and, above all, the countryside is generally open. Das Emas lies at about 3,000 feet on a gently rolling plain. Brazilians call plains *campos,* and their biologists distinguish among three types of *campos: campos limpos,* large open grasslands; *campos sujos,* grasslands in which shrubs have established themselves; and *campos cerrados,* plains interspersed with groups of trees, what we refer to as savannas. Das Emas is made up of all three types of *campos,* all more or less open countryside. In addition to these habitats, tall but narrow gallery forests line the banks of streams that drain the *campos.* These gallery forests are like narrow bands of rain forest winding through the plains, and they support animals more typical of rain forests than plains. The savannas of Das Emas support nearly 800 species of trees and shrubs, a quarter of which are typical of the Amazon Basin forests, and another quarter typical of Brazil's coastal forests. Thus, while Das Emas is essentially a savanna, it also contains flora and fauna normally found in tropical lowlands.

The plant formations result largely from a climate with a rainy season and a markedly dry season. Fires that sweep the *campos* during the dry season prevent the development of extensive forests, and year-round streams enable the gallery forests to survive droughts.

Apart from wildlife, the most interesting features of Das Emas are the termite mounds (*cupinzeiros*) that stretch as far as the eye can see in most of the park. Hundreds of thousands of brick-red mounds are more or less evenly distributed over the countryside, usually *campos limpos.* Most are as tall as a man, but some reach 10 feet. During the day they lend an unearthly aspect to the landscape, and at certain times of the year some acquire an eerie but spectacular aspect at night when they glow greenish blue, the result of phosphorescent larvae raised by the termites.

Wherever there are termites (and ants) in South America, there are sure to be anteaters, and these hundreds of square miles of termite mounds are happy hunting grounds for one of South America's stranger animals—the giant anteater (*Myrmecophaga tridactyla*). Nearly 6 feet long, including a long bushy tail, these animals are

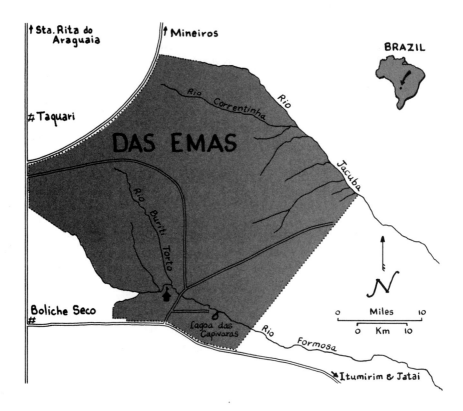

black with faint white stripes, and stand out conspicuously against the green grass of the *campos limpos.* They have a tiny mouth at the end of a long snout that houses the long sticky tongue with which they sweep up hapless insects. Their front paws are equipped with three strong curved claws well adapted to tearing apart rock-hard termite mounds, but poorly designed for walking. As a result, they are rather slow and may be easily approached. Despite their apparent clumsiness, however, they are not defenseless, and should not be molested. Do not try to pet a giant anteater.

The lesser anteater (*Tamandua tetradactyla*), an arboreal animal about the size of a housecat, specializes in raiding the countless termite nests lodged in trees of the rain forest. It too has a long snout for probing nests, plus a long, nearly naked prehensile tail well suited for life in the trees. Look carefully at branches in the gallery forest for this bizarre animal, for it is easy to miss. It freezes when alarmed, and its black, white, and brown pelage is excellent camouflage in the patches of sun and shade in the upper canopy.

Look (and listen) also for capuchin monkeys in the trees of the gallery forest.

Four species of armadillos have been identified in Das Emas, three of them identified by the number of narrow bands that enable them to flex their bony carapaces: three-banded, six-banded, nine-banded, and giant armadillos. The giant armadillo (*Priodontes giganteus*), 5 feet long and up to 100 pounds, is rare throughout its range, and may be on the verge of extinction. Visitors who spot these giants (or the extremely rare maned wolf) will be very lucky indeed. Nine-banded armadillos (*Dasypus novencinctus*) are commonplace in the park, however, and dart away from intruders with surprising speed. They scurry along smoothly on tiptoe, like tiny, animated Hovercraft, much faster than a man can run.

The pampas deer (*Ozotocerus bezarticus*), a graceful cervid about the size of the white-tail deer, was once extremely common throughout southern Brazil, Uruguay, Paraguay, and northern Argentina, but has grown scarce as a result of excessive hunting pressure. Fortunately, pampas deer are abundant in Das Emas: it is not unusual to see a dozen during a short walk.

Birdlife is also abundant; nearly 100 species have been identified in the park. In the *campos limpos* and *sujos,* keep an eye out for rheas (*Rhea americana,* similar to but larger than the lesser rhea of Patagonia), buff-necked ibis, southern lapwings, and several species of hawks and owls. Red-legged seriemas (*Cariama cristata*) are particularly common on the *campos sujos.* Large, long-legged birds easily distinguished by a pert crest, seriemas strut through the grass in search of insects, mice, and frogs, and usually run rather then fly from intruders.

Because of the gallery forests, Das Emas is a surprisingly good park in which to observe several birds more common in rain forests. In a true rain forest, observers can see plenty of birds, but because of the dense vegetation, usually only in brief glimpses as the birds fly past an opening in the leaves. At Das Emas, birds often fly *between* clumps of trees, and observers can watch several species of toucans, parrots, macaws, parakeets, and tyrants for several seconds as they move from one grove to another. Look for these birds in the scattered groves of Buriti (*Mauritia flexuosa*), where they seek the fruit of this palm. The Buriti is also used by man; its wood is hard enough to be used in construction, its leaves make excellent thatch and are a source of fiber for line, nets, and basketry, its sap can be made into a type of wine, and its nuts are edible.

Cupinzeiros (*termite nests*) *stretch as far as the eye can see across the* campos limpos (*grasslands*) *of Das Emas National Park.*

Visitor Facilities

At this time, Das Emas has no facilities for tourists. Park headquarters, 4 miles (6 kilometers) from the main entrance, house staff and family. Two additional houses provide lodging for visiting staff, scientists, or students. If the guest houses are not in use, IBDF staff in Brasilia may authorize tourists to use them. Camping is permitted only in the vicinity of park headquarters; all visitors wishing to overnight in the park must obtain permission from IBDF authorities in Brasilia. IBDF plans for the future of the park include providing limited facilities for non-intrusive tourist use of the park, but until these plans are finalized, visitors should contact park authorities in the Instituto Brasileiro de Desenvolvimento Florestal, SAIN, Avenida L-4 Norte in Brasilia.

A dirt airstrip for small planes lies near park headquarters. Several dirt roads and tracks cross the park from its headquarters. Three are recommended for walks or drives. The first heads east along the south side of the Rio Formosa for about 3 miles (5 kilometers) to the Lagoa das Capivaras (Capybara Lagoon), an oxbow lake formed by Rio Formosa. Follow the riverbank on foot to the lagoon, and watch for wildlife all the way. To reach the second road, turn right just after crossing the bridge over Rio Formosa. This road continues northeast toward Rio Jacuba, and reaches the park boundary in 9 miles (14 kilometers). To reach the third road, cross the same bridge, but keep left. This road proceeds northwest along the drainage of Rio Buriti Torto, and eventually curves west to the park boundary, 28 miles (45 kilometers) from park headquarters.

Visitors to Das Emas must be self-sufficient; bring all of your own food and supplies, including extra gasoline if you have a vehicle. Take plenty of water, food, and insect repellent on any hikes or drives in the park. Water in the park is potable.

The nearest town with full tourist accommodations (several hotels and restaurants) is Goiânia, 310 miles (500 kilometers) northeast of the park.

Recreation

Day hiking for birds and wildlife is unsurpassed. In September and October, the park is carpeted with scores of brilliant and strangely formed species of herbaceous wildflowers. Binoculars and spotting scope are useful. Bring protection from sun and insects, and wear high-topped boots and long pants in deep grass; several species of venomous snakes live in the park. The first people who somehow manage to float down one of the park's two rivers are going to have the wildlife experience of a lifetime. Although portions of the rivers are brushy, floating is permitted and is safe.

Historical and Cultural Aspects

Indians are known to have populated the region in ancient times. Primitive shelters, estimated to be nearly 11,000 years old, are evidence of the Indians' early existence here. No sites have yet been located within the park.

The first Europeans entered the area from Minas Gerais state in the 1870s, in search of diamonds. They did not find any, but a few stayed on. The park was set aside in the nick of time, for although the area is sparsely populated, enormous farms (*fazendas*) have gobbled up the region's last virgin forests and grasslands, and the area has become an important center of rice and soybean production.

Ironically, we owe this treasure of wildlife to the vision and initiative of a party of hunters. In 1960, A. T. Junqueira, a wealthy man from São Paulo, and a group of friends traveled and hunted for several weeks in the area with a rancher from the nearby town of Jatai. Astonished by the abundance of fauna and the wild beauty of the area, Junqueira suggested to government authorities that the area should be made into a national park. The Brazilian Park Service agreed, and in 1961 nearly 300,000 acres of land were set aside and Parque Nacional Das Emas was created.

Climate and Weather

The best time of year to visit Das Emas is June through August, when rainfall is light and wildlife is most abundant. The rainy season begins in December and lasts through March. Visits to Das Emas during the rainy season are not recommended; roads may become impassable for ordinary vehicles.

The temperature remains fairly constant throughout the year (about 72 degrees Fahrenheit) except for occasional cold snaps during the dry season, May to September. Frost makes an appearance every two or three years. Hike in mornings and evenings; the afternoons get hot and humid, and wildlife is not very active.

Location and Access

Das Emas is located in the southwest corner of the state of Goiás. It is a tough place to reach; at this time no public transportation goes all the way to the park. Ask at the IBDF offices for suggestions. The nearest place to rent a car is probably Goiânia, but it may be possible to hire a car or taxi in smaller nearby towns such as Jatai or Serranópolis. Regularly scheduled buses reach Jatai from Cuiabá, Belo Horizonte, Campo Grande, and Brasilia, but local buses in the vicinity of the park are less frequent. From Brasilia, the roads to the park pass through, in order, either Goiânia, Rio Verde, Jatai, Serranópolis, and Itumirím, *or* Jatai, Alto Araguaia, Coricho Seco, and Itumirím. Good luck.

Glossary

arara	macaw
borboleta	butterfly
cabeceinas	headwaters
capivara	capybara
cerrado	savanna
cupinzeiro	termite nest
mata ciliar	gallery forest
mata galería	gallery forest
pántano	marsh, swamp
papagaio	parrot
pássaro	bird
pegada	animal track
tamanduá bandeira	giant anteater
tamanduá mirím	lesser anteater
tatú bola	three-banded armadillo
tatú canastra	giant armadillo
tatú galinha	nine-banded armadillo
tucano	toucan
veado, cervo	deer
vereda de Buriti	grove of Buriti palms

♊ AMAZONIA:
Adventureland

Amazon.

The name alone stirs the imagination, and the establishment of this park provides all of us with a wonderful excuse to combine adventure with education. Although the park is easy to reach by South American standards, getting there can be an adventure if properly planned, and being there is a further adventure. A few risks are involved in visiting the park: there are plenty of things that bite or sting, and a few precautions are necessary to protect one's health. But risk is the essence of adventure, and after all, how often is it possible to hire a guide to lead you through a real jungle?

The word Amazonia refers to the region, not the river, and although this park is practically dead center in the Amazon Basin, it is not on the Amazon River, but rather on a major tributary, the Rio Tapajós. The Amazon is almost 150 miles downstream from the park. Visitors need not miss the mighty river, however, for one of the best ways to reach the park is by way of the Amazon itself.

The popular conception of the Amazon Basin is that of a vast, homogenous jungle. In fact, the basin supports a broad diversity of forest types, and visitors can see a variety of these ecosystems at the park. They may also see the following animals: collared and white-lipped peccaries, capuchin and tiny night monkeys; spider, howler, and cebus monkeys; bearded saki monkeys; giant river otters; giant and lesser anteater; tapirs; two species of sloths; ocelots; jaguars; mountain lions; capybaras; crocodiles; caimans; parrots; toucans; and most of the other animals one expects to find in the jungle.

Do not forget, however, that while faunal diversity is high in the tropics, populations are low. Many are small, arboreal, and, with the exception of some birds and primates, nocturnal; all of them are shy. Do not go to the park expecting to see or photograph every animal found in the Amazon Basin; it won't happen. But visitors who can get away from roads or take a small boat up a small river, and look and listen carefully, will see quite a few of them. Arise at daybreak as often as possible; it is cool at that time of day, and the chorus of frog noises, strange birdcalls, and roars of howler monkeys is incredible.

Amazonia, established in 1974, is Brazil's third-largest national park. Today it comprises 2.47 million acres, and IBDF authorities hope to increase its area to 3 million acres in the future, preserving 5,000 square miles of the rapidly shrinking Amazon forests. Because it is a zone of transition between the basaltic plateaus of the Brazilian Shield and the sedimentary basin of the Amazon, it is underlain by ancient Precambrian rock, basalt of volcanic origin, Paleozoic sedimentary rock, and Quaternary alluvium. The terrain is flat, broken only by a few low hills, but the combination of topography, climate, and complex bedrock have led to development of a variety of soils and therefore vegetation.

Although vegetation is diverse in the tropics, in Amazonia National Park diversity reaches its zenith. In general, sixteen to eighteen different tree species might be found on an acre of soil in the Amazon Basin, but in some areas as many as forty species per acre have been identified.

The sheer luxuriance of foliage is staggering. Years ago, some botanists decided to find out how many plants over 3 feet high grew in a patch of forest near Manaus. In one 44-by-44-foot square, they counted 1,652 plants, the equivalent of 23,000 plants per acre!

The forests can generally be divided into those that develop on dry land (*terras firmes*), and those that develop in marshes or lands subject to periodic flooding (*igapós*).

The dryland forests are the gloomy forests of legend and literature. Rich in hardwoods, they have the tallest trees, usually about 160 feet, although some giants reach 260 feet. The trees have fairly straight trunks, branching only near the uppermost canopy. The canopy is often completely closed; in some places as little as 1 percent of the light that strikes the canopy reaches the ground. As a result the floors of these forests are in deep shade, and relatively open. Ground cover is sparse, but epiphytes are abundant on upper branches, where they can get light. The northern part of the park is composed almost entirely of this type of forest. Although the park's forests appear to be pristine, the most valuable species have already been removed from much of its area. The pau rosa, which we call rosewood, is virtually gone, as are many of the palmitos and other species exploited for oils, incenses, and medicines.

In true *igapó* or marsh forests, undergrowth is thick, but not many of the plants are short. Trees, bushes, palms, and even ferns have buttressed root systems, or are supported on stilt-like prop roots.

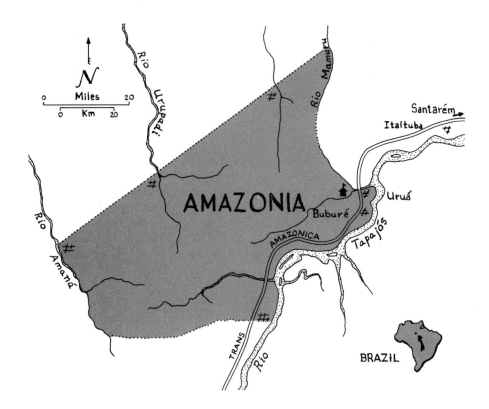

This collection of seeds picked up along a short trail illustrates the astonishing diversity of tree species in Amazonia National Park, Brazil.

Várzea forests are riparian forests inundated during annual floods, the gallery forests. Buriti and palmitos are common in these forests, and large epiphytes, lianas, orchids, and bromeliads are abundant.

In *cipós* forests the trees are short, but shrubby vegetation is dense. Lianas, flowering vines, ferns, bamboos, mosses, and fungi are abundant. It is a hot, dark, steamy forest, the "jungle" of adventure movies.

The predominant visual feature of the park is the Rio Tapajós, a clear river. In the Amazon Basin, rivers are characterized according to their color. Those that carry a heavy load of alluvium, usually clay, are the color of heavy cream or café au lait, and are called *rios brancos*. We would call such rivers roily. The other type of rivers, *rios negros*, carry heavy concentrations of dissolved organic matter that render the water the color of dark tea. Just downstream from Manaus, the dark Rio Negro enters the milky-brown Rio Solimoes, and the two types of rivers flow side by side without mixing for several miles (this is the famous meeting-of-the-waters, technically the point at which the Rio Amazon is born).

The Rio Tapajós is classified as a *rio negro*, but it is not usually tea-colored, and is even clear enough for snorkeling. It is one of the clearest of the Amazon's tributaries, and certainly one of the most attractive rivers in the entire basin. It has many rock outcrops, gentle rapids in its lower reaches, lots of islands, and mile after mile of clean, sandy beaches. Brazilians swim in virtually every river in the Amazon Basin, but most rivers do not appeal to foreigners (who knows what lurks in those murky depths?); the clear waters and sandy beaches of the Rio Tapajós positively invite a dip on a sweltering afternoon, although caution is still required.

Visitor Facilities

This is the real thing. No fancy hotels, no spotlights illuminating palm trees and swimming pool, no air conditioning, pet parrots, or waiters in black and white delivering iced drinks to your lounge chair. But travelers are welcome in the park even though facilities are not completed, and IBDF staff do whatever they can to make visits pleasant, comfortable, and interesting.

Administrative offices lie on the outskirts of Itaituba (ee-tie-TOO-bah), the closest town to the park (33 miles; 53 kilometers). Stop here for information and permission to enter the park.

Park headquarters is on the shore of the Rio Tapajós at Uruá, where park guards and maintenance personnel are housed. Facilities in Uruá include two guest cabins for visiting scientists and students. Tourists may use these cabins if they are vacant. Inquire at the administrative offices in Itaituba. Camping is permitted if the cabins are occupied.

Park staff have ambitious plans for facilities. They hope eventually to construct a visitor information center, roadside picnic areas, group campground, a research laboratory, and a series of interpretive trails. Interpretive programs are being designed to coordinate with riverboat trips and nature trails. The park owns two motor launches that may be available to visitors for travel on the Tapajós.

A pair of basic hotels and restaurants in Itaituba provide for the needs of visitors who do not wish to overnight in the park. Groceries can be purchased in the village, but the variety might be limited. Drink no water, including ice, without treating it. Wise visitors will arrive well stocked with water-purification tablets, a canteen, insect repellent, and, if they plan to backpack or camp, canned or dried food.

Recreation

Amazonia provides adventurous tourists with an opportunity to explore a rain forest without benefit of a tour or guide. Keep in mind, however, that it is very easy to get lost in these forests, and local residents will cheerfully (and cheaply) hire out as guides to take visitors on longer backpacking trips. Guided trips are not merely outdoor experiences; they soon become cultural experiences as you watch your guide brew up strange potions from plant leaves, fashion simple backpacks from branches and bark, point out medicinal plants and V-grooved rubber trees from the old days, and, without speaking your language, indicate what not to touch. Guides take great pride in their knowledge of jungle lore and know-how, and seem slightly amazed that ignorant as you are, you have survived for so long. Ask staff at the park office to recommend guides.

Until more trails are constructed, hiking in the park without a guide is limited to a 2- to 3-day trail leaving the road from kilometer post 80. This trail, maintained by locals who use it for annual pilgrimages to an isolated site with a small chapel, passes through several forest types and crosses a number of small drainages. Along the trail are small trees that bear a pear-sized fruit with a cashew-shaped appendage attached to its underside. They are indeed cashew (*cajú*) nut trees. Do *not* eat or taste the nuts; until processed, they are highly poisonous. Jungle trekkers should carry a hammock, a compass, and, yes, a machete. The machete is not for hacking a path through the jungle or killing snakes, but rather to blaze a trail through the vegetation, a common local measure that ensures safe return through otherwise indistinguishable terrain. The compass is a backup, in case you lose your machete. Once you notice the assortment of ants, scorpions, spiders, and centipedes that share the trail, you are likely to decide, like the Brazilians, that a hammock slung between trees is decidedly superior to sleeping on the ground.

The Rio Tapajós provides recreation in another form, and a different view of the park. In wetter months, when the river is high, it is easily navigated in a small boat. The park service may be able to provide rides; otherwise, boats can be rented in Uruá or nearby. The river is the temperature of a warm bath, and very inviting for swimming or snorkeling. **Caution:** Swimmers *must* take care to avoid piranhas, electric eels, stingrays, and snakes. Ask locals where to swim. Before stepping onto a sandy riverbed, scratch about with a stick to be sure that stingrays are not buried just beneath the surface. This may sound like a lot of hassle for a swim, but withering midafternoon heat will help overcome your concerns. Remember, too, that local settlers swim, bathe, and wash in the river every day, and only occasionally report injuries.

Climate and Weather

The climate at Amazonia is hot and humid. Temperatures and humidity are nearly constant all year. The mean annual temperature is about 80 degrees Fahrenheit, and it varies from 68 degrees to 95 degrees; humidity ranges from 75 to 90 percent. Rainfall is heavy, about 70 inches a year. The park experiences a rainy season and a dry season, but sudden rainstorms can occur at any time of year, so visitors should have raingear.

The dry season (summer or *verão*) lasts from the end of July to October, and is the best season to visit the park, for rainfall is light (2 inches a month), humidity is relatively low, and temperatures are moderate. The rainy season (winter or *inverno*) is February, March, and April, when 10 inches of rain falls every month, the humidity hovers at about 90 percent, and the heat is truly disagreeable.

Sleeping accommodations on small Amazon riverboats are comfortable, and most important, breezy.

Seasons are also marked by the appearance of biting insects. Tie or tuck in pant legs and wear long-sleeved shirts during daylight hours to avoid ticks and a small, biting blackfly that occasionally carries a dangerous parasite.

Location and Access

Amazonia lies south of the Rio Amazon in the state of Pará about midway between Manaus and Belém; it is located along the northwest shore of the Rio Tapajós, about 150 miles (240 kilometers) upstream from Santarém (pronounced sahn-TEEM).

These days travelers can get to the park by bus, boat, or plane; each of these modes of transportation offers a different perspective of the Amazon Basin, and a combination of travel methods is highly recommended.

Boats travel down the Amazon from Manaus to Santarém (about 36 hours), or upstream from Belém (2 days). From Santarém, there is a bus to Itaituba (8 hours), but the daily boat, which takes longer (24 hours), is far more interesting. Hitchhike or take a bus or taxi to the park from Itaituba. Check first at the administrative offices in Itaituba to see if they are sending staff or supplies to the park; they will gladly carry passengers to the park if space permits.

Travelers can easily return to Belém or Manaus on daily flights from Itaituba or Santarém. Make reservations early, for the planes are small, and flights are often full.

It is now possible to reach the park by bus from Belém, Manaus, Cuiabá, and Porto Velho via the Transamazónica Highway or its feeder routes. These trips are interesting, but tend to be long, hot, and strenuous. Delays as a result of muddy roads or washed-out bridges are inevitable during the rainy season.

AMAZON RIVER TRAVEL. In almost every circumstance, travel by river is preferable to travel by air or land in the Amazon Basin. Air travel is simply uninteresting, although it enables travelers to grasp the scale of the Amazon forests and the extent of depredation of the forest resource. Travel by bus is more interesting, but is arduous— dusty in the dry season, muddy in the wet season, and hot during all seasons. Riverboats are slow, but can be relatively comfortable and a fascinating way to travel. There are, however, a few tricks to learn.

Downstream travel is always faster, but the boats take advantage of the swifter midstream currents when traveling downstream, and you may be a mile or more from shoreside scenery. Upstream travel may take twice as long between points, but the boats are closer to shore, and the scenery is always better.

The food on boats is usually plentiful, but often monotonous, so take a supply of snacks. Do not drink river water; treat all water aboard the boat with purification tablets.

Bring a hammock (*rede*, pronounced HEY-gee). Sleeping accommodations on most boats consist of a pair of hooks from which a hammock is slung. Passengers are expected to bring their own hammock. Arrive well before departure time in order to select a place for your hammock that will maximize the breeze, provide good shelter from rain, and be away from engine-exhaust ports or galley ventilators. Avoid cabins that are not air-conditioned; they lack the breeze and are about as comfortable as an oven. Air-conditioned cabins are expensive, and besides, why miss most of the scenery and excitement of a river trip?

Classes on riverboats refer to the decks on which passengers sleep. First-class passengers sling their hammocks on the upper, which is to say breeziest, deck, and are usually first to receive their meals. Second class is the next lower deck, and so on. Third-class passengers travel on the lowest decks, which are often crowded, reek of diesel fumes, and may be loaded with such aromatic cargo as chickens, cattle, or crates of fish. Travel on riverboats is refreshingly casual; passengers generally have the run of the boat, and the flat roofs are popular places to while away the cool hours and visit with fellow travelers.

Tours or one-way trips on elegant boats that provide gourmet meals in air-conditioned cabins with television sets can be arranged from Manaus or Belém to several river ports. They are expensive and in my view less interesting than trips on public boats, which usually stop at several isolated sites along the river to load and unload cargo and passengers. To find a boat, simply go down to the docks. Boats will have chalkboards posted that indicate their destinations and estimated date and time of departure. Go aboard and speak to whomever is in charge. Shop around, for if a boat is not full as departure time nears, captains may reduce passenger fares.

Glossary

animais	animals
aves	birds
borracha	latex rubber
caboclo	slash and burn subsistence settler of the Amazon Basin; peasant
cachoeira	river rapids
carrapato	tick, chigger
chuva	rain
escorpião	scorpion
guía	guide
igapó	flooded forest
igarapé	stream
morro	hill
peixe	fish, pronounced PAY-shay
picada	trail
pium	biting blackfly
raia	stingray
ramal	long trail

5
CHILE

Chile is nicknamed "The Shoestring Country" for good reason: it is twenty-four times longer than its average width. In no place wider than 150 miles, it stretches nearly 2,700 miles, a span of latitude that encompasses parched deserts, fertile coastal plains, dense rain forests, and, finally, continental ice caps, fjords, and glaciers.

The one feature that unifies, indeed creates these zones, is the Andes, looming always in the background, a range that itself changes north to south from bare lofty rock to densely forested mountains to repositories of little but snow and ice. Of primary importance with respect to the scenery and morphology of Chilean parks are volcanos. Chile is indeed a land of volcanos; more than a thousand are strung like alpine pearls along the Cordillera, and no fewer than fifty are active. Nearly every Andean park in Chile contains one or more volcanos.

Northern Chile, from the Peruvian border to Copiapó, about 750 miles, encompasses a section of the parched Atacama Desert. Virtually no rain falls on these vast expanses of sand and rock, and wits describe this part of Chile as a naked mountain range next to an uplifted, deserted, 50-mile-wide beach. In these naked mountains high above the desert lies Parque Nacional Lauca.

The next 350 miles south is a zone of transition. Southward, stark desert gradually merges into a friendlier coastal plain. The transition zone is semi-desert, but light rainfall permits cactus and scrub communities to gain a foothold. Parque Nacional Fray Jorge lies on the coast within this zone.

The 400 miles from Illapel to Concepción lie in Chile's fertile Valle Central (Central Valley). A benign climate and rolling terrain favors intense cultivation, and has attracted nearly 80 percent of the country's population. The capital, Santiago, and several plush seaside resort cities lie within this zone.

Forest Chile begins south of Concepción. Rainfall is heavy in the zone, where dense stands of temperate rain forest alternate with expanses of hard-won farmlands. Chile's famed Lake District, a terrain of huge lakes interspersed amidst classic volcanos, lies in Forest Chile. The scenic qualities of the area are favorable for parks. Puyehue, Vicente Pérez Rosales, Los Paraguas, and Conguillío national parks are found here.

The zone ends abruptly at Puerto Montt, terminus of the railway system and, until recently, the highway network. At Puerto Montt, Chile's narrow coastal plain sinks into the Pacific, and the ice-carved west slopes of the Andes form the islands and fjords of Archipelagic Chile, a remote region of appalling weather that stretches southward 1,000 miles to Cape Horn. In this harsh and mysterious zone, nearer to Cape Horn than to Puerto Montt, lies the crown jewel of South American parks, Torres del Paine.

Everybody enjoys Chile. Virtually every traveler to South America is impressed by the warmth and generous hospitality of the Chilean people. Rich or poor, busy or idle, Chileans always have time for a smile and a friendly word with visitors, and many chance encounters in Chile blossom into full-fledged international friendships.

The park system is flourishing in Chile. By 1987, Chile had set aside thirty-four national parks from one end of the country to the other. They total nearly 23 million acres (as a comparison, Yellowstone comprises 2.2 million acres) and range in size from 200 to 6.5 million acres. In addition, Chile has preserved nearly 10 million acres as national reserves and natural monuments.

The system, however, is more advanced conceptually than physically. A few parks have a well-developed infrastructure, including visitor centers, professional staff, interpretive trails, descriptive brochures, and so on, while others have been set aside legally, but at this stage of development are little more than lines on maps. In addition, following recommendations of UNESCO, Chile has assigned certain of its public lands into one of several functional categories, such as national parks, natural monuments, national reserves, pristine reserves, nature sanctuaries, genetic reserves, biospheric reserves, and protected zones. Visitors therefore encounter a full range of parks and reserves, from those with well-developed facilities to those with no facilities whatsoever.

Chile's parks and reserves are administered by the Corporación Nacional Forestal y de Protección de Recursos Naturales Renovables or National Forest and Protection of Renewable Natural Resources Corporation (CONAF). CONAF has sophisticated and progressive management objectives for the lands under its control; if these plans can be brought to fruition, Chile and humanity in general will have a magnificent network of parks and reserves in perpetuity. The objectives include preservation of each species of Chilean flora and fauna as well as representative or unique examples of the many Chilean ecosystems. CONAF budget allowances usually fall far short of what is

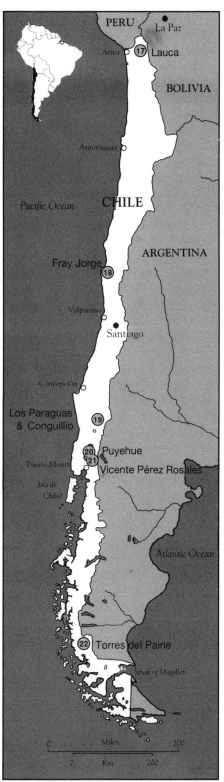

needed to meet its objectives, but its invariably gracious and helpful staff makes heroic efforts to make ends meet.

⊡ LAUCA:
Park at the Top of the World

Chile is divided into twelve political subdivisions called regions, each designated by a name and a Roman numeral. The northernmost of these subdivisions is Region I, Tarapacá.

Within this region are two national parks (Lauca and Isluga Volcano), one natural reserve (Las Vicuñas), and a national monument (Salar de Surire). One of the parks, Lauca, is relatively easy to reach, fairly well developed, and well worth a visit by any travelers who find themselves in the extreme north of Chile. The park has abundant wildlife, spectacular scenery, and is a splendid representative of the high altiplano ecosystem. The park's features are considered so important that in 1981 UNESCO declared Lauca to be a Biospheric Reserve, global acknowledgment of the importance of the park and its attributes.

One of the most interesting attractions associated with Lauca is simply getting there. Visitors who start from the Chilean coastal town of Arica begin their trip at sea level, and after a short journey find themselves standing on a lakeshore at 15,000 feet, not far from the volcanic summits of the Andes. From Arica, within three hours, visitors progress through a breathtaking cross-section of ecological zones: open sea, desert littoral, coastal foothills, interior desert, precordillera, and, finally, the Altiplano.

Chile originally set Lauca aside as a forest reserve in 1965, redesignated it as a national park in 1970, and set its final boundaries in 1983. The park is large (460,000 acres) and high (10,000 to 20,000 feet). Its geomorphology includes cinder cones, volcanic calderas, lava fields, hot springs, and fumaroles. Ten peaks within the park exceed 16,000 feet.

Lauca is an excellent park in which to see wildlife difficult to find elsewhere; such as huemuls, vicuñas, viscachas, and the giant Andean coot.

The road to Lauca from Arica first crosses the dry littoral plains, then enters the Lluta Valley, climbing first through a succession of lifeless, hill-sized sand dunes that range in color from alabaster to chartreuse, and later through a zone of tall candelabra cactus.

The first point of wildlife interest is near Putre, a tiny town on the western outskirts of the park. Putre lies at about 11,500 feet, and the steep mountainsides that flank the town receive sufficient rainfall to support groves of queñoa trees (the *Polylepis incana* of Peru's Parque Nacional Huascarán). These groves provide food and hiding places for the secretive huemul or Andean deer (*Hippocamelus antisensis*).

The huemul (also called guemal or taruca), once common in high mountains from northern Ecuador to southern Argentina and Chile, was hunted to the verge of extinction, and now survives only in isolated pockets in which it is protected. Nearly every Andean park includes huemuls, a prestige animal, among its wildlife, but Lauca is the only park in which they are sufficiently abundant to permit a casual visitor to catch a glimpse of this rare deer. The huemul, about the size of a small mule deer, and dark gray to dark brown, is not a particularly spectacular animal; the pleasure in sighting it derives more from the animal's rarity than its appearance.

To the consternation of local farmers and delight of visitors, huemuls frequently wander at dusk and dawn into the cultivated fields that surround Putre, there to graze calmly, more like domestic livestock rather than an endangered species. The final leg of the road into the park from Putre climbs through more queñoa groves, and huemuls may also be spotted on the mountainsides that precede arrival onto the altiplano. In 1988, park staff estimated that Lauca supported a steadily increasing population of about 700 huemuls.

After a 5-mile (8 kilometers) climb, the road reaches the high plains of the park proper, and the visitor has arrived on the Altiplano. Snowcapped peaks and bands of vicuñas immediately come into view.

Lauca is the only readily accessible park, apart from Pampa Galeras in Peru, in which vicuñas may be seen in large numbers at close hand. Soon after Peru began its vicuña rehabilitation program, Chile recognized the peril and importance of its own herds, and took steps to protect and augment existing vicuña populations. With the assistance of UNESCO, the World Wildlife Fund, and a number of vicuñas from Pampa Galeras, a herd of 400 animals was established at Lauca by 1971. Hunting was prohibited, poaching controlled, and the program became a resounding success. By

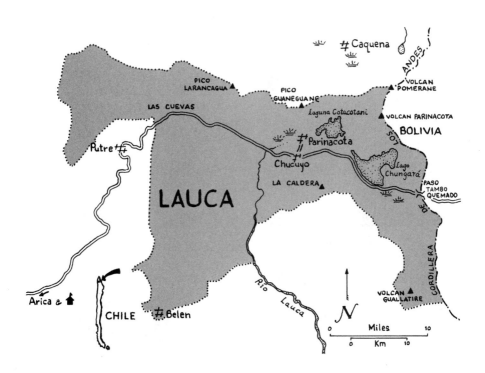

1976 more than 3,000 vicuñas were counted, and by 1988 about 22,000 of these once-rare animals roamed the grasslands of Lauca.

In some respects, vicuña habitat at Lauca is superior to Pampa Galeras. Water and grass are more abundant, and seasonal variations less extreme. Most of the park's vegetation is the characteristic altiplano bunchgrass, predominantly hardy *Festuca* and *Stipa* grasses (*ichu*), but snowmelt and abundant springs provide Lauca with features relatively rare in altiplano parks: extensive bogs (*bofedales*). Lush sedges and several species of herbs and wildflowers proliferate in and near these bogs, preferred grazing areas for vicuñas. Look also for guanacos and rheas in the vicinity of the bogs. Now protected, populations of these animals had increased to 1,600 and 600, respectively, by 1988. Ask the park ranger for permission to bathe in the hidden hot springs in the large *bofedal* near the Las Cuevas ranger station.

Near Las Cuevas, the road is cut through a 50-yard-long heap of boulders on the margin of a large *bofedal*. On rainless days, arrayed amongst the boulders, indeed all over the gravel roadway, dozens of gray, rabbit-sized animals bask in brilliant sunlight. These are mountain vizcachas (*Lagidium peruanum*), rodent relatives of chinchillas and guinea pigs. Unlike the plains vizcacha of lowland Argentina, which is strictly nocturnal, mountain vizcachas are active during daylight hours. They appear logy

Tufted-ear entertainers, mountain vizcachas are common in rocky areas of Lauca National Park, Chile.

when basking and will permit a fairly close approach, but they are very agile, and disappear into the rocks in an eyeblink when alarmed. Often erroneously compared to rabbits, vizcachas have long fluffy tails, tufted ears, high-pitched whistles, and absurdly long tactile whiskers that make them vaguely spectacular little animals—far more interesting than mere rabbits, and worth a pause to investigate.

Scattered on several hillsides between Las Cuevas and the turnoff to the village of Parinacota are curiously shaped bright green humps and domes that range from basketball-size to 10 feet wide and 3 feet high. By all means stop to investigate, for they are alive, and among the oddest members of the plant kingdom: llaretas (*Laretia compacta*). From afar, llaretas appear to be a single, spongy plant that covers and rounds off the outlines of rocks on which they grow. Closer inspection reveals that they are thick, granite hard, and comprised of thousands of individual plants that produce tiny, pale yellow flowers. The plants have extremely long roots that bind together to form a compact, resinous mass. This growth form helps to protect the plants from the temperature extremes of the altiplano. Unfortunately, the llareta also makes good firewood when broken up into smaller pieces. Supply cannot keep up with demand because llaretas grow extremely slowly—a large llareta may be several centuries old—hence, these curious plants of the altiplano are now rare where unprotected.

Parinacota lies 12 miles (19 kilometers) from Las Cuevas. On nearing the village, llamas and alpacas come into view, domestic stock herded by the few dozen townspeople, most of whom are Aymaras, descendants of the Indians who have peopled the southern Altiplano for centuries. Stop to inspect the church (its frescos were painted in 1699), and try an alpaca steak dinner at the village's only restaurant (cheap and delicious). Travelers who wander through the village will see scarves, sweaters, vests, and other knitted alpaca and llama goods hanging from doorways on display to passersby. Some residents will knit a sweater overnight on request. Quality ranges from good to excellent, but bargain hard so as not to be considered a dunce. CONAF maintains quarters and a small visitor center in Parinacota, easy to find. A nearby interpretive trail is in disrepair.

Ten miles east of Parinacota, the road skirts the edge of Lago Chungará, one of the world's highest lakes of its size (14,800 feet). CONAF has built an office, campground, and picnic area on the shore of Chungará, a good site from which to explore the lake and its surroundings.

Keep an eye out for flamingos. Ornithologists estimate that 435 species of birds inhabit or pass through Chile, and Region I, Tarapacá, has recorded more—237—than any other region. Flamingos illustrate this abundance nicely. Four species of flamingos are found in South America, one of which, the American flamingo, reaches the southeast United States. All three of the other species are found in or near Lauca National Park. The Chilean flamingo, *Phoenicopterus chilensis*, is the widest-ranging bird, found in lakes and marshes at all elevations from Ecuador to Tierra del Fuego. It may be encountered in any lake or pond in the park. The other flamingos are strictly inhabitants of the altiplano. The Andean flamingo (*P. andinus*), the largest flamingo, and the Puna flamingo (*P. jamesi*), the smallest, are more common in the salt marshes (*salars*) south of Lauca, but both have been observed within the park.

The most conspicuous bird in Chungará is the giant coot, *Fulica gigantea*, called tagua gigante in Spanish. This slate-black bird, nearly the size of a turkey, is the only coot with red bill, legs, and feet. Giant coots build huge nests of weeds on cones of small stones and matted vegetation, or floating nests made of the same vegetation that they eat. Some of these nests may be 8 feet or more in diameter.

Other birds associated with the altiplano are abundant and easy to observe in Lauca. The black-headed Andean gull, *Larus serranus,* is especially common on Lago Chungará. Look for the glossy black Puna ibis, *Plegadis ridgwayi,* and the Andean avocet, *Recurvirostra andina,* in *bofedales* near Parinacota. The avocet, a long-legged white bird with dark brown wings and tail, is distinguished by its long, sharply upturned bill with which it probes the beds of ponds and marshes.

Visitor Facilities

The widest choice of accommodations for visitors outside the park is at Arica, Chile's northernmost seaport. A dune-fringed, bustling town of 150,000, Arica is 100 miles (161 kilometers) from the park, and has about two dozen hotels and *residenciales,* and plenty of restaurants. Check at the tourist office (Calle Arturo Prat 375) for a list of hotels and prices, and for information on transportation to the park. Check in also at the CONAF office (Maipú 333) for information on getting to the park, and to obtain permission to stay overnight at CONAF facilities within the park.

Because of the abrupt and extreme change in altitude between Arica and the park, some visitors spend a night at Putre (11,500 feet) to acclimatize to the elevation before proceeding to the park itself. There is only one hotel and restaurant in Putre, but visitors may be able to stay at the small office and sleeping quarters maintained by CONAF with prior permission from the office in Arica. Accommodations at CONAF facilities are limited and on a space-available basis; priority is naturally given to CONAF staff. Bring your own food, drinking water, and sleeping bag to all CONAF facilities. CONAF staff are sometimes unable to get to Arica for long intervals, and appreciate whatever fresh fruits or vegetables you might spare. A visit to the small handicrafts school on the edge of town is worthwhile. Putre is the last place to obtain groceries before entering the park; stores close early.

The only overnight accommodations within the park are at CONAF facilities at Las Cuevas, Parinacota, and Chungará. Basic kitchens are available at each, and camping is permitted nearby.

On high elevation: Visitors entering Lauca from La Paz, Bolivia, may already be acclimatized, and therefore suffer no ill effects from oxygen deprivation. Travelers arriving directly from Arica, however, will climb nearly 15,000 feet in about 4 hours, and may indeed experience altitude sickness (*soroche* or *mal de puna*). To avoid becoming ill, follow a few precautions: (1) Deliberately slow down your usual rate of physical activities, avoid running, and forget your morning jog or calesthenics; (2) Eat light meals; (3) Avoid alcohol and tobacco; (4) Get plenty of sleep.

Those who are susceptible to *soroche* would be wise to spend a night at Putre before entering the park. Susceptibility to altitude sickness varies widely from one individual to another. Some people are not affected at the elevations of Lauca; others are. It is rarely fatal, but can be uncomfortable and frightening. The most common symp-

Rock-hard llaretas, among the oddest of altiplano plants in Lauca National Park, assume their strange form as a means of protection against drought and cold. Because they are a good substitute for firewood on these high, treeless steppes, they are becoming extinct where unprotected.

tom is a moderate to severe headache, but shortness of breath and nausea may also develop. Aspirin might help. Leaves of a small bush called chachacoma (*Senecio graveolens*) are offered to visitors as a local remedy. The leaves may be chewed—they are peppery—or made into strong tea. The surest cure for *soroche* is to get back to lower elevations, where symptoms quickly disappear.

Recreation

Scenery and wildlife are Lauca's primary attributes. Binoculars, spotting scope, and both wide-angle and long camera lenses are useful. Short hikes facilitate wildlife observation; backpack only if acclimatized to the altitude. The many peaks in the park invite mountaineering, but prior authorization from CONAF is required. Climbers are advised that the park is remote with respect to support and medical facilities. Boating is possible on the several lakes, but you must bring your own boat. Unlikely as it seems, in 1989 Lake Chungará became the site of the world's highest sailboat regatta when fourteen members of Arica's yacht club hauled their boats to the lake and raised their sails in the thin air.

Historical and Cultural Aspects

Descendants of Lauca's original Aymara Indian inhabitants still live in the park, and speak their own language. Crumbling reminders of their ancestors are scattered widely throughout the park: ancient houses, vicuña traps, trailside cairns, pictographs of vicuñas and huemuls, and old hunting camps. Ask rangers for directions to these ruins.

Climate and Weather

Lauca may be visited year-round. The nearby Monumento Natural Salar de Surire and Reserva Nacional de Vicuñas Pampa Galeras are accessible only from March through November. Rain or snow may fall at any time of year.

At all times, however, you must protect yourself from sun, wind, and cold. Bring warm clothing, gloves, headwear, sunglasses, and sun-block cream. Sunny days may be hot, but as soon as the sun drops below the horizon, temperatures fall dramatically. Lightweight sleeping bags should be supplemented with a blanket, if possible. Even in summer (December through February) temperatures drop well below freezing nearly every night.

Location and Access

Lauca is in the extreme northeast corner of Chile, close to Peru and adjacent to the Bolivian border. The overland route between La Paz and Oruro, Bolivia, and Arica passes through the park, so those traveling from one country to the other can arrange a stopover in the park without undue inconvenience. Buses that pass through the park leave Arica for La Paz and Oruro twice weekly. Stop off at one of the CONAF facilities and hope that the bus that passes through after you have seen your fill has room for you. Check for tickets and times at the bus station on Avenida Puerto Montt in Arica.

It is possible to hitchhike to the park, but traffic can be light; Sundays are the best days for hitching rides.

Several tour companies (Turismo Payachatas, Jurasi, and Huasquitur) arrange one-day tours to Lauca from Arica in cars or Volkswagen vans. Prices range from $12 to $16 (U.S.) per person. Since driving time from Arica to Lago Chungará is nearly 5 hours, one-day tours tend to be rather hurried affairs. Two or three days, with overnights at CONAF quarters, are much more satisfactory. Schedules and itineraries are somewhat flexible, so it is possible to work out longer trips with tour companies, whose friendly staff do their best to accommodate visitors.

A good alternative for a small group is to rent a jeep from one of the two or three car rental agencies in Arica, and do your own tour. If your budget permits, with your own vehicle it is possible (from March to November) to make a loop trip that passes through Parque Nacional Lauca, Reserva Nacional Las Vicuñas, Monumento Natural Salar de Surire, and Parque Nacional Volcán Isluga, returning to Arica via Highway 5, joined near the town of Huara. CONAF facilities are located along this route in Guallatire, Surire, and Enqualga. Roads are rough and gasoline scarce, so travelers who rent cars *must* carry extra gasoline, and have good tires and a good spare. Ask the rental agency to have the carburetor adjusted for high-altitude driving, and be sure that the engine contains antifreeze.

Distances and driving times from Arica to several points of interest are as follow: Putre—93 miles (150 kilometers), 3 hours; Las Cuevas—99 miles (159 kilometers), 3.5 hours; Parinacota—112 miles (180 kilometers), 4 hours; Chungará—124 miles (199 kilometers), 4.5 hours; Guallatire—143 miles (230 kilometers), 5.5 hours; and Surire—174 miles (280 kilometers), 7 hours.

Glossary

apachetá	road, trail, or pass marker (cairn)
caití	Andean avocet
caminata	hike
campo de lava	lava flow
chaco	vicuña trap
cono cinérico	cinder cone
cuervo de pántano	Puna or Andean ibis
cumbre	peak
cuy	guinea pig (pronounced KWEE)
gaviota Andina	Andean gull
guardería	ranger station
ñandú or *suri*	lesser or Darwin's rhea
parina	Quechua word for flamingo; Parinacota means "lake of flamingos"
tambo incaico	Inca house (ruin)

🗝 FRAY JORGE:
Garden by the Sea

Occasionally a South American country will set aside a small, out-of-the-way tract of land, call it a park, reserve, or monument, and then get on with the business of developing larger, more spectacular parks with bigger budgets and higher public profiles. These small parks are usually of little interest, but occasionally exquisite little gems are hidden away in the countryside. Parque Nacional Fray Jorge is one of these hidden treasures.

As one travels south in Chile, the brutal sterility of the Atacama Desert moderates ever so slightly. Life appears, in the form of thirsty-looking scrub brush and cacti, but make no mistake, until reaching the approximate latitude of Illapel, the land is in the harsh grip of a semi-desert.

Not far from La Serena, however, in the midst of this semi-desert, a curious set of circumstances has created conditions that permit a small, temperate rain forest to flourish at the edge of the sea. The principal attraction of Fray Jorge is this pocket forest, a textbook example of the Valdivian or Chilean rain forest.

The park contains neither glaciers, volcanos, nor exotic wildlife, and your understanding of South American natural history would not suffer appreciably if you missed Fray Jorge altogether. Nevertheless, if you have been traveling for several hundred miles through desert Chile, the sight and feel of Fray Jorge is as refreshing to the spirit as an ice-cold lemonade on a hot summer afternoon.

The coast at Fray Jorge is reminiscent of Marin County, north of San Francisco. The bluffs are high, and the sea rough. Gale-force winds blow inland constantly, and shrubbery that persists at the sea edge is carved by the wind into bizarre shapes. The forest persists in small clumps scattered over the hills that face the sea, dense thickets of moss-draped trees that sprout from damp soil. In some places the forest is impenetrable, but instead of being continuous, it is spread in wave-like patches along the rolling seafront hillsides. The spaces between forest clumps are covered with huge moors of heath and wildflowers.

Most of the understory plants within the forest proper are friendly; few have spines or thorns. The one exception is a dull-green nettle, whose sting is sharper and more persistent than that of its North American cousins; you will know when you sit on one. Yet around the margins of the entire forest are the familiar, formidable desert plants, attractive in their own way but armed with every form of spine, hook, and thorn imaginable.

How, you may ask, it is possible for a rain forest to exist in the middle of this semi-desert, where annual rainfall may be as little as 3 inches? Part of the answer is fog. For most of the day, great, ragged patches of fog swirl in from the sea and sweep through the trees, leaving a thin film of moisture on everything in their path, including hikers. The fog lends drama to Fray Jorge, for the scenery of the park changes constantly as patches of fog and intervening periods of bright sunshine alternate throughout the day. Botanists comparing the amounts of moisture contributed to the forest by rain and by fog find that whereas annual rainfall may vary from 3 to 10 inches, the fog consistently provides the equivalent of from 24 to 36 inches of rain—just enough for a rain forest.

But fog is only part of the answer to the puzzle. Why is the forest limited to Fray Jorge's 38 square miles? Why are there no forests along the sea to the north or south of the park? Chilean botanists believe that when the quaternary glaciers advanced westward from the Andes, temperature and moisture regimes permitted the Valdivian forest to flourish far north of its present boundaries. When the glaciers retreated, temperatures increased and moisture decreased. The forests were also forced into retreat, to be replaced by the semi-desert that now surrounds the park. The forests of Fray Jorge are therefore relict survivors of vast forests of this earlier, less austere period. Many theories have been proposed to explain why the forests survived here and not elsewhere, but most botanists agree that they survive in this one spot on Chile's central coast only because the nearby Río Limari discharges relatively warm water into the cold Pacific to create the fog that brings the forest the moisture it requires.

The forest has held men's interest for centuries. It was described in about 1627 by Franciscan monks, who used its wood to construct the bell tower of the San Francisco Church in the city of La Serena. The interest of botanists of international stature in

The desert that surrounds Fray Jorge National Park, Chile, in spring bloom

the forest and its origins predates establishment of the park. A resolution calling for protection of the forest was passed by a Pan-Pacific Scientific Congress in 1933, and similar concerns for its preservation were expressed at ensuing conferences and symposia. In 1941, Chile responded to these concerns, and created Fray Jorge. More recently, the park has been designated a Biospheric Reserve, the most important UNESCO category of wildlands, and a clear declaration of its uniqueness among the world's parks.

Visitor Facilities

The forest is a living classroom, and facilities reflect that purpose. In a grove of eucalyptus trees, an administrative center has been constructed that includes a laboratory, classroom, living quarters, interpretive trail, and exhibit room. A few stuffed animals, maps, and scores of pressed plants are on display in the exhibit room. The forest lies a few miles past the administrative center, toward the sea. Obtain permission to pass through the gate that blocks the road at the park offices. For the first 3 miles (5 kilometers), the dirt road climbs through a narrow valley of scrub and cactus. The last 2 miles (3 kilometers) are steep and rocky, and the road soon enters the forest proper. The road ends at the head of an interpretive trail, unmarked but distinct, that winds for about 1 mile (1.6 kilometers) through the trees and meadows above the sea. Several good campsites are located along the trail, which loops back to the road. From several sites, it is possible to see the snowcapped Andes far to the east and foam-fringed rocky islets in the sea to the west.

No streams lie near the trail; campers should take plenty of drinking water. Beware the biting flies, enormous but slow-witted, that hover about the slopes and follow you along the trails.

The best time to visit Fray Jorge is during the austral spring, October through December, when both forest and desert flora are in riotous bloom.

Location and Access

Fray Jorge lies on the coast in Region IV, just off Chile's principal highway, Ruta 5. Ovalle, the nearest town, lies 25 miles (40 kilometers) to the northeast of the park, and has several hotels and restaurants. Several buses travel between La Serena/Coquimbo and Ovalle daily. It is possible to hitchhike to Fray Jorge from La Serena, Ovalle, or points south, but traffic from Ruta 5 to park headquarters may be light. During summer months, competition with students can be stiff.

Visitors can stay at the CONAF facilities when space is available. Since Fray Jorge sees nearly 2,000 visitors a year, it is advisable to contact CONAF staff in La Serena before arriving at the park. Check at the tourist office on the Plaza de Armas, next to the post office, or at the kiosk at the corner of Avenida Prat and Calle Matta.

🖳 LOS PARAGUAS AND CONGUILLIO: Lava, Snow, and Monkey Puzzle Forests

Forest Chile, with its well-known Lake District, begins at the city of Temuco. East of Temuco, between the towns of Curacautín and Melipeuco, lie Los Paraguas and Conguillío national parks. Although administered as two units, the parks are adjacent, and from the perspective of the visitor are a single unit. The two parks plus the forest reserve of the upper Río Bio-Bio have been recently nominated by the Chilean government for Biospheric Reserve status as representatives of Chile's Nothofagus (beech) forest.

The parks are dominated by snowcapped Llaima Volcano (10,250 feet), a lively volcano with double craters and permanent smoking fumaroles. The mountain is seldom out of sight, and its frequent eruptions—the last occurred in 1957—are responsible for the character of the parks. Dozens of stark black lava flows cross the landscape, and the three major lakes in the park have been formed by lava flows and slides that have dammed watercourses.

The most dramatic floral features are extensive groves of araucaria trees that cover the slopes of Llaima Volcano and the Sierra Nevada peaks in Conguillío. North Americans know the araucaria or pehuén (*Araucaria araucana*) as the monkey puzzle tree, so-called because of its stiff and sharp leaves. *Paragua* means umbrella in Spanish, and one of the parks is named for the curious parasol shape of the araucaria. These two parks, with a combined area of over 114,000 acres, contain the most extensive remaining accessible stands of these magnificent trees in Chile. They should not be missed by visitors.

The araucarias are the largest, tallest, and most striking trees, but the forest of these parks is a beech forest, in which no fewer than four species flourish at different elevations. In the lowest, more humid sections of the parks, the coihue (*Nothofagus dombeyii*), a tall evergreen beech, is the dominant tree, and is often found in association with the false beech or roble (*N. obliqua*). At higher levels, the coihue is associated with the raulí (*N. alpina*); at the highest elevations, the high beech or lenga (*N. pumilio*) dominates.

Annual rainfall is abundant, but not sufficient to support the lush growth of bamboo, ferns, mosses, epiphytes, and vines characteristic of the Valdivian forests along

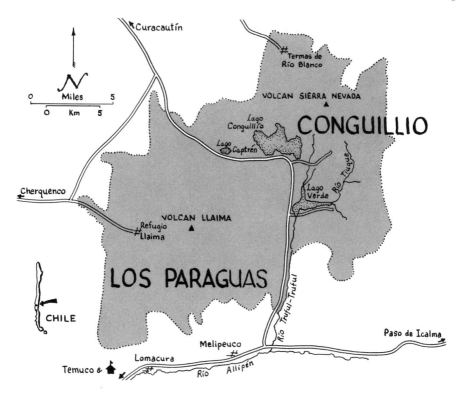

Pampas grass is one of the first plants that take root in fresh lava flows from Llaima Volcano. Conguillío National Park, Chile

the coast of southern Chile. This is good news for hikers and backpackers for whom the term Valdivian forest is often synonymous with impenetrable thickets. The Nothofagus forests at the latitude of Los Paraguas and Conguillío are open woods that lend themselves well to cross-country travel even without trails, and because of the conspicuous volcanic landmarks it is nearly impossible to get lost in these parks.

Los Paraguas/Conguillío is one of the more advanced parks in South America with respect to provision of services to assist the public in gaining an appreciation of

park features. Visitor centers, for example, are replete with exhibits and graphic lessons for the public on protecting and appreciating environmental resources. Interesting biological and geological features along the well-marked nature trails are clearly explained and interpreted. And during the summer season (November to March), visitors may avail themselves of the following typical sorts of ranger-led informative activities at the visitor center at Lago Conguillío: Tuesday—hike to Sierra Nevada (10 hours), slide show on Chilean national parks; Wednesday—boat trip to Saltos de

Conguillío (3.5 hours), fireside talk on ecology; Thursday—hike to Lago Captrén (6 hours), slide show on regional fauna; Friday—hike for children (4 hours), slide show on regional flora; Saturday—nature-trail hike (1.5 hours), slide show on Parque Nacional Conguillío; Sunday—lecture on Chilean birds.

Approaching the park from the south, visitors first ascend the narrow valley of the Río Truful-Truful. Near the south-entrance office and information kiosk, about 1 mile (2 kilometers) within the park, an outstanding short nature trail winds along above the river and leads to an enormous outcrop of columnar basalt. Many of the columns have fallen away, creating huge piles of symmetrical, hexagonal building blocks. The trail also affords excellent views of 100-foot cuts made by the river through the soil and subsoil of the slopes of Llaima Volcano. The cuts have exposed dozens of multicolored strata of ash, mud, and volcanic dust, as much as 20,000 years old, with which the volcano periodically blankets the region. A set of waterfalls along the trail is of particular interest because as the lip of the falls has eroded upstream, a hollow basin with high walls of basalt has been formed. Within the basin, spray has created a zone of very high humidity colonized by a large variety of flowers, some found nowhere else in the park—a classic example of microclimate and microhabitat.

Winding north, the road crosses immense open lava fields and scattered open stands of araucaria and beech. Many of the lava fields are so recent that the process of plant succession has not yet begun or is in its earliest stages; many of the rocks are bare or plated with colorful lichens just beginning to establish a presence. One of the more picturesque and surprising early invaders of the lava fields is pampas grass. Scores of 6-foot clumps of the giant bunchgrass stand surrounded by nothing but fine black sand.

The first lake the road reaches is Laguna Verde, a lovely contrast to the eerie setting of lava flows and mountains. The lack of vegetation on recent lava flows lends the lake a rather barren atmosphere, but it has a picnic and camping area, a pleasant 0.5-mile (1 kilometer) trail, and good fishing.

North from Laguna Verde, the road passes an administration center on deep blue Lago Arco-Iris (Rainbow Lake), and soon reaches Lago Conguillío, the park's centerpiece lake. Scenery on the road between these lakes is exceptional, due largely to the striking silhouettes of araucaria trees standing well above the forest understory against a backdrop of bright sky and snowy peaks.

A full range of visitor facilities is available at Lago Conguillío, and it is recommended as a base camp for hikers, backpackers, fishermen, or those who simply want to spend a few days watching clouds drift over a beautiful spot. Lago Conguillío lies in the midst of a mature araucaria forest, and is a peerless place to get a feel for these unusual trees—the heft of their enormous cones and seeds, the birds that inhabit them, where they grow and how densely, and the sound of the wind drifting through them. Visitors can even live for a few days in ingeniously designed and comfortable circular cabins that have been constructed—without harming the trees—around the trunks of several enormous araucarias. The lake is a place to fish, swim, hike, daydream, sunbathe, and socialize—in a word, dawdle.

A dense auracaria forest lies between Lago Conguillío and the next lake east, Laguna Captrén. Captrén is much smaller than Lago Conguillío, but no less beautiful, and has a well laid out campground and picnic area situated in a grove of huge coihue and araucaria trees.

Los Paraguas and Conguillío have interesting fauna, but the most commonly seen animal is an introduced species, the European hare (*Lepus europaeus*). Mountain lions (*Felis concolor*) have been sighted near Laguna Arco-Iris and Lago Conguillío, and family groups of the spaniel-sized pudú (*Pudu pudu*) have been observed near the mouth of the Río Tiuque at Laguna Verde and in nearby woods, and near Cerro Colorado in Los Paraguas. Both of these animals are extremely shy, however, and difficult to observe in the wild.

Not so with the parks' birds. Look in Laguna Verde and Lago Conguillío for the great grebe (*Podiceps major*). Largest of the grebes (30 inches long), this blue-and-white diving bird is at once distinguishable by its 4-inch bill, and is usually seen alone or in pairs. The crested grebe (*Podiceps occipitalis*), gray and white, is common on Lago Conguillío and Laguna Captrén in groups of ten to fifteen birds. Glossy black neotropic cormorants (*Phalacrocorax olivaceus*) may be seen on all lakes in the park, alone or in small groups. Dark-brown patches around the eyes distinguish the spectacled duck (*Anas specularis*), not common in the park but nearly always present near the falls of the Río Truful-Truful. The most common duck in Lago Conguillío is the Chilean pintail (*Anas georgica*), a brown-and-white bird with a sharply pointed tail.

The most impressive forest bird is the Magellanic woodpecker (*Campophilus magellanicus*), a large bird (15 inches long) with red head, blue-black body, and white bill. This bird has become extinct over much of its range because it requires mature forests for its survival and cannot survive in logged-over landscapes. Fortunately, it is relatively abundant in Chilean parks, and may be sighted in Los Paraguas/Conguillío in older beech or araucaria stands near Lago Conguillío, Laguna Captrén, near the Río Blanco, and along El Contrabandista, the Smuggler's Nature Trail, near Lago Conguillío.

Visitor Facilities

Campsites and picnic areas are located at several points on the shores of Lago Conguillío and lagunas Verde and Captrén. All facilities, including bathrooms, rain shelters, and tables, are provided. Some campgrounds are free; others are available at a nominal charge.

Near Playa Curacautín on Lago Conguillío is a visitor center, store, and amphitheater. Rustic but charming cabins are available, and rowboats may be rented.

Trails are abundant through the park. Most trailheads and nature trails are located at or near the parks' three largest lakes.

Recreation

The parks' summer season runs from November to March; January and February are the most crowded months.

Los Paraguas and Conguillío are excellent hiking and backpacking parks during summer months (December through February). Hikes range from easy to difficult. Visitors interested in climbing volcanos can take trails to either the Sierra Nevada or the smoking craters of Llaima from Lago Conguillío. Llaima may also be ascended from the west, by entering the park through the village of Cherquenco. CONAF and a private concessionaire maintain basic huts (*refugios*) on the volcano. Obtain detailed information at the CONAF offices in the parks.

Fishing, boating, bird-watching, and swimming are the other summer activities appropriate for Los Paraguas and Conguillío.

Conguillío closes in the winter, as snow piles up to depths of 10 feet, but Los Paraguas is a winter recreation park, well known for its skiing. Chair lifts, warming huts, and other winter facilities are located on the lower west face of Llaima Volcano, approached from Cherquenco. The winter season is from May to October.

Historical and Cultural Aspects

These parks are part of the ancestral home of the Araucanian or Mapuche Indians, most of whom have now intermarried with non-Indian Chileans and have been absorbed into the general population. It was love rather than warfare that finally pacified the Araucanians, for they, along with North America's Seminoles, were the only indigenous tribes in the western hemisphere that could not be subjugated by military might. Neither the Spanish conquerors nor, later, the government troops of Chile could decisively defeat them in battle. After countless unsuccessful attempts to conquer the Araucanians, whose last uprising was just over a century ago—about the time General Custer was making his last stand—the Chilean government wisely sued for peace, agreeing to make citizens of the Araucanians and not to confiscate their lands.

More than 100,000 descendants of these hardy people still live on remnants of their ancestral lands south of the Río Bio-Bio. Most are now farmers and herdsmen, but some still keep many of their old customs, and are skilled craftsmen who earn a living by making silver jewelry, weavings, leather goods, and pottery.

Climate and Weather

During summer months, light clothing is adequate. Take a sweater, as evenings can grow chilly, and raingear too, for rainstorms, though brief, are common year-round. Tough boots are necessary to withstand hiking on the hard and sharp-edged lava. The average temperature of the warmest month is about 60 degrees Fahrenheit.

Location and Access

Los Paraguas and Conguillío are in Chile's Region IX, at the northern end of the Lake District, about 30 miles (48 kilometers) east of Temuco.

At this writing, public transportation does not go all the way to the parks, but frequent buses go to Melipeuco and Curacautín, the two towns nearest the parks, from Temuco. Hitchhiking the last few miles to (and within) the parks is easy. To climb the west face of Llaima Volcano, take a bus from Temuco to Cherquenco, and hitchhike or hike the 13 miles (21 kilometers) to the ski lodge. Visitors may also rent a car in Temuco and make a pleasant 130-mile (290 kilometers) loop trip through Chilean farmlands and the parks.

Visitor facilities at Lago Conguillío include rustic cabins constructed around the trunks of araucaria trees. Conguillío National Park, Chile

Local CONAF staff often make trips in cars and trucks to parks within their jurisdiction, and if they have room will take passengers. Check at the CONAF office in Temuco (Manuel Montt 1151).

Glossary

blanquillo	crested grebe
cañadón	steep, usually deep canyon
carpintero negro	Magellanic woodpecker
caseta de control	control station, entrance
cuervo	cormorant
huala	great grebe
letrina	latrine
pato anteojillo	spectacled duck
pato jergón	Chilean pintail duck

⊞ PUYEHUE:
Room with a View

Chile's Lake District, between Temuco and Puerto Montt, encompasses eight large lakes and scores of smaller ones nestled in rolling Andean foothills in a patchwork of forest and farmland. A quaint town or village and several inns lie on the shores of virtually every lake. The eastern backdrop for this countryside is the densely forested Andes and a series of volcanos, many active, that create a genuinely picture-postcard atmosphere for this part of Chile. It is little wonder that the Lake District attracts visitors from all over Chile, South America, and the world.

Perhaps the best place from which to actually view this area is from a place called Antillanca, in Parque Nacional Puyehue. From Antillanca, it is possible to see, in one breathtaking glimpse, lakes Puyehue, Llanquihue, Bonito, Toro, Paraíso, and Rupanco, *and* the following volcanos: Puyehue, Casablanca, Puntiagudo, Osorno, Calbuco, and Tronador. There is much more to see in Puyehue, but it is worth a trip to the park for this single astonishing view.

Puyehue is one of seven national parks, old and new—four are described in this book—that have been established in the uplands of the Lake District. A large park (265,000 acres), Puyehue is one of Chile's first, established in 1941, well before the national park movement took firm root.

In the Araucanian tongue, a *puye* is a small freshwater fish, and *hue* means place, so *puyehue* means place of puyes. It is more than that, however, being a splendid conglomeration of forests, mountains, volcanos, lakes (over twenty), rivers, and hot springs. All of these features have been made readily accessible to visitors in tasteful fashion by the Chilean Park Service and private concessionaires, even though only two roads pass through the park.

Four areas are developed in the park, each of which merits a visit: Playa Puyehue, Aguas Calientes, Antillanca, and Anticura.

PLAYA PUYEHUE. Playa Puyehue is at the western edge of the park, on the shores of Lago Puyehue. Several inns, restaurants, and picnic areas lie near the lake, but the primary attraction, well worth a visit even if you do not bathe, is farther up the road: the Gran Hotel Termas de Puyehue. The hotel and adjacent buildings are devoted to hot springs in the grand old European fashion, and it is all reminiscent of turn-of-the-century spas of the Austro-Hungarian Empire. The hotel is an immense stone structure, surrounded by well-tended lawns, flower gardens, and gravel pathways. Bathers visit not only for fun, but for reasons of health. The waters of Puyehue Hot Springs are reputed to cure or ease symptoms of everything from rheumatism to impotence, and clients can avail themselves of a variety of treatments—from mud baths to therapeutic massages—under the supervision of resident physicians. Pools range in size from bathtub to family-size to Olympic. The Gran Hotel Termas de Puyehue is located at the intersection of Rutas 215 and 485. Chilean Ruta 215 is an international route that enters Argentina at Paso Puyehue, 60 miles (96 kilometers) from Osorno. At the hotel, a side road, Ruta 485, heads south to Aguas Calientes and Antillanca.

AGUAS CALIENTES. Aguas Calientes lies a few miles farther up the road from the hotel, and is clearly intended for the use of the general public. A hostel, store, CONAF administrative center, and a score or so of A-frame cabins have been constructed, but campgrounds and picnic sites are available. Lectures and slide shows on natural history topics are given at the CONAF visitor center. An excellent self-guiding nature trail has been laid out near the visitor facilities, but the most popular attractions are the hot-spring pools, one outdoor pool along the edge of the Río Chanleufu and a larger covered pool at the level of the road. So much hot water seeps through the rocky banks of the river that many bathers simply dig themselves a tub-sized hole at the river's edge to create their own private thermal pool.

Aguas Calientes is located in a thickly forested valley. Two types of Valdivian forests exist in Chile: the coastal Valdivian forest represented at Fray Jorge and common in Archipelagic Chile, and the Andean Valdivian forest, which flourishes in drier and higher locations. Puyehue's forests are Andean Valdivian at lower elevations, but range upwards to stunted communities of coihues and lengas near treeline. Vegetation is exuberant at lower elevations, where higher humidity permits the vigorous growth of mosses, lichens, and ferns characteristic of the Valdivian forest. Cross-country hiking would be most difficult in the dense understory.

ANTILLANCA. About 10 miles (16 kilometers) past Aguas Calientes, the road ends at Antillanca, a site situated near treeline on a shoulder of Casablanca Volcano. It has been observed that the treeline in this part of Chile is one of the few in the world com-

From the slopes of Casablanca Volcano behind Antillanca, a view of Osorno Volcano on the right, and Puntiagudo Volcano on the left; in the foreground is a side crater of Casablanca Volcano.

posed of deciduous trees. Antillanca is a ski resort, but open to summer use. Overnight accommodations are available at either the ski lodge or at a ski hut and warming huts operated by a climbing club. A trail from Antillanca leads to nearby Casablanca Volcano. Bring your own food in summer (November to February) in case the lodge restaurant is closed. The best views from Antillanca are from readily accessible Casablanca Volcano or from the bare ridge behind the ski tows.

ANTICURA. The Río Gol-Gol and its tributaries drain most of the central portion of Puyehue, including the high country near the Argentine frontier. Ruta 215 follows the river valley toward the border, and on this road, 10 miles (16 kilometers) east of the Gran Hotel, lies Anticura (Shining Rock, in Araucanian). Picnic and rest areas, campgrounds, rustic cabins, a hostel, and a small store have been built at Anticura. The visitor center features permanent exhibits with slide shows on ecological topics shown daily at the height of the summer season (January and February). Several trails start at Anticura, one of which leads to a refugio and hot springs on the slopes of Puyehue Volcano (4 hours).

Another of the trails is perhaps the finest interpretive trail through the Andean Valdivian forest in Chile. About 45 minutes are required to hike this 0.5-mile (1 kilometer) trail. Nearly all of the dominant trees and shrubs typical of the Valdivian forest are identified for the visitor, including three species of the native American bamboo (chusquea), a surprising sight in these temperate latitudes. The trail eventually leads to a waterfall in the Río Gol-Gol, Salto del Indio. Legend has it that a group of Araucanians escaped from Spanish captivity and hid from their pursuers in the large cave behind the cascade. A primary attraction along the trail is *el abuelo*, the grandfather, an enormous coihue tree that was already old when the New World was discovered. *El abuelo* is 800 years old.

Wildlife is scarce in Puyehue. Pudús, foxes, and mountain lions have been sighted in the park, but the only wildlife likely to be seen by casual visitors are mountain vizcachas, common above treeline and in volcanic areas. Waterfowl, including torrent ducks, coots, and Chilean pintails, are common on lakes and watercourses. Magellanic woodpeckers may be seen (and heard) in mature forests; hikers are likely to see condors near the volcanos.

The geomorphology of Puyehue is a result of intense glaciation as well as vulcanism. The valleys of the Gol-Gol, Pescadero, and Chanleufu rivers are classic U-shaped valleys carved by ice. Terminal and lateral moraines are visible along the eastern margin of the coastal plain outside the park, and glacial erratic boulders are strewn about hay fields on the margins of Lago Puyehue. Casablanca Volcano and several nearby craters appear to be inactive, but Puyehue Volcano and the Caulle chain of peaks have erupted relatively recently. In 1960, a series of eruptions opened twenty-nine small craters on the northeast face of Puyehue Volcano. Lava and volcanic ash were expelled from the craters and nearby fissures for a week.

Recreation

Puyehue is essentially a hiking and backpacking park. Although lower sectors are dense forest, CONAF has constructed and maintained numerous trails for visitors. Puyehue is a good park in which to try to climb a volcano. Puyehue (7,450 feet) and Casablanca (6,600 feet) are relatively low and accessible peaks, and are not dangerous climbs for prudent, experienced hikers. Puyehue Volcano is reached from Anticura, and Casablanca from Antillanca. Mountaineers should register their plans with CONAF staff in Anticura or Aguas Calientes prior to ascents.

Fishing is good in the rivers and lakes, and no visitor should leave without jumping into a hot-spring pool.

Climate and Weather

The best summer months to visit Puyehue are December to March, during which the average temperature is about 55 degrees Fahrenheit. Valdivian forests are humid, evergreen temperate rain forests, and rain is what keeps them green. Over 160 inches

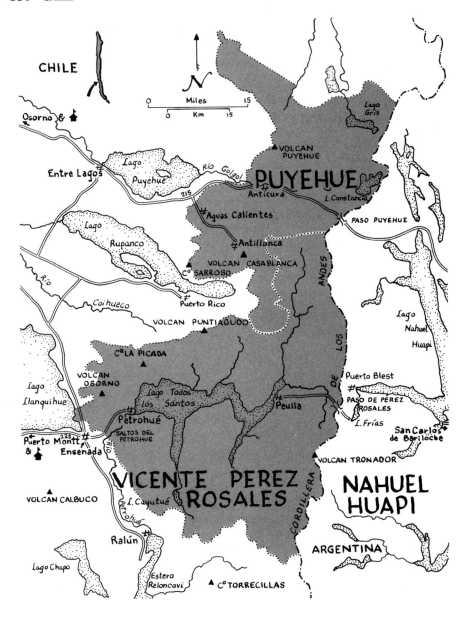

of rain falls each year at Aguas Calientes, so bring raingear. January and February are the driest months of the year. Bring good windbreakers for hiking above treeline, good boots for hiking on lava and snow, plus sunglasses, sunblock cream, and a good hat.

Most of the facilities at Aguas Calientes and Gran Hotel Termas de Puyehue are open year-round. The skiing facilities at Antillanca are extensive. Five lifts have been constructed, and the hostel sleeps 200 people. The ski season extends from August to October.

Location and Access

Puyehue is in Region X east of Osorno on the Argentine frontier.

Ruta 215 is the main overland bus route between Chile and Argentina's Lake District and the resort town of Bariloche. Those traveling from one country to the other can make Puyehue a convenient stop in either direction.

Buses leave Osorno daily (in summer) for Aguas Calientes and for Argentina via Anticura and Paso Puyehue. Most buses depart from the station at Errazuriz 1400, near the municipal market. Hitchhike to Antillanca from Aguas Calientes. It is possible to hitch to the park (and to Argentina) from Osorno, but competition with students in summer is intense.

The tourist office in Osorno (O'Higgins 671) is very helpful. Check also for maps, information, and a possible ride at the CONAF office in Osorno (Mackenna 674).

Glossary

alojamiento	lodging
andarivel	chair lift
centro de visitantes	visitor center
la caza está prohibida	hunting prohibited
piscina techada	covered pool
se prohibe la caza	hunting prohibited
sendero de historia natural	natural history trail
siempreverde	evergreen

VICENTE PEREZ ROSALES:
Thoroughfare through the Andes

At about the fortieth parallel, nature and history have been exceptionally kind to Chile and Argentina. The two nations share the Andes, and at this latitude each has its own remarkable region of mountains, forests, lakes, and streams. Each country has established a national park on its own side of the border, Nahuel Huapi in Argentina, and Vicente Pérez Rosales in Chile. And because of the unique topography of the Andes in this area, travelers may cross the mountains by road (through Parque Nacional Puyehue) or by a unique combination of road and lake transportation through Parque Nacional Vicente Pérez Rosales. Each country's gateway to the other passes through an area of outstanding scenic beauty, a wonderful introduction to Argentina from Chile or to Chile from Argentina.

Vicente Pérez Rosales is Chile's oldest park, and the largest north of Puerto

Montt. The park was established in 1926, and expanded in 1950 to its present 620,000 acres. It is named for an early settler of the region who organized the immigration of German settlers to the area in the 1850s.

Like Puyehue, the park has been shaped by a combination of glaciation and vulcanism. U-shaped valleys and deep mountain lakes were left behind when the last glaciers retreated. Then Osorno Volcano arrived on the scene, changed the face of the park, and created a lacustrian highway through the Andes.

Lago Todos los Santos, 28 miles (45 kilometers) long, is surrounded by the park, which also borders the third-largest natural lake in South America, Lago Llanquihue (286 square miles). These lakes formed a single unit in early interglacial epochs, but lava from the eruptions of Osorno and Calbuco in the post-glacial epoch divided it. Osorno's eruptions are also responsible for the wild character of the Río Petrohué, which drains Todos los Santos, for the river churns and boils through a long series of formations of black basaltic lava that have crept down the sides of Osorno over the centuries.

Vicente Pérez Rosales is a true rim-of-fire park. Osorno (8,730 feet) is the most prominent volcano in the park, but several other large volcanos dominate the park's skyline: Pantoja (6,044 feet), Picada (5,610 feet), and Puntiagudo (8,170 feet). Casablanca (6,496 feet) is shared with Parque Nacional Puyehue, and the highest, Tronador (11,352 feet), is shared with the Argentine park Nahuel Huapi. Puntiagudo (Sharp-pointed) Volcano is the most dramatic of the peaks because of its steep sides and sharp summit, but Osorno is matchless for classic symmetry. Three snowcapped volcanos—Osorno, Calbuco, and Tronador—are visible from Petrohué, the village at the west end of Lago Todos los Santos.

The mountains of Vicente Pérez Rosales support Andean Valdivian forests, similar to those of Puyehue, but there are also extensive meadows and marshes on the deltas of the many rivers that flow into Todos los Santos. A larger variety of shorebirds are therefore found in Vicente Pérez Rosales than in Puyehue. Ferns, mosses, and arboreal lianas—up to a foot in diameter—are abundant in the forests at lower elevations, and fuchsias splash the woods on all sides with bright purple.

Three areas in the park are developed for visitors: Ensenada, Petrohué, and Peulla.

ENSENADA. Ensenada, at the east end of Lago Llanquihue just outside the park, has several small German-style hotels and inns. From Ensenada, hitchhike or hike to two *refugios* on the southern route to the summit of Osorno (4 hours). To reach the northern approach to the volcano, take a bus or taxi from Ensenada or Puerto Octay to the road that goes to La Picada ski area. Hitch a ride to La Picada, where an alpine club maintains three climbing huts. Hut maintenance is erratic; be sure to take your own food. Prior to departure, check for information at the tourist office in the Gran Hotel in Osorno or at the Hotel Ensenada in Ensenada. **Note:** Only experienced climbers should attempt to reach Osorno's summit. Rope, ice-axe, and crampons are required.

The road from Ensenada to Petrohué ascends the valley of the Río Petrohué. The park entrance and an information office are located 3 miles (5 kilometers) from Ensenada. One mile (2 kilometers) farther are the Petrohué Falls (Salto de Petrohué), where the river drops over a recent lava flow. A 0.5-mile (1 kilometer) nature trail along the river is maintained at the falls. A campground and picnic site are located nearby and at several other spots along the river.

PETROHUE. The road reaches Lago Todos los Santos at Petrohué, 9 miles (14 kilometers) from Ensenada. Todos los Santos is said to be Chile's most beautiful lake, and may well merit its reputation. The lake is startlingly blue, tinted slightly with rock flour from the vestiges of glaciers tucked into the mountains along the frontier. It lies directly between Osorno and Tronador volcanos. Situated at low elevation (560 feet), Todos los Santos is a warm lake, well sheltered from prevailing west winds, and is popular for swimming and water sports. Most boat traffic is for tourists, but other boats carry cargo, for along with a summer-home population, the more than 300 families who live around the lake can reach the road system only by boat. Most of the families operate dairies, and produce cheese. During the school year, their children live and attend classes in Petrohué.

A visitor center and several campground and picnic areas are operated by CONAF and private concessionaires. Overnight accommodations and meals are available at the Hostería Petrohué, several private homes, and at a small *refugio*.

A trail (actually a jeep road) leads from Petrohué to the slopes of Osorno, and ul-

Several launches such as these ply the waters of Lago Todos los Santos, carrying thousands of tourists each year through the Andes from Chile to Argentina and vice versa. Note the luggage. Vicente Pérez Rosales National Park, Chile

timately to the ski area at La Picada. Check at the CONAF visitor center for current information on trails, and especially bridges.

Motor-launch excursions to the end of the lake and back are available through the Hostería.

PEULLA. Peulla is the isolated hamlet at the east end of Todos los Santos, the last accommodations available before reaching the Argentine frontier. The hotel Peulla (expensive) is the only regular hotel in the village, but lodging may be available at several private homes along the lake. Camping is allowed near the CONAF office.

A short hike takes visitors to the Cascada Los Novios (Sweetheart Falls), where a spirited little stream tumbles over a cliff through dense stands of bamboo.

Unless you plan to stay at the hotel, bring your own food. A tiny shop at the hotel carries only a few groceries. Meals and rental boats are available at the hotel.

Recreation

Vicente Pérez Rosales is a sightseeing park. Go there for the views. If you climb any of the volcanos, the views simply get better.

Trout fishing is excellent in the streams and lakes of the park. The season is open from mid-November to mid-April, and a license is required. Boats may be rented on *lagos* Llanquihue and Todos los Santos, and drift-boat trips may be arranged on the lower reaches of the Río Petrohué.

Climate and Weather

Although the park is open year-round, the nicest time to visit is from December through March, when the average temperature is about 60 degrees Fahrenheit, and rainfall is relatively low. Eight months of very rainy (or snowy) weather make up the rest of the year. This is mountain country, so be prepared for rain at any time.

Rain is not as serious a threat in the park in summer, but bugs are. Petrohué means "place of petros" in Araucanian, and petros are small, persistent blackflies that love to dine on human beings. Even worse are gigantic horseflies called tábanos, which, if permitted, will chew as big a piece of flesh from a passerby as they can carry away. Be sure to take bug dope.

Location and Access

Vicente Pérez Rosales lies on the Argentine border in Region X, immediately south of Parque Nacional Puyehue, and 42 miles (67 kilometers) northeast of Puerto Montt. The park is a principal tourist thoroughfare between the loveliest portions of Chile and Argentina.

A number of short journeys in South America, ranging from easy to difficult, are considered by seasoned travelers to be so unique that they should not be missed. Among them are the bus/train trip from Cuzco to Machu Picchu (easy); the Inca Trail to Machu Picchu (a long hike); the train trip from La Paz to Arica, Chile (arduous); the boat trip down the Amazon from Iquitos, Peru, to Manaus, Brazil (hot); the boat trip from Puerto Montt to Punta Arenas, Chile (rainy and sometimes rough); and the bus/boat trip through the Andes from Puerto Montt to Bariloche, Argentina (easy).

Most travelers find the notion of floating across the Andes on a boat not only intriguing, but irresistible. Thousands of tourists make the trip each year, mostly between October to April, and few are disappointed.

There are three basic ways to make the international crossing: one-day organized trip, two-day organized trip, or leisurely trip on your own schedule. All three follow the same route, and use the same mode of transportation: a bus from Puerto Montt to Petrohué; a lake steamer across Lago Todos los Santos to Peulla; a bus from Peulla across the border to Puerto Frías, Argentina; a lake steamer across Laguna Frías; a short bus ride from Laguna Frías to Puerto Blest; another lake steamer down a long arm of Lago Nahuel Huapi to Puerto Pañuelo; and finally a bus ride into Bariloche. Presto! You've crossed the Andes.

ONE-DAY ORGANIZED TRIP. The trip is relatively cheap—about $40 (U.S.). Check at the tourist offices in Puerto Montt (corner O'Higgins and Varas, or at the railroad station or bus terminal) or at Andina del Sud (Varas 437) for schedules and prices. The drawback of this option is that it is generally an inflexible package tour, a rushed trip through country in which one should linger. The one day can be very long, for buses leave Puerto Montt early, and arrive in Bariloche late. Schedules are tight, and there is little time to dawdle. If the day happens to be rainy or cloudy, you may well miss the extraordinary mountain scenery that is the primary reason to make the trip (the bus trip across Paso Puyehue is also scenic, but cheaper and quicker). Try to avoid this option.

TWO-DAY ORGANIZED TRIP. This trip follows the same route as the one-day trip, but with an overnight stop at the hotel in Peulla. The trip costs more because of lodging and meals, but since travelers can wait for later boats and buses, the two-day trip permits a longer stay in many parts of the park. In addition, a good meal and a night's rest are most welcome after several hours on buses and boats.

YOUR OWN SCHEDULE. Following your own schedule permits you to inspect and pick the best boats and the clearest days for the lake trips, an important choice since the best vantage points are usually the lakes. You can travel, point to point, to nearly all of the destinations mentioned above at your own pace, spending the night where you wish. Make reservations at Hotel Peulla if you are traveling during the height of the season, however, for the hotel fills up quickly when boats arrive. If camping, take your own food. It is possible to hitchhike to Petrohué from Puerto Montt, but you must pay for transport across the three lakes, and either pay for a bus ride or hike from Peulla to Puerto Frías and from Laguna Frías to Puerto Blest.

Don't fret over the options, for whichever trip you choose will take you through the heart of some of the most beautiful alpine terrain on the continent. What more can a traveler ask?

Paine Towers, Central (left) and Monzino (right), Torres del Paine National Park, Chile

回 TORRES DEL PAINE:
Jewel of the Crown

If fate gave you an opportunity to experience one and only one of South America's panoply of national parks, it would have to be Parque Nacional Torres del Paine.

Torres del Paine is not a mere park, but a park of parks, a destination of travelers to whom a park is more than a place in which to be entertained, but rather an experience to be integrated into one's life. Torres del Paine is the sort of park that changes its visitors by setting standards of sheer sensory impact against which all other parks are thereafter measured.

The factor that launches Torres del Paine into a world-class park, to be compared in the same breath only with the likes of Yellowstone, the Everglades, Gates of the Arctic, or Glacier, is its completeness. It has every feature that the most demanding visitor to a temperate-zone park could expect. A portion of the southern Andean ice cap is included within its borders; its glaciers are massive and dynamic, yet reasonably accessible. Its mountains are rugged and photogenic, and range from gentle forested hills that anyone can explore to spires of sheer stone that severely and regularly test the skills of the international climbing community. The park encompasses a series of lakes and ponds of varying sizes and colors connected by waterways that range from meandering meadow streams to full-blown rivers replete with waterfalls and cascades. The park's flora is relatively insignificant; it contains no trees, shrubs, or flowers of more than passing interest. But its fauna is extraordinary, easy to observe, and cannot fail to rivet the attention of visitors.

CONAF staff at Torres del Paine are professionals, proud of their park, and well aware of the extraordinary value of the resources they watch over. Exceptionally courteous and helpful to those who have journeyed from all over the world to reach Torres del Paine, they have managed to make the park accessible to visitors without impairing its wild and scenic character. Visitor accommodations and services are designated and constructed in good taste and nonintrusive fashion. The road system is adequate, no more than is needed, but the network of trails and refuges that reaches into every corner of the park is matched by no other temperate-zone park in South America. *Refugios,* for which at this writing no charge is made, put Torres del Paine well within reach of the budgets of poor travelers.

Finally, like all truly great parks, Torres del Paine has that indefinable element in its character to which visitors eventually respond. Whatever this element is, it causes hikers to stop in midstride, veer off the trail, and sit alone to gaze into the blue depths of the mountains or across a distant ice cap, contemplating some aspect or other of nature and life.

Torres del Paine is large (450,000 acres), and one of those parks, like Yellowstone or Glacier, that can be enjoyable explored for several weeks. One-day tours are offered to tourists in the nearest town, Puerto Natales, but resist the temptation, for your appetite will only be whetted by a short visit. Make every effort to arrange your schedule so as to spend at least a day or two in the vicinity of the two hotels, and three or four days using the trails and *refugios.* A week should be enough for most visitors, a month for aficionados.

The first thing to learn about this park is how to pronounce its name correctly: TOR-ehs del PIE-nay. Torres del Paine means "Paine Towers." The towers are conspicuous enough, but there is some mystery about the derivation of their name. Some say they were named for an early settler in the region, a woman named Paine, and others say the region was given its name by Tehuelche Indians who once inhabited the area.

The park was born with little fanfare in 1959 as a 15-square-mile plot of terrain named Parque Nacional Lago Grey. Three years later, when the region was still known to only a handful of climbers and travelers who specialized in out-of-the-way places, the park was expanded to include the principal mountains, and was given its present name. International recognition soon followed, and the park was expanded again. In 1978, Torres del Paine was declared a Biospheric Reserve by UNESCO.

Ironically, the park's reputation grew more quickly abroad than in Chile. Thousands of tourists began to visit the park each season, mostly from Europe, North America, Australia, New Zealand, and Japan. But eventually the Chilean public became aware of their park far to the south. In 1988 the number of Chilean visitors finally exceeded the number of foreigners.

A good place to start is the *sede administrativa* (administrative center), a cluster of buildings at the edge of Lago del Toro, about 20 miles (32 kilometers) from the park entrance. But for the flocks of rheas wandering calmly about, an American visitor might mistake the *sede* for a dude ranch with its painted wooden buildings, barns, outbuildings, corrals, and grazing horses. Purchased by the Chilean government, the center is in fact a ranch whose buildings have been converted into CONAF offices, living quarters, and support buildings, which include a small hotel and dining room, store, boat house, stables, and *regufio*. A modern visitor and information center with exhibits and a relief map of the entire park has been added; begin orientation here. The rangers who staff the visitor center are knowledgeable and accustomed to visitors who do not speak Spanish. The park brochure includes a map on which trails and locations of *regufios* are clearly indicated. The relief map in the visitor center allows visitors to plan a trip in accord with their own schedule, taste, and skills.

Spend a day or two at the *sede*, within strolling distance of three rivers, or spend an easy day hiking to Laguna Verde (4 hours). The park is laced with streams that at flood stage may be too dangerous to cross or may wash out bridges, so check with park staff about the condition of trails and footbridges before setting out on long hikes. Floods are not the only hazard; the wooden bridge on the road to Lago Grey from the Administrative Center was burned down by a careless smoker in 1988, temporarily stranding a car, a bus, and several tourists on the wrong side of the river.

Among the more interesting features of life at the *sede* are the other visitors. Many of them will be backpackers (*mochileros*), and on any evening the *refugio* will be sheltering men and women from two or three continents and a dozen or so different countries. The *refugios* are linguistic towers of Babel, of course, but communication somehow occurs, and information on the best cheap hotels and restaurants within a thousand miles of the park is eagerly sought and readily exchanged.

THE PAINE MASSIF. Torres del Paine lies between the central spine of the Andes, nearly buried under a massive ice cap, and the steppes of southern Patagonia, which

Above: Salto del Indio (Indian Falls), created when a flow of lava from Osorno Volcano crossed the path of the Rio Gol-Gol, is on one of the interpretive trails in Puyehue National Park, Chile. **Right:** River banks relate much of the geological history of Conguillio National Park, Chile. Strata exposed by the Truful-Truful River show layers of volcanic ash, mud, and lava laid down by successive eruptions of nearby Llaima Volcano.

Above: Ñandús (Darwin's rheas) in Torres del Paine National Park, Chile. **Left:** Photographer's Bane: guanacos often strike wooden poses that lend them the appearance of stuffed animals, Torres del Paine National Park, Chile. **Opposite:** During spring runoff, this lava flow from Osorno Volcano creates a 60-foot waterfall, Vicente Pérez Rosales National Park, Chile.

Above: Access to a mangrove swamp is provided by the elevated interpretive trail at Isla de Salamanca National Park, Colombia. **Left:** Under moss and lichens, a carved face with headdress; Pueblito, Tayrona National Park, Colombia. **Opposite, top:** Colorful Inca terns (Larosterna inca) are some of the many animals associated with the Humboldt Current. **Lower left:** Blooming puyas (Puya raimondii) can produce as many as 8,000 blossoms on a single enormous spike, Huascarán National Park, Peru. **Lower right:** Valley of Puyas: the Pochacota River Valley in the south of Huascarán National Park, Peru.

Opposite, upper left: Howler monkeys (Alouatta seniculus) in Brownsberg Nature Park, Suriname. **Upper right:** Rainforest symmetry; climbing vines in Brownsberg Nature Park, Suriname. **Bottom:** Scarlet ibises and herons in the mangroves of Morrocoy National Park, Venezuela. **This page, right:** Near the páramos, five-needled pines struggle for existence, Sierra Nevada National Park, Venezuela. **Below:** World of Epiphytes: every tree in the cloud forest furnishes anchorage for these plants of the air, Henri Pittier National Park, Venezuela

Most of the trails in the Sierra Nevada National Park, Venezuela, are well designed and well maintained.

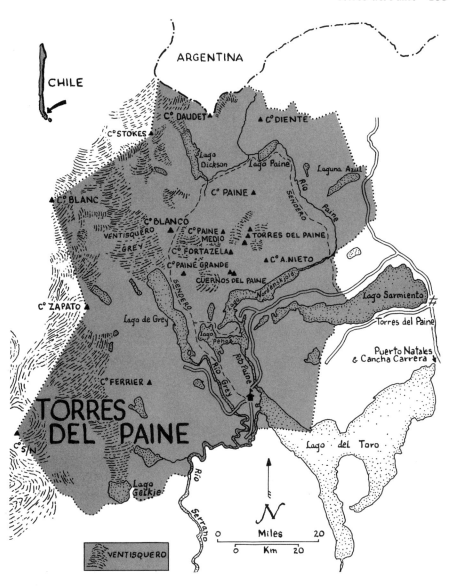

gradually descend eastward to the Atlantic. Its mountains are the remnants of a batho-lith thrust upward by tectonic forces that millions of years ago forced the southern continents apart. To the east of the park a series of rolling hills dotted with small ponds of glacial origin marks the transition from mountains to steppes.

The mountains that comprise the Paine Massif are not high for the Andes, but they are precipitous. Paine Grande (10,007 feet) is the highest, but most of the other peaks range from 8,500 to 9,000 in elevation. What makes individual mountains so dramatic is that from most places in the park entire peaks can be seen—from base to summit—and they appear to leap into the clouds from the floor of the valley.

The classic views of the Paine Massif are from the south. These views rival or surpass the well-known vista of the Grand Tetons from across Jackson Hole. The most conspicuous mountains are the Cuernos del Paine (Paine Horns, 8,530 feet), two massive peaks of pinkish gray granite made exceptionally striking by caps of several hundred feet of jet-black slate. Gemlike, the mountains have distinct facets, steep and slightly concave, scooped from their sides by glaciers. The Cuernos block the view of all but the tips of the three towers, which lie north of them and are best seen from the park entrance, from trail 1, which approaches the towers, or from trail 3, which leads from the park entrance to Lago Paine. Seven small glaciers nestle in the deep recesses of the massif, two of which bracket the three towers. In the United States, the towers would probably be called needles, for they are far more steep and sheer than the word "tower" suggests.

The best way to see all of the peaks of the massif, as well as the large glaciers descending from the ice cap, is to hike the loop trail from the park entrance to the Pehoé guard station (*guardería*). The hike is long—6 to 7 days—though not especially steep, but it is one of the best scenic walking tours in South America. The trails pass seven major lakes, skirt two large glaciers, and connect five *refugios*.

One of the most popular shorter hikes (8 hours) is a portion of this loop trip, from the Pehoé *guardería* to the *refugio* at Lago Grey. This *refugio* is near enough to Grey Glacier that on windless nights visitors can hear from their sleeping bags the thunder of ice blocks plunging from the face of the glacier into Lago Grey.

The glaciers of Torres del Paine are in full retreat. Ventisquero Dickson (Dickson Glacier), for example, is known to have receded by as much as 56 feet a year for the last ninety years. This rate of recession provides visitors with an opportunity to observe at close hand the process of plant succession from bare rock to Magellanic forest along the margins of the lakes that usually form at the ends of the glaciers.

GUANACOS AND RHEAS. The region that is now Parque Nacional Torres del Paine was severely overgrazed by sheep and cattle prior to being taken over by the government. Much of its forestland was logged, and fires set to create more pasture were permitted to rage unchecked. Local ranchers relentlessly hunted most of the region's birds and animals for food or to reduce predation on their livestock. When protection of park resources arrived with CONAF, the region's flora and fauna were clearly in need of recuperation.

The forest of Torres del Paine still show signs of overexploitation that will not be healed for decades, but the more resilient wildlife populations have vigorously responded to protection. Torres del Paine is one of the few parks in the world in which visitors will have a better than average—though still slim—chance to see a mountain lion. It has also become by far the best place in South America to see two of the continent's more interesting animals: guanacos and Darwin's rheas.

When Charles Darwin landed in Patagonia in 1832, he was greeted by the sight of "an elegant animal—with long slender neck and fine legs" in herds that reached the size of several hundred individuals. The tawny brown-and-white animals he saw in Patagonia and later in Bolivia were guanacos (*Lama guanicoe*), one of the two wild cameloids of South America. The ancestors of the guanaco and its cousins, the vicuña and domesticated llama and alpaca, reached South America by crossing the Panamanian isthmus thousands of years ago; they then died out in North America. Guanacos, the tallest South American mammal, were very successful migrants. Their only enemy, except for man, was the mountain lion, and their range extended from Bolivia to the Straits of Magellan, including most of the pampas and Patagonia.

From the time the first Spanish colonists and their seventy-two horses landed on the shores of present-day Argentina in 1535, the guanaco herds were doomed. The animals had been hunted by Indians for food, skins, and bones for implements, but increased hunting pressure and competition with sheep and cattle for habitat proved to be too much, and the herds dwindled. By 1900, only a few family bands survived in remote forests and mountains. When Torres del Paine became a park, no guanacos were known to be in the area.

Today several hundred guanacos inhabit Torres del Paine, and the guanaco is one of the park's star attractions. Small herds defend choice meadows and small ponds throughout the park. Unlike their counterparts outside parks—which, while usually protected, are subject to poaching—the guanacos of Torres del Paine have grown accustomed to vehicles and hikers. In motion, guanacos are graceful and fleet. They permit close approaches, but tend to strike frozen, statue-like poses that frustrate photographers of wildlife. As a result, tourists often leave the park with scores of photos of what appear to be stuffed museum specimens. They stare at intruders with haughty intelligence and erect ears. Flattened ears indicate displeasure; if you get too close, you may be splattered with a noxious gob of half-digested grass, for guanacos, like llamas, spit when irritated.

Guanacos have keen eyesight and acute hearing. Their long necks serve them well on flat and rolling grasslands, and they are considered by some biologists to be ecological equivalents to the pronghorn antelope of the western Great Plains.

A similar long neck, but less graceful fleetness of foot are characteristic of a second animal that has also made a remarkable recovery under protection—the ñandú, called Darwin's rhea or the lesser rhea in English (*Pterocnemia pennata*). Ñandús were hunted for sport, feathers, and food (imagine the drumsticks), and their populations had declined drastically. Their eggs, up to 6 inches long, are still considered delicacies.

Two species of this enormously entertaining ostrich-like bird inhabit South America. Only experts can distinguish the American rhea, which inhabits the plains of southern Brazil, Uruguay, Paraguay, and northern Argentina, from the smaller rhea of the highlands of the southern Andes and Patagonia, including Torres del Paine. South Americans use several common names interchangeably for both birds—suri, avestruz, and ñandú—but ñandú (pronounced nyan-DOO) seems to be most widespread. They have a curious social structure. At nesting, males defend a harem of from four to six females, who lay all their eggs in the same well-camouflaged nest, which can contain as many as fifty eggs. The male then drives off the females, incubates the eggs, and guides and defends the chicks until they can manage on their own. Their natural predators are mountain lions, foxes, and feral dogs, but they are not as helpless as they appear. If cornered, they can deliver powerful slashing blows with their clawed feet.

Like the park's guanacos, ñandús are habituated to vehicles and people, and will permit visitors to get remarkably close. They are most common in the relatively arid rolling hills along the eastern border of the park, but flocks routinely peck their way through the grounds of the *sede* as calmly as overgrown chickens.

Because of the variety of habitats available in the park, the avifauna is rich. Sheldgeese, buff-necked ibis, black-necked swans, southern lapwings, and neotropic cormorants are the most common birds, but backpackers are likely to see flamingos in the marshes and smaller ponds, Magellanic woodpeckers in the stands of lengas, and peregrine falcons and condors on the mountain slopes.

Visitor Facilities

The nearest overnight accommodations outside the park are in Puerto Natales, 70 miles (113 kilometers) from the park entrance, but two hotels within the park offer complete services and are moderately priced. The more elegant of the two is the Hotel Pehoé, built castle-like on a tiny island in Lago Pehoé and connected to shore by a footbridge. The hotel faces the Cuernos and Paine Grande, and the view over the lake from the hotel is stunning. Even if you do not stay at the hotel, you should linger over a drink or meal on the terrace on a sunny afternoon or clear evening. Hotel Pehoé is about 14 miles (22 kilometers) within the park.

The second hotel is the Posada Río Serrano, near Lago del Toro at the *sede administrativa*, 22 miles (35 kilometers) from the park entrance. The Posada is a bit more rustic, less formal, cheaper, and somewhat friendlier than the hotel, but is quite comfortable. Each evening, stories of the day's adventures are recounted over beers or bottles of superb Chilean wines in its pub-like bar.

Note: Because of the growing popularity of Torres del Paine, these hotels are often full during the summer season, especially when organized tours arrive. Visitors who plan to stay at one of the hotels should be sure to reserve a room in advance in Punta Arenas or Puerto Natales. For Hotel Pehoé, go to Turismo Pehoé (21 de Mayo 1460) in Punta Arenas; for Posada Río Serrano, contact Serco Ltda. (telephone 23395) in Punta Arenas, or go to the office on Arturo Prat 270 in Puerto Natales. An alternative is to contact the CONAF office (near the hospital on Avenida Carrera) in Puerto Natales to see if a reservation can be arranged by shortwave radio; it's not guaranteed, but worth a try.

Car camping is growing popular in Chile, but camping along the road system is restricted to established sites. One campground is located near Lake Pehoé, and another is on the banks of the Río Serrano 1 mile (2 kilometers) south of the *sede*. CONAF maintains developed campgrounds on Laguna Azul and Laguna Amarga.

Three *refugios* are located on the road system: one at the *sede*, one at Laguna Amarga, and one at the north end of Lago Pehoé. Accommodation at all of the *refugios* is basic, but free. Most of the *refugios* have wooden bunks, a wood stove, and water nearby. They also have burgeoning populations of famished mice, so protect your food. The *refugios* tend to be small, dark, and smoky, but they quickly fill with good cheer when groups of backpackers arrive.

Note: Although most hikers of the loop trail can get from one *refugio* to the next in a day, some of the distances are better suited for two short days of hiking. Furthermore, the number of backpackers sometimes exceeds the capacity of a *refugio*. All backpackers should therefore be appropriately equipped to spend a night or two in the open. Tent and camp stove are essential. Safe drinking water is abundant, but backpackers and campers should bring all of the food they will need from Puerto Natales. A small store at the Posada Río Serrano has some groceries, but it is expensive and the choice is limited.

The park brochure map is adequate for experienced hikers, but backcountry trails are not as well marked as North Americans are accustomed to. Distances and approximate hiking times are indicated in tables. Locations of *refugios*, roads, ranger stations, and major peaks, rivers, and streams are shown. You won't get lost.

Recreation

Torres del Paine is clearly a fine place to backpack, but there are other ways to enjoy the park. Plenty of rewarding destinations lie at the end of day hikes and short strolls, and the road system itself passes many of the park's highlights. Every visitor will have frequent opportunities for bird-watching and wildlife observation. Horseback rides from the *sede* to backcountry sites, including Ventisquero Grey, can be arranged at the Posada Río Serrano.

The Paine Massif is a destination for climbers from all over the world, and every season parties ranging from solo climbers to fully equipped expeditions attempt the summits of the Cuernos and, more particularly, the towers themselves. Climbers should note that the weather on the peaks is usually abominable, as one storm after another marches through. Gale winds can last for weeks on end. Note also that park authorities frankly advise climbers that because of the remoteness of the peaks and the rugged character of the terrain, prompt help or technical assistance in case of emergency cannot be relied upon. Park rangers are trained in first aid and will provide as much assistance as possible, but the park does not maintain a mountain rescue team. At one time, climbers needed permission from the Ministerio del Interior in Santiago as well as from park authorities in Torres del Paine before they could make a climb. It would be wise to check with CONAF in Puerto Natales before leaving for the park. Write Director, Administración Parque Nacional Torres del Paine, Corporación Nacional Forestal, Puerto Natales, Región XII, Chile.

The Río Serrano and other streams in the park support resident trout as well as runs of large salmon. Fishermen will need a permit from the Servicio de Agrícola y Ganadería; inquire at the CONAF office in Puerto Natales.

Boats may be rented on Lago del Toro at the *sede,* and organized launch tours now approach Ventisquero Grey from a dock at the southern end of Lago Grey. Despite the remote location of the park, it is likely that Torres del Paine will become an international kayaking center in years to come. The streams of the park offer kayaking opportunities ranging from easy to nearly impossible, and the interconnected lakes and streams provide routes through the park that kayakers will find irresistible. The location also makes it feasible to combine river trips with sea kayaking, for the Río Serrano flows into a narrow fjord that leads to Puerto Natales and onward. The trip should not be attempted by inexperienced kayakers, for gale winds can suddenly rage through the straits and fjords, and on some reaches of the route, long stretches of sheer cliffs provide no means of getting safely ashore. One kayaker, an American, has al-

Ñandús (Darwin's rheas) are making a remarkable comeback in Torres del Paine National Park, Chile.

ready disappeared without a trace in these waters. It may be necessary to obtain permission from the port captain in Puerto Natales (Calle Pedro Montt, near the waterfront) prior to setting out.

Cultural Aspects

Chile has one of the most progressive park services in Latin America—and perhaps the western hemisphere—with respect to park philosophy and ethics of conservation. Despite the chronic budget shortfalls that plague all Latin American park services, and the obvious inability to put enough staff in the field to prevent depredations in some parks, CONAF has developed a farsighted philosophical underpinning for its parks that could serve well as a model for all other countries.

Chile conceives of her parks not only as repositories of valuable natural resources, but as national classrooms in which sophisticated conservation attitudes can be instilled into the public consciousness. CONAF defines national parks as areas, generally extensive, that contain diverse habitats, unique or representative of the country's ecological diversity, are not significantly altered by human activity, are capable of self-perpetuation, and in which species of flora or fauna or geological formations are of special educational, scientific, or recreational interest. This definition represents an admirable ideal that does not merely exist on paper, but is consistently reinforced by CONAF visitor services and emphatically demonstrated by the unbridled enthusiasm of CONAF staff for parks under their stewardship. Exhibits, slide shows, and talks at visitor centers tend to be educational rather than simply informative.

This attitude is also reflected in park rules and regulations, and some of the regulations (*prohibiciones*) at Torres del Paine illustrate the point. Visitors to this park are warned—not requested—not to:

♦ deposit garbage, rubbish, or chemical products from any source or in any volume into any waters or at any place not intended for such deposits;

♦ overnight (except in emergencies), picnic, or light fires in any part of the park not intended for such use;

♦ remove or extract soil, leaves, humus, mud, sand, gravel, or rocks from any part of the park;

♦ frighten, molest, capture, or injure any of the park's fauna;

♦ cut, pull up, remove, or mutilate any of the park's flora;

♦ destroy nests, reproduction or rearing sites, or take actions that might interfere with or impede the reproductive cycle of the park's fauna;

♦ collect eggs, seeds, or berries;

♦ introduce exotic species of flora or fauna into the park; or

♦ bring about visual or acoustic disturbances.

These may sound to North Americans like prosaic admonishments, but in the context of centuries-old Latin American traditions that hold that resources of public lands are basically there for the taking, they are revolutionary prohibitions that seem to be taking root quickly, especially among young Chileans.

Climate and Weather

An anecdote will illustrate the problem at this park. On a fine Monday afternoon in January, the author enjoyed a pleasant swim in Lago Pehoé and spent all of the following day draped in winter clothing.

The weather in Torres del Paine is, to say the least, subject to rapid change, even through a single day, and is virtually unpredictable. Be ready for anything, especially in spring and fall, when the snowcapped mountains are at their dramatic best.

The park is open all year, but the best time to visit is from October to April, during which the average temperature is about 50 degrees Fahrenheit. Rain is common in summer, and snow and rain in winter, when drifts may temporarily block roads. Temperatures also fluctuate widely. Sunny summer days can be quite warm—shirtsleeve weather—but chilly rainstorms can blow in at any time of the day, and evenings can grow cool enough for sweaters or coats.

For a visit to Torres del Paine, provide yourself with adequate raingear and water-resistant boots.

Location and Access

Torres del Paine lies in Chile's Region XII, Magellanes Province, 55 miles (88 kilometers) north of Puerto Natales; it is not easy to reach. Not only is it a long way from North America, it is a long way from most of South America, since it lies near the curling tail of the continent, only about 240 air miles (386 kilometers) from Cape Horn.

Once you reach the general vicinity, however, it is not difficult to get to Torres del Paine. If you are making a grand tour and have reached Argentina's Parque Nacional Los Glaciares, you are only about 35 air miles (56 kilometers) from Torres del Paine, although to reach the park by bus, you must go through Río Gallegos and El Turbio, a road trip of nearly 400 miles (644 kilometers). A new international gravel road connects Calafate, Argentina, with the park, but no public transportation currently travels this road. A similar shortcut to the park from Calafate, not yet served by public transportation, is through Esperanza, Argentina, to the border crossing near Cerro Castillo, Chile. Travel agencies in Calafate will have the most recent information on public transportation, if any, over these routes. Hitchhiking is possible, although traffic is light in summer and practically nonexistent in winter. Be prepared for *long* waits, and have your passport and visas in order. There are scheduled flights between Calafate and Río Gallegos or Ushuaia.

Most travelers visit Torres del Paine on their way to or from Ushuaia, Argentina, or Punta Arenas, Chile. From Ushuaia, you can reach Punta Arenas by bus or plane. Puerto Natales, which has a score of hotels, inns, and restaurants, is a 160-mile (257 kilometers) ride on fast, comfortable buses from Punta Arenas; it can also be reached by boat every ten days or so from Puerto Montt (check at the offices of Navimag, Terminal Transbordadores Angelmo, on the waterfront at Puerto Montt).

Once you reach Puerto Natales, there are a number of ways to reach the park. Hitchhiking is possible, although traffic is heavy only during the summer (December through February), when there is lots of competition. Visitors can also try to catch a ride from the CONAF offices on one of their buses or trucks; it's cheap but not regularly scheduled. A scheduled bus leaves Puerto Natales several times a week during the summer (Buses Sur, Baquedano 534 in Puerto Natales, José Menendez 565 in Punta Arenas); taxis can be hired at any season, although they are more expensive if costs are not shared. Package tours from either Punta Arenas or Puerto Natales include a number of itineraries and lengths of stay; inquire at Buses Fernandez (Eberhard 555 in Puerto Natales, Chiloé 930 in Punta Arenas).

Glossary

cabalgata	horseback ride
caminata	hike
capitanía del puerto	port authority
escorpión	scorpion, found in drier sections of the park
leña	firewood
mochila	backpack
mochilería	backpacking
mochilero, -a	backpacker
portería	entrance, access
sede administrativa	administrative headquarters
sendero, huella	trail

Frailejones or tall friars is the descriptive term Colombians give to the espeletias that are characteristic of the humid uplands of northern South America—the páramos. *Puracé National Park, Colombia*

🌀 6
COLOMBIA

South America is called the Bird Continent by ornithologists for good reason: about 40 percent of all bird species known in the *world* are represented somewhere in South America. And if there is a heaven for ornithologists, it is surely in Colombia, for nearly half of the birds in South America can be found in this one country, which has over twice as many species as all of North America north of the Mexican border.

Complex topography is one reason for the remarkable variety of birds and other animals in Colombia. The country is extremely rugged, for in Colombia the Andes have spread out into three separate ranges divided by deep valleys, high plateaus, and tropical lowlands. North and east of the mountains are the Caribbean coast and the grassy lowlands (*llanos*) of the Orinoco headwaters, to the southeast are the *selvas*, the upper Amazon rain forests, and to the southwest are the tropical lowlands along the Pacific coast.

A second reason for this variety of wildlife is complex climate. Climatic zones change with altitude, and Colombia has a hot zone (*tierra caliente*) from sea level to 3,500 feet, a temperate zone (*tierra templada*) from 3,500 to 6,500 feet, and a cold zone (*tierra fría*) above 6,500 feet.

The third reason is Colombia's position at the southern edge of the land bridge between North America and South America. Many forms of birds and other wildlife had developed in isolation in South America before the Central American land bridge

rose to connect the continents. When the bridge appeared, a host of new animals invaded from the north; many of them found a spot in Colombia that met their needs, and stayed on.

This diversity of landforms and habitats has endowed Colombia with a rich potential for national parks; over twenty-six areas have been set aside for this purpose, most in recent years. National parks in Colombia are administered by the División Parques Nacionales y Vida Silvestre (National Parks and Wildlife Division) of the In-

stituto Nacional de los Recursos Naturales Renovables y del Ambiente (National Institute of Renewable Resources and Environment), called by its acronym, IN-
DERENA. If you are beginning your Colombian travels in the capital city, stop in the
INDERENA offices in Bogotá at Avenida Caracas, No. 25A-66, and request maps
and printed information on Colombia's national parks.

Despite the best efforts of INDERENA, social and political turmoil over the last
decade has forestalled the development of an adequate infrastructure for a network of
national parks in Colombia. In addition, Colombia has become somewhat dangerous
for travelers in recent years. Some visitors travel for several weeks through the country
with no problems whatsoever; many others, more careless perhaps, have been robbed
or cheated. Colombia has become the cocaine capital of the world, and has fallen heir
to the violence associated with that drug.

This does not mean that you should not visit Colombia. It does mean that wherever you go in the country, you must guard your belongings zealously, be prudent with
respect to your activities, circumspect in your dealings with strangers, and have nothing to do with drugs of any kind.

Given these circumstances, three of Colombia's parks warrant a visit. Each is
within easy reach of a major city, and each represents a facet of South American natural history found in few other national parks of the continent.

🖾 PURACÉ:
Páramos and Rare Wildlife

As we have seen, the altiplanos of Bolivia, Peru, and Chile are austere plateaus
that support scattered clumps of bunchgrass and dry scrub. These plateaus are cold, but
it is not so much low temperatures as lack of moisture that limits plant growth and
lends a beautiful but bleak aspect to these high grasslands called *punas.*

Venezuela, Ecuador, and Colombia also have high, cold plateaus, but instead of
being arid, many are drenched in a clammy, penetrating mist that leaves every surface
dripping wet. The high humidity and almost continuous year-round drizzle have created the *páramo,* a completely different type of grassland than that found in the southern Andes. And one of the best places to see *páramos* is in the mountains of Parque
Nacional Puracé in southwestern Colombia.

In Quechua, language of the Incas, *puracé* means "mountain of fire," and this
park encompasses not only splendid *páramos,* but also snowcapped volcanos that exceed 15,000 feet, and thermal features in a setting distinct from the more southerly
highlands. In one sense, Puracé is the roof of the continent, for it is the birthplace of
rivers that drain three watersheds and flow into the Pacific, Atlantic, and Caribbean.
The Río Patía flows west to the Pacific, the Río Cauca and Río Magdalena join and
flow north to the Caribbean, and the Río Caquetá flows east to disappear into the vast
embrace of the Amazon.

Established in 1968, comprising nearly 215,000 acres, and ranging from 8,200 to
15,400 feet in elevation, the park provides refuge for some of South America's strangest and most elusive wildlife.

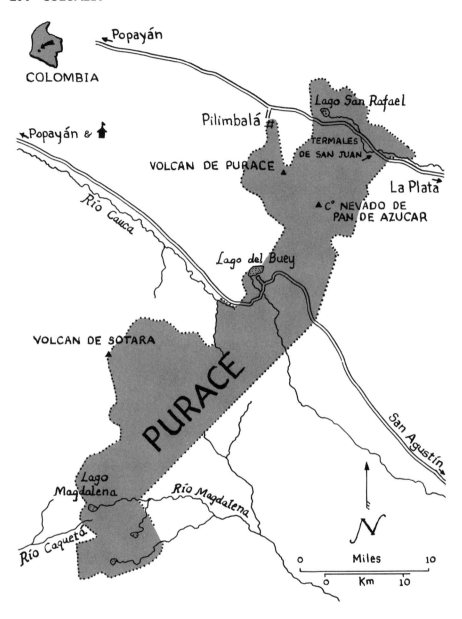

Páramos are characterized by a dense mixture of grasses and low-growing herbaceous plants. The variety and abundance of strangely formed bright flowers in these grasslands and their forest fringes have been noted since they were first described. Most herbaceous plants of the *páramo* are compact, and grow close to the ground or assume cushion or mat forms in order to reduce heat loss. The most characteristic plant of the *páramo*, an exception to this rule, is the espeletia, or frailejón.

Frailejón means "tall friar," and the word describes these strange plants well. Espeletias are members of the daisy family, which includes sunflowers, goldenrods, and thistles, but they bear no superficial resemblance to their familiar relatives. Like many *páramo* plants, they have leaves arranged in rosette fashion around a thick central stem. As the plant grows and lower leaves drop off, a trunk-like stem reminiscent of some palm trees forms, and the plant assumes a tree-like appearance. Some adults even reach tree-like dimensions—20 feet in height—but most are about as tall as a man. With their rosettes of hairy gray-green leaves they indeed resemble tall clerics striding with divine purpose through the mist, with sodden blankets draped over their shoulders.

Puracé is not exclusively *páramos.* Below 10,000 feet, the slopes are covered with a luxuriant growth of forests usually covered by thick clouds. These dripping forests have a dense understory that is home to three rare South American animals seen so seldom that little is known of their life histories: the mountain tapir, spectacled bear, and Andean pudú.

The first mountain tapir (*Tapirus pinchaque*) was sighted and described in the Puracé area in 1829. Like its lowland cousin, the mountain tapir lives near water, and makes tunnel-like trails through the undergrowth. It is similar in appearance and habits to the lowland tapir, but is distinguished by long, dark, sometimes curly hair on its sides and shoulders that is responsible for its original name, hairy or woolly tapir. The animal has long been hunted for meat, and its primary range is now restricted to mountainous regions of southern Colombia and northern Ecuador. The mountain tapir is difficult to observe because of the heavy cover in which it chooses to live. Although it has been sighted at elevations ranging from 6,500 to 14,500 feet, it will likely become even more rare outside the park as its forest habitat is destroyed by logging and agricultural development. For this reason, those who come across its trails in the forests of Puracé would be wise to linger in hopes of sighting the animal, for its days may be numbered.

The Andean spectacled bear (*Tremarctos ornatus*) is the only bear found in South America. It is black, and often has dull yellow patches on its cheeks and around its eyes that account for its name; South Americans call it oso negro or oso de anteojos, literally black bear or spectacled bear. It is medium-sized—an adult male weighs about 140 pounds—and makes a nest for itself of branches and leaves. Its usual habitat is high forests, including *páramo* areas, but like other bears it is nomadic and highly adaptable, and has a wider range than once believed. Signs and sightings of bears have been made in semi-arid desert areas near sea level in Peru. Regrettably, the spectacled bear is considered by hunters to be the prime trophy animal of South America, and it is hunted relentlessly wherever it is not protected. In some parts of the lowlands east of the Andes, it raids croplands and is also hunted by farmers. The bear is notoriously difficult to sight in the wild, but if you get away from the road, keep your eyes open, your mouth shut, and your fingers crossed—you may get a look at one of these bears in Puracé.

The third rare mammal found in Puracé is called venado conejo, or rabbit deer, by the Colombians—the Andean pudú (*Pudu mephistopheles*), smallest of the cervids. This toy-like deer, about a foot high, is a different species than the pudú found in lowland forests of Chile and Argentina, and even more shy than its southern brethren. It has tiny, spiky antlers, and though it is hard to imagine why, the Andean pudú is also a highly sought hunting trophy. Habitat destruction and settlements are probably the greatest threats to this tiny animal.

About 200 species of birds have been identified in the park, among them such rare birds as the quetzal, condor, and cock-of-the-rock. The cock-of-the-rock (*Rupicola peruviana*), of special interest to ornithologists because of its complex communal courtship display, is about a foot long, and makes its home in dense thickets, usually near streams. The male has black wings, but the rest of its plumage including a tall crest, is flaming orange.

Visitor Facilities

The most convenient hotels and restaurants outside the park are at the city of Popayán, 35 miles (56 kilometers) from the park entrance, but accommodations are available within the park.

Start your visit at the tiny village of Pilimbalá at the park entrance. Stop first at park headquarters to look at maps and obtain printed information, and then inspect the other facilities. The village is located near several hot springs, and several pools have been constructed for visitor use. Meals may be obtained at a restaurant-bar, and overnight accommodations are available at several rustic cabins. The average annual temperature at Pilimbalá is only 48 degrees Fahrenheit, and nights are cold, so when not soaking in a hot spring, travelers will need the comfort provided by the wood stoves in the cabins.

Two hikes from Pilimbalá are recommended. A 4- to 5-hour climb from the village will bring you to the crater of Puracé Volcano (13,000 feet). Good boots and warm clothes are necessary for this climb, which is best made during the dry season—December, January, and February. Guides are available, but not required. Keep an eye out for condors; it is estimated that six pairs nest in the vicinity of Puracé and adjacent Pan de Azucar volcanos.

A small lake, Laguna San Rafael, lies just north of the road to La Plata, about 6 miles (10 kilometers) from Pilimbalá. The highest point on the road, about 11,000 feet, lies just beyond the lake. An easy early-morning or evening downhill walk from the overlook near this high point back to Pilimbalá will take hikers through an extensive *páramo* and past the lake. An hour or so spent sitting quietly on the lakeshore with binoculars at hand will be rewarded with sightings of birds and other wildlife. Report all sightings of rare wildlife to park rangers at the San Juan or Pilimbalá ranger stations.

About 8 miles (13 kilometers) toward La Plata from Pilimbalá lie Termales de San Juan (San Juan Hot Springs), a group of more than 100 sulfurous springs that erupt in a forest clearing and form a series of warm streams that drain off, steaming, into the forest. Many of these springs eject boiling water, and their runoff channels are splashed with parallel bands of algae and bacteria mats whose colors vary with temperature in a fashion reminiscent of the hot springs of Yellowstone. The hot springs are just off the main road, and an interpretive trail leads through the thermal areas. Swimming is not permitted, and bathing in the springs is prohibited.

About 1 mile (2 kilometers) past Termales de San Juan, a 1-mile (2 kilometers) road leads to the Saltos de San Nicolás (Saint Nicholas Cascades). The cascades are of indifferent interest, but the road is not heavily used and affords excellent opportunities for bird and wildlife observation.

The visitor center at Termales de San Juan blends well with its surroundings at Puracé National Park, Colombia.

Recreation

Wildlife observation (and incidental hiking) is the principal attraction of Puracé. Visitors should not, however, visit the park fully assured that they will see its rare wildlife; some patient, hardworking, and lucky visitors will see a tapir, bear, or pudú, but many more won't see any of them.

Puracé is a good park in which to relax, in which to take a break from an extended journey. Its cool temperatures are a refreshing contrast to Colombia's *tierra caliente,* and long soaks in its hot springs are guaranteed to ease tight muscles and repair travel-frayed nerves.

Climate and Weather

Rainfall occurs all year in Puracé, but is somewhat reduced from December through February. Even in the absence of rain, clouds keep the forests damp, so good raingear, including water-repellent boots, are useful all year. Evenings are chilly, and nights cold. Warm sweaters are a must. If you climb Puracé Volcano, you must protect your skin with some form of sun block.

Location and Access

Puracé is located 35 miles (56 kilometers) southeast of the city of Popayán in southwestern Colombia.

Stop at the tourist office (Carrera 6, no. 3–74) in Popayán for maps, location and prices of hotels, and bus schedules; the staff is very helpful. Several buses a day leave Popayán for Puracé (2 hours) from the new bus terminal near the airport. Ask for a ticket to Parque Nacional Puracé (not simply Puracé) or Pilimbalá, for the town of Puracé lies 10 miles (16 kilometers) short of the park. Hitchhiking is possible to and within the park, but traffic is light on weekdays.

Glossary

aguas termales	hot springs
altura	altitude
azufrada	sulphurous
gallo de roca	cock-of-the-rock
gavilán	hawk
nevado	snowcapped mountain
población	village, small town
venado	deer

🄴 ISLA DE SALAMANCA:
The Sea Jungle

Several large rivers reach the ocean along the northern coast of South America—in Brazil, the Amazon; in Guyana, the Essequibo; in Venezuela, the Orinoco; and in Colombia, the Magdalena. These rivers and a succession of smaller ones discharge enormous amounts of fresh water into warm seas and are partly responsible for development of the vegetative community that lines hundreds of miles of South America's northern coastline—mangrove swamps.

In the popular imagination, the reputation of mangrove swamps is similar to that of Amazon jungles: disease-ridden; unbearably hot; full of quicksand; endless, impenetrable thickets at the edge of the sea. The mangroves around Devil's Island and its nearby coasts were, after all, hostile environments into which men simply disappeared, and were far more efficient at holding prisoners than mere gun-toting sentries. Mangroves, of course, do not quite live up to their grim reputation, and they are of great interest to naturalists, but there is a measure of truth associated with their reputation that concerns students of natural history and all other visitors. Mangrove swamps, not quite land and not quite water, are indeed difficult to move around in. In this respect, mangroves are like rain forests: it is easy to get to the edge of a mangrove, but difficult to get within it.

Only a few sites in South America are situated and developed in such a manner as to help a visitor experience this unique habitat and its denizens. One of the best such sites is Parque Nacional Isla de Salamanca on the Caribbean coast of Colombia.

The park, established in 1964, occupies 52,000 acres of mangrove swamps at the mouth of the Río Magdalena. It comprises a long, coastal sand spit that lies between the open sea and a huge brackish lagoon, the Ciénaga Grande. The spit is laced with a maze of channels that connect smaller *ciénagas* and weave through hundreds of islets and mud flats that provide food, shelter, and nesting areas for thousands upon thousands of birds and a smaller group of aquatic and semiaquatic fauna.

Park managers have neatly solved the visitor access problem in two ways. They have constructed a series of boardwalks that extend nearly a mile into the mangrove forests and provide access by foot into the swamps, and have also mapped out a series of channels through the park that visitors can explore by water. The park service even provides boats with which to explore the waterways.

Biologists have long realized that mangrove swamps (*manglares*) are among the most productive ecosystems in the world. Red mangroves are known to drop over three tons of leaves per acre into their habitat every year, and the swamps trap and recycle nutrients borne to the sea from land by rivers. They thereby provide food for enormous numbers of microorganisms, which are in turn food sources for larger creatures, and on up the food chain to the last links in the chain in this park: birds, crocodiles, and mammals.

Isla de Salamanca is a relatively small park, and its habitat, though complex, is relatively homogeneous. Nevertheless, more than 200 species of birds have been listed for the park, and the sheer number of birds approaches the incredible populations of the guano islands of Peru and the penguin rookeries of Patagonia. Some of the highest densities of birds in South America, indeed the world, are found at Isla de Salamanca and nearby.

The organism that holds this system together is the mangrove tree. Three types of mangroves flourish in the park under chemical and aquatic conditions that discourage nearly all other forms of terrestrial plant life: the black, white, and red mangrove. The black mangrove (*Avicenna germinans*) requires the driest sites, and can reach a height of 100 feet. The white mangrove (*Loguncularia racemosa*) tolerates wetter sites, and

Herons and egrets are so abundant at Isla de Salamanca National Park that they share roosts; upper right, little blue heron (Florida caerula); *lower left, cattle egret* (Bulbulcus ibis).

mature trees may reach 60 feet. The toughest of the three, the red mangrove (*Rhizophora mangle*), forms a solid, dark-green forest that usually extends farther seaward than the other species.

Mangroves seem to lack central trunks, and are instead supported by scores of branch-like prop roots that extend into the water and hold the tree 3 or 4 feet above the surface as if on bended elbows. Some of these strange roots, especially characteristic of white mangroves, are air roots or pneumatophores, structures rare in the plant world. Nature had to figure out a way to prevent mangroves from simply drowning in a wasteland of shifting channels and fluctuating water levels; the answer was pneumatophores, roots that are negatively geotropic. These roots do not respond to the pull of gravity, but instead grow up out of submerged ground, rise above the surface of the water, and surround clumps of mangroves with thousands of short spikes, vegetative pincushions that provide adult plants with an opportunity for gas exchange in the atmosphere.

A mature red mangrove tree produces banana-yellow flowers in spring, and about 300 seeds. The seeds, pencil-shaped and about a foot long, are sharp-pointed. If they fall into shallow water, they can strike bottom and become imbedded in the sediment, where they take root. But they also float, and if they are not deposited in a suitable place when they drop from the tree they can drift with the tide for hundreds of miles, and stay alive for up to a year. Eventually, the rooting end of the seed becomes waterlogged, and the seed moves on, semi-submerged, until it dies or finds an appropriate place to take root.

As they set down roots, drop leaves, and catch detritus carried back and forth by

the tide, mangroves create suitable habitat for themselves and for many other creatures. They shelter marine invertebrates, provide safe nurseries for fish, and support
huge populations of such birds as jacanas, ibises, herons, screamers, anhingas, cormorants, egrets, kingfishers, frigate birds, pelicans, parakeets, skimmers, gulls, and
terns—a true cornucopia of seabirds and shorebirds.

The ubiquitous neotropic cormorant (*Phalacrocorax olivaceus*) is one of the most
common birds in the park, but one of the strangest of the mangrove birds is the wattled jacana (*Jacana jacana*), a foot-long black bird with a red wattle and yellow wingtips. Jacanas are distinguished by feet with extremely long, thin toes and nails. When
extended, their feet, nearly as long as their bodies, enable them to run over floating
vegetation and debris as if weightless. Herons, ibises, and egrets, called garzas by Colombians, are especially abundant, among them snowy white cattle egrets (*Bulbulcus
ibis*), white great egrets (*Casmerodius albus*), which stand nearly 4 feet tall, and the
slate-gray-and-white tricolored heron (*Hydranassa tricolor*). You may see as many as
three species of kingfishers in the park.

Crabs, shellfish, and other mollusks are abundant in the quiet waters created by
the mangrove islands, and so are the animals that feed on them. Among the smaller
animals are two that the Colombians call zorros (foxes) and we call raccoons: the common raccoon (*Procyon lotor*) and the similar, but semiaquatic, crab-eating raccoon
(*Procyon cancrivorus*), called zorro cangrejo.

Two of the larger denizens of the mangroves are caimáns, and manatees or sea
cows. Only one true crocodile is found in South America; though much reduced in
numbers, they are found exclusively in the Río Orinoco system. All the rest of the
crocodile-like reptiles in South America are caimáns, which differ from alligators only
in minor anatomical details. Some caimáns are equally at home in salt water or fresh
water, and although they are not common in the park, they do pass through. They are
quick, and do not permit intruders to approach closely during the day. However,
caimáns are more active at night and can be easily detected by their red eye-shine if
you are out after dark with a flashlight.

Many of the channels between the islands are stained rusty brown from tannins in
the mangrove bark, but other channels are kept clear by tidal action, and in these
channels lucky visitors might catch sight of a small group of manatees (*Trichechus
manatus*), sluggish aquatic mammals that range in size from 7 to 13 feet, and weigh up
to half a ton. They are strictly vegetarian, and not dangerous. If you hear persistent
gurgling noises, and see a commotion in shallow water, investigate at once, for it may
be manatees. If you see a manatee dive, do not assume that it will surface again
nearby, for they can stay under water for half an hour.

Although the primary attraction of the park is its mangrove forests, the upland
portions of the park are dry deciduous forests that support deer, capybaras, and even
howler monkeys.

Visitor Facilities

No overnight accommodations are available at the park, but none are needed;
the park is only a mile or two (2 kilometers) from Barranquilla, a major port city with
dozens of hotels and restaurants. Check locations and prices at the tourist office (Carrera 72, No. 57–43, Oficina 401).

The two centers of activity at the park are Los Cocos and Cangarú. Los Cocos, at kilometer 10 on the Carretera Barranquilla-Ciénaga, is an obligatory stop, for it is the site of a wooden, 1-mile-long (2 kilometers) interpretive causeway built into the mangroves and *ciénagas*. Placards at strategic locations along this elevated "trail" indicate names and characteristics of local flora and fauna. Allow at least an hour for a leisurely stroll. As always, early morning and late evening are best for seeing birds and wildlife.

A visitor center at Los Cocos includes a collection of mounted animals native to the park, dioramas, and photographic exhibits on natural-history topics. The park service has also constructed pools that are microhabitats for caimáns and manatees. Meals are available at a bar-restaurant.

One of the most pleasant ways to spend a day at Isla de Salamanca is to explore the park with one of the pedal-powered boats (*bicicletas marinas*) that can be rented at Los Cocos. Pack a camera, lunch, binoculars, swim gear and towels, mask and snorkel, sunglasses, insect repellent, and plenty of water or beer, then pedal to a beach on the open sea, bird-watching all the way. It may be possible to arrange a longer tour of the waterways by motorboat with a park service guide (*inspector*) to sites of special interest. Overnight camping is not permitted at Los Cocos.

The second center of activities is at Cangarú, about 10 miles (16 kilometers) east of Los Cocos. A small coffee shop, picnic area with thatched shelters, barbecue pits, tables, fresh water, bathrooms, and showers are available. Overnight camping is permitted at Cangarú with permission from park authorities in Barranquilla (Carrera 44, No. 40, 20 Piso 9) or Santa Marta (Calle 17, No. 4–88). Cangarú provides access to Playa Grande, a 10-mile-long (16 kilometers) beach of white sand fronting the Caribbean and backed by mangroves. Because of the cooling breezes and opportunity for dips in the surf, the beach is a pleasant place to spend a hot afternoon. The wind is fairly constant, but if it dies bathers will need to protect themselves well from zancudos, jejenes, and tábanos, each a different type of biting fly.

Between May and September, visitors may run across curious, scallop-shaped tracks running up the beach from the surf. These are the tracks of marine turtles, which lay their eggs in the sands of Playa Grande during this period.

Recreation

The availability of boats makes wildlife observation more fun and less work in Isla de Salamanca than in many other parks. Visitors can also swim in the sea, snorkel in the sea and the *cienagas*, and beachcomb at this park.

Climate and Weather

Temperatures are hot during the day and warm in the evening. Humidity is always high. The average annual temperature is about 82 degrees Fahrenheit. Visitors soon learn that sea winds significantly moderate the temperature, and make efforts to keep themselves in a stiff breeze.

Two seasons prevail at Isla de Salamanca, a dry season (*tiempo seco*) from December to July, and a wet season (*tiempo mojado*) from August to November. The best time to visit the park is during the dry season.

Location and Access

Isla de Salamanca is located on the Caribbean coast of Colombia, on the eastern outskirts of the city of Barranquilla.

The main highway between Barranquilla and points east runs the length of the park. Construction of this highway has unfortunately blocked the flow of fresh water into several *ciénagas* on the seaward side of the road, and by increasing the salinity has killed off many acres of mangroves. Several buses a day leave Barranquilla for the cities of Santa Marta or Ciénaga. Most of the bus stations are near the intersection of Calle 34 and Carrera 45. Watch your belongings!

Glossary

agua dulce	fresh water
babilla	cayman
caño	canal or channel
caimán	cayman
ciénaga	brackish lagoon
garza	ibis, heron, or egret
garza real	great egret
manatí	manatee
manglar	mangrove forest or swamp
mangle	mangrove
mangle amarillo	white mangrove
mangle rojo	red mangrove
mangle salado	black mangrove
pato cuervo	cormorant

TAYRONA: Ancient Trails

Not far from Isla de Salamanca, near the city of Santa Marta, is another national park on Colombia's northern coast. This park, Tayrona, occupies over 37,000 acres, and lies along 53 miles of the Caribbean. Established in 1964, it ranges from brown hills covered with cactus and thorny scrub at its western margins to subtropical forests in its central and eastern zones. Like Iguaçú, Parque Nacional Tayrona offers a rare opportunity for visitors: well-maintained trails that wind through dense tropical forests. One major difference between Tayrona and Iguaçú, however, is that the trails in

A carved face with headdress is plated with moss and lichens. Pueblito, Tayrona National Park, Colombia

Tayrona were built and used for several hundred years by a pre-Columbian civilization that has vanished. Visitors hike these trails with the ghosts of the Tayrona Indians.

Little is known about the Tayronas, but in several respects their accomplishments were superior to the celebrated works of the Incas. Their remaining ruins prove that they were skilled engineers and agriculturists, for many of their canals, bridges, and staircases are still in use. They built permanent villages, as the stone foundations, corrals, and rechanneled drainages indicate. And they were artisans, for they adorned stone grottos with artwork, and carved figures into rocks along the trail.

The Tayronas were clever in their selection of a homeland, for the park is an island of greenery on an otherwise arid coast. About 90 percent of the park is virgin forest. Most of the remaining 10 percent is land that has been converted to coconut plantations. The plantations are along the beaches, but the Tayronas planted some trees near their villages, and it is not unusual to find coconut trees today in forests 1,000 feet or more above sea level.

Wildlife in Tayrona is usually more audible than visible. In the morning, the eerie roaring of howler monkeys is likely to bring visitors bolt upright in their hammocks. Brocket deer also roam the park, but the most visible animals are small reddish-brown squirrels that seem to inhabit every other tree in the park. From June to September, the green turtle (*Chelonia mydas*) and the loggerhead (*Caretta caretta*) turtle nest on the many beaches of Tayrona.

The avifauna of Tayrona is typically Colombian; the chorus of early-morning birdcalls is astonishing. Some of the most visible of the 300 species listed for the park are pelicans, gulls, woodpeckers, parakeets, and kingfishers. The park is one of the best places in Colombia to see the beautiful keel-billed toucan. Point your binoculars in any direction, and you are likely to see a bird you have never before seen.

Visitor Facilities

The principal center of activity is Cañaveral, at which visitors will find sanitary facilities, water, showers, a small restaurant, campground, and hammock hooks. Overnight camping is permitted. Visitors will be favorably impressed with the tastefully rustic developments in the recreation complex. Mosquitos are a problem. Visitors should use a flashlight when walking about the campground at night; several species of venomous snakes inhabit the park.

Two trails from Cañaveral are recommended. A 3-mile (5 kilometers) trail to the east leads to several small beaches that are usually deserted. A more scenic trail—it passes through rain forest and coconut plantations, crosses rocky headlands with marvelous views, and parallels long white beaches—is the 4.5-mile (7 kilometers) trail that heads to Arrecifes and Pueblito. The first stretch of this trail is inland, and passes through a dense forest that can be strangely silent during midday hours. The trail returns to the coast at Arrecifes, where there is a small ranger station and a welcome re-

Well constructed and well engineered, centuries-old stone pathways of the vanished Tayrona Indians wind through the forest of Tayrona National Park, Colombia.

freshment stand, then continues along the coast for 1 mile (2 kilometers) or so, and connects with the trail constructed by the Tayrona Indians. The Tayrona trail heads inland again, following a small creek upstream through the forest for 1.5 miles (3 kilometers) to Pueblito, the principal archaeological site in the park, about 1,500 feet above sea level. Ruins are marked, and explanatory placards are posted about the site. A park ranger is usually in residence in Pueblito, and will sometimes escort visitors around the area, to point out objects and structures of particular interest.

The round-trip distance from Cañaveral to Pueblito is about 9 miles (14 kilometers), and can be made in one day if you get an early start. There are many inviting places to camp along the way. Carry plenty of drinking water, and sleep in hammocks, not on the ground.

Recreation

A wider variety of recreation than usual is available at Tayrona: short or long hikes, day hikes or overnight backpacks, swimming, skin diving, saltwater fishing, bird-watching, wildlife observation, exploring ruins.

Caution: Coral reefs offshore from many beaches, including Cañaveral and Arrecifes, provide for exceptional skin diving during the dry season, when the water is not roily from river runoff. The surf can be rough on some beaches, however, and rip-tides occur. Sharks have been observed in these waters. Be cautious, and do *not* swim alone. Beaches in the vicinity of Tayrona are reported to be used at night as transfer points for drugs. Visitors are cautioned to avoid these beaches after dark.

Climate and Weather

Tayrona has a dry season (January to April) called summer, and a wet season (August to October). The best time to visit is during the dry season. Thunderstorms occur all year, so bring a light raincoat.

Location and Access

Tayrona is in northern Colombia, its western margin a few miles east of the city of Santa Marta. Cañaveral is 3 miles (5 kilometers) from the main highway between Santa Marta and Riohacha, called Carretera Troncal del Caribe. The turnoff to Cañaveral from the highway is at El Zaino, 22 miles (35 kilometers) from Santa Marta.

To reach the park from Santa Marta, take a Maicao or Riohacha bus from the ter-minal at Carrera 8 and Calle 24, get off at El Zaino, and walk or hitchhike 3 miles (5 kilometers) to Cañaveral. A direct, but more expensive bus goes directly to Cañaveral from the Hotel Zulia in Santa Marta. Hitchhiking from Santa Marta to El Zaino is possible, but not recommended.

Glossary

anfiteatro	amphitheater
arrecife	coral reef
buceo de observación	skin diving, snorkeling
calzada lítica	stone pathway
cimientos viviendas	house foundations
cocotero	coconut palm grove
piedra del sol	stone of the sun altar
plazoleta ceremonial	ceremonial square
tortuga marina	marine turtle
vida silvestre	wildlife

Back from the brink of extinction, a young vicuña (Vicugna vicugna) *stays alert at Pampa Galeras National Vicuña Reserve, Peru.*

PERU

Peru is rich in paradoxes that result in fascinating natural history.

For half the year, Peru's narrow coastal plain is shrouded by *La Garúa,* a dense, clammy mist that blocks sunlight and creates cool, humid days. Yet in many places the plain beneath this moist fog has not felt the touch of rain for centuries, for it is the most arid region known to man—a northern extension of the Atacama Desert.

Above the Atacama, not far from the Pacific Ocean, a tiny stream escapes a small lake and threads its way through high Andean peaks. But rather than heading for the nearby Pacific, it turns east. Four thousand miles later, it discharges the rainfall of half a continent into the muddy swells of the Atlantic Ocean. The brook born at the edge of the Pacific has become the Amazon.

A few miles west of the sterile Atacama, life thrives in the waters of the Peru Coastal Current, also known as the Humboldt Current—a cold, upwelling sea-river so rich in nutrients that marine phytoplankton can turn the water into thick organic soup. Tiny crustaceans graze on the phytoplankton, and in their turn are scooped up by enormous shoals of small fish—silversides, herrings, and anchovies. These fish support the most dense concentration of marine avifauna on earth. From 20 million to 25 million cormorants, boobies, pelicans, and other seabirds live along Peru's seacoast— the teeming margin of a lifeless desert.

Such biological and geographical curiosities result from Peru's diverse landforms: the coastal desert, the mountainous Cordillera, the Andean highlands, and the Ama-

218

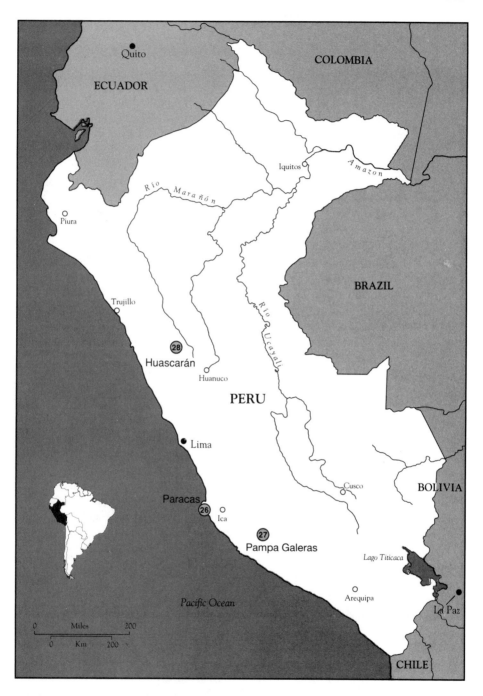

zon Basin. Peru now has well-established parks in three of these zones: on the desert
seacoast, Reserva Nacional Paracas; on the edge of the Altiplano, Reserva Nacional
de Vicuñas Pampa Galeras; and in the high Andean Cordillera, Parque Nacional
Huascarán.

🄿 PARACAS:
Desert Wastes and Teeming Seas

One hundred fifty miles south of Lima, a barren, toadstool-shaped peninsula juts into the sea from Peru's straight coastline. The peninsula is a part of Reserva Nacional Paracas, home to an unusual combination of scenery, archaeology, and wildlife.

Despite forbidding wastes, bright desert colors characterize the reserve. Drab cliffs glow brown and blood red at sunset. Pink, buff, and violet sand dunes change color as gusts of wind shift sand of different weights and colors. Purple and brown strands of kelp and seawrack strew brick-red beaches.

For much of the year *La Garúa* dominates the sky, softening stark horizons, and obscuring silhouettes. At Paracas, it distorts the surf's roar and transforms the clamoring of sea lions and seabirds into eerie moans and wails.

On a day's walk along the reserve's coastline, visitors may sight sea lions, ospreys, flamingos, whales, penguins, vultures, Inca terns, condors, dolphins, cormorants, boobies, pelicans, and a score of other species of seabirds. Yet life effectively stops at the high-tide line, for except for vagrant birds and an itinerant fox or two, most of Paracas Reserve is a beautiful, trackless wasteland of sand, gravel, saltpan, and exposed bedrock. The transition from biotic to nearly abiotic terrain is abrupt, a matter of a few feet, the first thing noted by the errant naturalist.

A good place to start is the observation point overlooking the main sea lion rookeries at Punta El Arquillo. The last mile of the trail to the overlook skirts the edge of cliffs several hundred feet high. Bright red lichens adorn the cliffs in this area—virtually the only plants found on Paracas Peninsula. Below, on ledges just above the surf, sea lions array themselves in comfortable crevices and folds.

What we call sea lions, South Americans call lobos marinos (sea wolves). Two species frequent Paracas: lobo chusco (*Otaria flavescens*) and the southern fur seal (*Arctocephalus australis*), locally called lobo fino. As many as 4,500 can be found at sites near Punta El Arquillo, where bedlam prevails. A constant din rises from the ledges as they maneuver for preferred positions. The rookeries are visible, but nearly inaccessible from shore. With permission, rope-wielding visitors can reach them by making use of steel belaying pins driven into the rocks a few yards to the east of the overlook.

Near the rookeries, observers might spot Humboldt penguins (*Spheniscus humboldti*). Their presence a few degrees from the equator is startling, for they are popularly associated with the ice caps of Antarctica and the southernmost coasts of South America. Their presence is explained by the Humboldt Current, which provides both food and the cold waters the birds require. Humboldt penguins normally breed only on offshore islands, and Paracas is one of the few locations on the mainland to see them, for they associate closely with the sea lions and seldom wander far from the rookeries.

The Inca tern (*Larosterna inca*), perhaps the most beautiful of the Paracas seabirds, is also associated with the Humboldt Current and often found in the company of sea lions. This cliff-nesting tern looks like a small gull, with blue-gray body, a sturdy

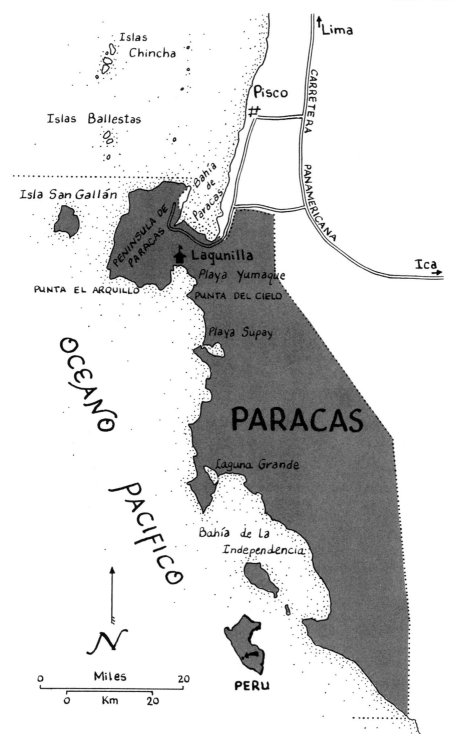

Lima

Islas
Chincha

Islas Ballestas

Pisco

CARRETERA

PANAMERICANA

Bahía
de
Paracas

Isla San Gallán

PENINSULA DE
PARACAS

Lagunilla

Playa Yumaque

Ica

PUNTA EL ARQUILLO

PUNTA DEL CIELO

Playa Supay

OCEANO

PARACAS

PACIFICO

Laguna Grande

Bahía de la
Independencia

N

Miles

0   20

PERU

0   Km   20

tomato-red bill, and matching feet. Its most striking characteristic, a narrow white face stripe, curves beneath the eyes and down the neck, ending in an upsweep of jaunty mutton chop sideburns.

The Paracas seacoast is also a prime location to observe a bird usually associated with high mountains—the Andean condor (*Vultur gryphus*). Strong onshore breezes create a standing wave of air over the sea cliffs at Paracas. Condors, as well as other soaring birds, ride the crest of the wave along the coast, in search of meals swept in by the tide. Turkey vultures (*Cathartes aura*), recognized by their red heads, and black vultures (*Coragyps atratus*) perch on clifftops with wings outstretched in the cooling breeze. The condor, however, cannot be mistaken for a vulture. Adult condors, with wingspans of up to 10 feet, dwarf vultures, and even at a distance the white collar at the base of their necks is distinctive. They often soar on the edge of the cliff tops, and to have one of these gigantic birds whisk by a few steps away is an eye-popping experience. February to April are the best months to look for condors in Paracas, for sea lions are calving and the birds concentrate near the rookeries to feed on placental remains.

All three birds responsible for Peru's renascent guano industry—cormorants, boobies, and pelicans—populate the shores of Paracas Reserve. Huge amounts of nitrate-rich guano, the Quechua Indian word for "excrement," were once removed from several islands not far from Peru's coast. Ten miles north of Península Paracas lie the most famous of the guano repositories, the Chincha Islands. Businessmen ignored conservation in earlier days, and by 1910 the guano was nearly gone and the industry dead. Eventually the government stepped in, and instituted strict regulation and protection measures. Since then, the industry has in large measure revitalized.

Two cormorants, the Peruvian or guanay cormorant (*Phalacrocorax bougainvillii*) and the red-legged cormorant (*Phalacrocorax gaimardi*), frequent Paracas. The

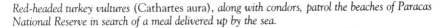

Red-headed turkey vultures (Cathartes aura), *along with condors, patrol the beaches of Paracas National Reserve in search of a meal delivered up by the sea.*

Peruvian cormorant is responsible for two-thirds of the Chincha Island guano deposits, but red-legged cormorants are more common at Paracas. Both birds may be seen resting in small groups on rocks just above the surf or perching on tiny ledges in the cliffs.

Peruvian or variegated boobies (*Sula variegata*) have preposterous blue bills and feet, and share cliff-side roosts with cormorants. Boobies are dive-bombers; like kingfishers and pelicans, they drop straight into the sea for fish. Peruvians call them piqueros (lancers).

The third guano-producing bird is the familiar brown pelican (*Pelicanus occidentalis*), "alcatraz" in Spanish. Much larger than the other two birds, this great aviator entertains onlookers throughout the reserve, and is one of the most common birds along the entire length of the Peruvian coast.

Beaches are inaccessible near Punta Arquillo, so beachcombers should visit Punta del Cielo, 4 miles (6 kilometers) southeast of Lagunilla. In the afternoons, large flocks of gray gulls (*Larus modestus*) and Franklin's gulls (*Larus pipixcan*) face the eye of the strong wind on Yumaque and Supay beaches. Black skimmers (*Rhycops nigra*) glide along the surf, and several species of terns wheel overhead, from swallow-sized Peruvian terns (*Sterna lorata*) to the gull-like elegant terns (*Sterna elegans*).

Every summer, flocks of visiting whimbrels rummage through detritus on these beaches with their long, decurved bills. The American oystercatcher (*Haematopus palliatus*) and the slightly larger black oystercatcher (*Haematopus ater*) race up and down the wet sand, probing with their thick red bills for shellfish and marine worms. Kelp gulls (*Larus dominicanus*) and band-tailed or Peruvian gulls (*Larus belcheri*) squabble over tidbits, and the ubiquitous pelicans glide over wave tops.

Marine algae washed up on beaches near Punta del Cielo attract one of the few terrestrial animals found in Paracas—shiny buff-colored lizards. Up to a foot long, they scurry over heaps of pungent kelp, and dart in and out of crevices in the cliffs behind the beaches.

Beachcombers should look for the yard-wide tracks of marine turtles in damp sand: a double row of half-moons connected to a broad line between them, in appearance like the skeleton of a snake.

Tinier tracks belong to the coastal fox (*Dusicyon griseus*), which patrols the beach in hopes of ambushing unwary lizards, seabirds, or one of the large purple crabs that scuttle among tideline rocks. These small foxes seldom emerge during daylight hours, but their tracks on the beaches indicate a busy nightlife. They are shot on sight near mainland guano repositories, but are remarkably tame under some circumstances. How these foxes slake their thirst along this barren and waterless coast is a perplexing biological riddle.

At the northern end of Supay (Quechua for "devil") Beach is a curious geological feature known as La Catedral (cathedral). To reach it from the road, descend the steep slope of sand to the beach and walk north toward the cliff that ends the beach. At the cliff's base, a small opening pierces the jutting headland to give access to a large, nave-like grotto—a cool, dim amphitheater with a vaulted, 30-foot ceiling. The surf roars in this natural echo chanber, and filtered light illuminates the grotto's interior and casts shimmering shadows on the curved walls. **Caution:** The grotto is only accessible via the cave, and only at low tide.

The shallow southern reaches of Paracas Bay and several salt marshes near the sea provide excellent habitat for the Chilean flamingo (*Phoenicopterus chilensis*). "Flamenco" in Spanish and "parihuana" in Quechua, the flamingo has a wide distribution, ranging south from Ecuador, Bolivia, and Brazil to Tierra del Fuego. Through that range, this unusually adaptable bird struts through warm saline marshes at sea level, along the margins of cold lakes and ponds in the Andean highlands, and along the banks of rivers in the steppes of southern Patagonia. The population of flamingos at Paracas fluctuates through the year from several dozen to several hundred. June to August is the best time to see large flocks of the birds.

Visitor Facilities

The first stop for all visitors should be the park's administration center, a small building in the village of Lagunilla, both office and living quarters for park staff. The director knows the whereabouts of local wildlife and will orient visitors on large-scale maps. Visitors with their own vehicles should consult park authorities before settting out to explore, for few roads are marked, many are dangerous (deep sand and steep grades), and some areas are closed to vehicular traffic. Few signs guide the visitor.

The park has no developments or tourist facilities. Visitors planning to spend considerable time in the reserve should bring everything they need with them, including water, firewood or fuel, and shelter. Camping is allowed in the reserve. Visitors can buy fresh fish or eat at a tiny restaurant in Lagunilla.

Two comfortable hotels overlook the east shore of Bahía Paracas, not far from the reserve. One, Hotel Paracas, offers trips by motor launch to the nearby Ballestas Islands. The 4-hour trip enables visitors to see at close range the astonishing density of nesting birds on guano islands. Several hotels in Pisco offer cheap accommodations, and taxis can be rented there for a trip to Paracas.

Recreation

Paracas is primarily a wildlife observation area. Although wildlife is abundant and easily observed, binoculars or spotting scopes are useful. Walks along the high cliffs overlooking the sea and beachcombing sorties in isolated coves are exceptionally rewarding activities. Seeing Paracas requires desert hiking, and visitors should carry plenty of water and protect themselves from sun and heat. Morning is the best time to explore, for afternoon winds can be fierce.

Historical and Cultural Aspects

Paracas has an ancient cultural legacy. Archaeologists have recovered hundreds of well-preserved mummies from the necropolis of a civilization that flourished in the area nearly 1,600 years ago. The Museo Julio Tello, near the entrance to the reserve, contains weavings and tapestries, tools and household utensils, and several dioramas of reconstructed dwellings of this early civilization. The dining room of the Hotel Paracas houses an excellent collection of pre-Inca ceramics.

On the northern tip of Península Paracas, a series of lines traced into a hillside facing the sea form El Candelabro, the candlestick. Some authorities believe the 50-yard-long pre-Inca figure represents the tree of life of early cosmologies. The *candelabro* is too large to be appreciated from the ground, but the launch trip to the Ballestas Islands provides an excellent sea view of the ancient stick figure.

Modern as well as ancient man has left his mark on Paracas. A number of hillsides bear marks of motocross, an off-road racing sport now banned within the reserve. Hunting of birds, sea lions, and marine turtles and their eggs is also banned.

Climate and Weather

Paracas has a desert climate: hot during the day, cool at night, chilly in early morning. From November to March, the *garúa* blankets the desert, but during spring and fall it burns off by midday. Strong winds are a regular feature of the weather pattern. With respect to climate, any time of the year is a good time for a visit.

The combination of sun, sand, and wind dictates the use of sunglasses, a good hat, and sunscreen lotion for those prone to sunburn. Take a sweater and light windbreaker for chilly mornings and evenings.

Location and Access

Paracas is the most accessible of Peru's major parks. It lies 150 miles (241 kilometers) south of Lima, near the small town of Pisco, just off the main coast road, Ruta 1-S. A paved secondary road leads to the entrance to the reserves, 7 miles (11 kilometers) southwest of Pisco. Just past the Museo Julio Tello, a narrow dirt road to the left leads 3 miles (5 kilometers) south to the reserve headquarters. The junction is not marked.

Glossary

ballena	whale
delfín	dolphin
garúa	coastal fogbanks, common along the Atacama Desert
gaviota	gull
gaviotín	tern
guardaparque	park ranger
mirador	overlook, observation point
pingüino	penguin
puesto de vigilancia	roughly, ranger station
Quechua	Indian language commonly spoken in Peru, Bolivia, and Ecuador
zorro	fox

🔲 PAMPA GALERAS:
Last Stand of the Vicuña

The landscape is austere on the western edge of the Andean Cordillera—high, open, rolling terrain interrupted by scattered boulders and by small gullies carved by intermittent streams. This bleak countryside is home to the vicuña (*Vicugna vicugna*), perhaps the best known of Andean wildlife, the animal responsible for the creation of Reserva Nacional de Vicuña Pampa Galeras.

In several respects, the history of the vicuña parallels that of the North American bison. Both animals lived in reasonably stable balance with indigenous peoples who made use of their meat and fur. As a result of European colonization, both were hunted to the brink of extinction by the thoughtless exploitation of wildlife that ensued. And both were saved, at the last minute, by creation of national reserves in which they were protected from hunters by force of law.

More than 2 million vicuñas populated the Peruvian altiplano in the year 1500. The Incas utilized and managed them brilliantly, and took principles of conservation far more seriously than any modern state—poachers were put to death.

Soon after the Spanish conquest, however, exploitation of the vicuña began in earnest. Hunters poisoned waterholes and used trained dogs to run down the newly born. Ultimately, as prices for vicuña wool skyrocketed, they used automatic weapons to bring down the animals. Under such relentless pressure, the population fell to about 250,000 by 1950. Despite a ban on hunting vicuñas, poaching continued, and by 1967 only a few thousand harried individuals survived. The end was clearly in sight.

The same year, Peru established Pampa Galeras, and employed armed guards to protect the 800 vicuñas on the reserve. Vigilance was scrupulous and enforcement strict. The reserve soon became Peru's Wild West: gun battles between guards and poachers cost seven lives during the program's early years. But the results of vigorous protection were spectacular: within five years the population of vicuñas had reached 7,500. By 1977, the population was 31,000, and Pampa Galeras had become a model wildlife refuge.

Encouraged by the project's success, the government launched an ambitious program to repopulate 16 million acres of altiplano grassland—lands barely marginal for other uses—with more than a million vicuñas by the year 2000. The long-range project is complex, involving habitat improvement, utilization of the vicuña for meat and wool, continuous scientific and economic studies, education programs, and the integration of other altiplano wildlife of economic value (guanacos, vizcachas, and several birds). The program affects several dozen communities and many tracts of communally owned land, so political problems persist and funds are scarce. But hopes are high for continued success, and conservationists the world over keep an attentive eye on Pampa Galeras.

Pampa Galeras lies at an elevation of over 13,000 feet in the zone of open arid grasslands known as the *pajonal de puna,* or simply *puna.* Scattered clumps of coarse grasses collectively referred to as ichu characterize the treeless *puna.* Small herbaceous plants grow among the clumps of spiky ichu, and in drier areas, resinous tola bushes predominate.

Vicuñas (Vicugna vicugna) *are one the few wild animals that can not only survive but flourish on the harsh grasslands that comprise the high-altitude* punas *of Peru, Bolivia, and Chile. Pampa Galeras National Vicuña Reserve, Peru*

Puna plants are hardy, for the physical environment is harsh. Erratic precipitation, severe winds, and temperature extremes prevail. "Grassland" is a highly optomistic term for *puna,* for wide expanses of *puna* comprise little more than patches of gravel and bare soil, over which are scattered thin tufts of ichu. Indeed, workers at Pampa Galeras complain that boots wear out quickly on the rough cobbles that cover the ground, and that walking is difficult.

Although closely related to them, vicuñas and their South American relatives are not camels. The South American form of camels—llamoids—evolved from the same stock as Old World camels, and share the long neck and long ears, short tails, and short tempers of their Asian cousins. Smaller than camels, they lack humps, and have adapted successfully to an environment that even the toughest camels would not easily survive.

The four South American llamoids are llamas, alpacas, guanacos, and vicuñas. Two are domesticated: llamas (*Lama glama*), largest and most colorful of the four species, and alpacas (*Lama pacos*), usually pure brown, black, or white. Travelers commonly see llamas and alpacas herded to and fro over the altiplano laden with firewood or other cargo, and wearing gaily decorated ear tassels, collars, and packsaddles. The wide-ranging guanaco (*Lama guanicoe*) is wild, and though common in some Argentine and Chilean parks, is rare in Peru. The vicuña is also wild, and although herds exist elsewhere in the Andes, one of the best places in the world to see this animal today is Pampa Galeras.

Color and size distinguish the vicuña from the other llamoids. The vicuña is the color of light caramel, shading to white ventrally and on the inside of the legs. A prominent patch of long white fur adorns its breast like a bib. Vicuñas are the smallest of the llamoids, the size of North American antelope. Their habit of staring directly at intruders and flattening their long ears when irritated lends males a demeanor of imperious intelligence. Females, with enormous eyes and long eyelashes, are the unmistakable coquettes of the *puna.*

Scores of vicuñas come into view during the course of a short walk from the administration center to the top of any of the low hills nearby. Groups and individuals ander in every direction over the countryside. Some animals move resolutely away if visitors come too close, but most seem to wander aimlessly as they graze.

Surprisingly, what appears to be a random dispersal of vicuñas over the *puna* is actually the result of highly structured social behavior that determines with remarkable precision the location of the animals. Prominent clues to this rigid social life are scattered over the *puna* in the form of trampled circles some 6 feet across. In the center of each circle, like a tidy heap of olive pits, lies a mound of the pellets voided by the vicuñas. These circles are *estercoleros,* the common voiding places peculiar to all four species of llamoids. The landscape is dotted with *estercoleros,* sometimes dispersed, but often arrayed in long, nearly straight lines that stretch for hundreds of yards across the *puna.* These lines mark the boundaries of vicuña real estate, areas vigorously defended by their owners and invaded by other vicuñas only at considerable risk.

Vicuñas live in two distinct social groups. The first, the family group, comprises an adult male, from three to eight females, and recently born young. This group presides over a feeding territory and a resting territory, which the male defends from intruders by aggressive posturing and, if necessary, by kicking and biting.

When the young vicuñas in a family group reach several months of age, they are expelled, creating room for the next generation. The expelled females join other family groups elsewhere, but expelled males take up a wandering life as members of the second social group—the bachelor herd.

Life changes drastically for a young male joining a bachelor herd. The herds do not maintain territories, and may roam several miles a day in search of rangeland not already claimed and defended by a family. Bachelor herds lack leaders, and as many as forty or fifty males may eventually join a herd. A male generally stays with a bachelor herd for two to three years, after which it acquires a family of its own and begins to defend its own territory.

Unraveling the complex social life of the vicuña required years of tedious field work, much of it done at Pampa Galeras. The reserve is not a zoo, and except for a few free-roaming pets near the administration center, the vicuñas are not tame. But they are habituated to the sight of humans on foot, and to all appearances they carry on their lives as usual.

Observers can quickly identify family groups and bachelor herds, and distinguish between ever-vigilant males, docile females, and playful youngsters. Eventually, visitors may see adult males chase off trespassing members of a neighboring family, or see an adult respond to a challenge by an ambitious member of a bachelor herd.

Grazing vicuñas are often startled by passing vehicles, and take flight alongside the road or in the roadbed. While passengers scramble for cameras, the vicuñas trot along at 15 miles an hour with the peculiar rolling gait of camels and llamoids. If the driver speeds up, so do the vicuñas. The necks stretch out, the ears flatten, and these ungainly and ill-proportioned creatures suddenly transform themselves into tawny thoroughbreds, loping smoothly across the rough *puna* at speeds in excess of 35 miles an hour.

Vicuñas not only achieve this speed with ease, but sustain the pace for miles at altitudes few animals can even tolerate. In the most literal sense, they are born speedsters. Newly born vicuñas are large and precocious. On their feet within fifteen to twenty-five minutes of birth, they can outrun a man within the day. Furthermore, though continuing to nurse, they begin to nibble at grasses and herbaceous plants on the second day of life.

Few animals are as well adapted to a specific habitat as the vicuña is to the *puna.* Its enlarged heart and lungs compensate for the disadvantages of thin air. Its blood contains an exceedingly high proportion of red corpuscles, maximizing the oxygen-carrying capacity of its circulatory system. Special water cells in the stomach absorb water from plant food that might otherwise be lost, and thus help the vicuña to cope with the arid conditions of the *puna.*

Unfortunately, the fine wool that protects them from both frigid temperatures and high-altitude radiation also brought them to the brink of extinction. Some fibers are one-seventh the diameter of human hair. Garments woven from vicuña wool were the royal ermine of the New World prior to the Spanish conquest, worn exclusively by the Inca nobility. More recently, wool and pelts fetched absurdly high prices that encouraged the poaching that nearly exterminated the species.

Much of the *puna* is unsuitable for grazing domestic animals. Sheep and cattle fare poorly, and quickly deplete the limited range resources, for plants grow slowly in the thin, poor soils. Vicuñas, however, are uniquely adapted to the submarginal range conditions of the *puna.* The soft pads on their feet do not damage plant life as do the sharp hooves of foraging domestic animals. In addition, the vicuña has specialized dentition that results in lifelong maintenance of razor-sharp lower incisors. Thus, a grazing vicuña nips off portions of small, low-growing plants that later recover, rather than tearing them out of the soil, roots and all.

Visitor Facilities

The *sede administrativa* (administration center), located on the main Nazca-Puquío road, houses several professionals, their offices and laboratories, and a museum and visitor center. The reserve does not yet have facilities for tourists, but the staff appreciate public interest, and will orient and inform visitors. Camping is permitted near the *sede,* where water and sanitary facilities are available. Rooms may be offered on a space-available basis.

The small colonial town of Nazca, 3 hours by road to the west, offers the most suitable overnight accommodations.

Climate and Weather

High altitude is the major modifying factor in the climate of Pampa Galeras. Daily temperature fluctuations can range from 90 degrees Fahrenheit under scorching sun to well below freezing at night. Winds may be severe, freezing in winter and desiccating in summer. Although Pampa Galeras receives from 10 to 20 inches of annual precipitation, virtually all of it falls from December to March, usually as hail, sleet, or snow. The rest of the year is dry.

A hat, sunglasses, chapstick, and sunscreen lotion are absolutely essential for protection from ultraviolet radiation at this elevation. Warm clothes are a necessity.

Historical and Cultural Aspects

The vicuña's fine wool has been highly prized since the days of the Incas. At *chacus*, great hunts held every three to five years, hunters killed only as many animals as needed. Officials noted the condition of the remaining animals, counted them, and released them. The crumbling ruins of a vicuña trap on the reserve indicate that centuries ago these hunts took place on the present site of Pampa Galeras. The present government plans to restore and use the old trap, an ironic link between modern and ancient conservationists.

Location and Access

Pampa Galeras lies 340 miles (547 kilometers) south of Lima, on the Nazca-Puquío-Cuzco road. At Nazca, a dirt road leaves the paved Carretera Panamericana, and climbs eastward into the Cordillera. The 65-mile (104 kilometers) trip to Pampa Galeras from Nazca takes about 3 hours on a rough, narrow road. Although the road climbs over 12,000 feet in 40 miles (64 kilometers), grades are gentle, for dozens of switchbacks are engineered into the road. Traffic is light; hitchhiking is not recommended.

Several buses pass Pampa Galeras weekly, en route west to Nazca or east to Abancay or Cuzco. Schedules are irregular.

Glossary

cría	young animal, usually nursing
grupo familiar	family group
hembra	female animal
macho	male animal
tropilla de solteros	bachelor herd

HUASCARAN: In the Mountains' Lap

Parque Nacional Huascarán is Peru's showpiece, an outstanding South American alpine park. Immense, it encompasses many of the highest peaks in the Andes; scarcely a corner of the park lacks a dramatic view of towering peaks.

The scenic characteristics of Huascarán stem from its unique position in the Andes. In central Peru, the Andes divide into two distinct ranges separated by a densely populated valley, the Callejón de Huaylas (Huaylas Corridor). To the west lie the stark, relatively low peaks of the Cordillera Negra, a range influenced climatically by the coastal desert. Often shrouded in mist, the Cordillera Negra receives little rainfall, and is a treeless, somber range. But east of the Callejón lies a range of higher mountains composed largely of pale diorites—the Cordillera Blanca, a range of titanic, perpetually snowcapped mountains, with dozens of peaks higher than any found in the contiguous United States.

Huascarán embraces more than 100 linear miles of the Cordillera Blanca, takes in the entire eastern margin of the Callejón de Huaylas, and includes portions of nine Peruvian provinces. A true mountain park, Huascarán contains twenty-seven peaks higher than 19,500 feet. From the central plaza of Huaraz, the largest town in the Callejón, twenty-three peaks with tongue-twisting Quechua names are visible: Jatunmontenpuncu, Oxshapalca, Chekiaraju, Huanashraju, and so on. Each exceeds 16,000 feet.

Pico Huascarán, at 22,205 feet, is the highest point in Peru. Each year its summit is the goal of climbing expeditions from all over the world. The mountain enjoys a significant place in the annals of mountaineering as the first major peak climbed by a woman. Annie Peck, an intrepid American mountaineer, reached its summit in 1908.

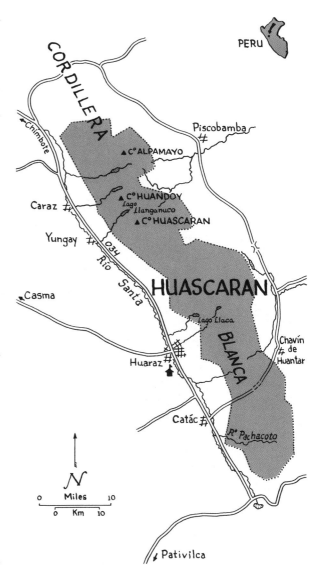

It is also a killer mountain.

Squarely in the center of the restless Andes, Huascarán is often near the epicenter of those inescapable facts of Peruvian mountain life, violent earthquakes. Several times in the last 40 years, residents of the Callejón have suffered from the effects of earthquakes. Pico Huascarán was directly involved at least twice. In 1962, a tremor nudged a monstrous landslide from its slopes that obliterated the small village of Ran-

Killer mountain: every few decades, avalanches or landslides thunder down the sides of Mount Huascarán to obliterate villages or small towns. Huascarán National Park, Peru

rahirca. Eight years later, when a quake of catastrophic intensity struck the entire Callejón, resulting in over 50,000 dead and injured, a landslide once again thundered down the slopes of Huascarán, this time to bury the town of Yungay and most of its 20,000 inhabitants.

Not far from the unpredictable Huascarán lies Alpamayo, a steep, nearly symmetrical pyramid. This striking peak attracts international attention, and enables Huascarán to lay legitimate claim to a unique distinction. Alpamayo was declared by the

1966 World Conference on Scenic Beauty to be "the most beautiful mountain in the world." Happily for visitors who enjoy hiking, it lies close to a popular loop trail, described below.

The lower elevations of the Cordillera and the extreme southern end of the park resemble the arid *puna* of Pampa Galeras. But because the range receives more rain than the *puna*, some authorities classify the area as *páramo*, a humid subalpine vegetation zone more characteristic of Colombia and Ecuador than Peru. Indeed, low shrubs and a rich variety of grasses and forbs cover every slope. Orchids grow on rocky hillsides, and pineapple-like bromeliads occupy exposed sites, even sheer cliffs. Heaths, sedges, and sedums proliferate in high alpine tundra, and above that, rocks, lichens, snow, and ice.

Microclimate and elevation dramatically affect plant distribution. While the dry southern valleys are essentially treeless, a few moist valleys in the northern and central areas of the park support some rather curious trees. The trees are not imposing—about 15 feet tall—and it is easy to overlook the fact that by all reckoning they should not even exist in the thin air at these elevations. They are, in fact, the highest trees in the Andes, polylepis (*Polylepis incana*), able to flourish up to 14,500 feet. Called quenal by Peruvians, polylepis do not form forests, but exist in isolated groves in sheltered, well-watered canyons. Peeling layers of parchment-like reddish bark cover their gnarled trunks and limbs. Host to many arboreal plants—bromeliads, orchids, and thick encrustations of golden, cream, and russet foliose lichens—they form colorful exceptions to the normally drab alpine vegetation. They grow slowly, and are losing the battle for survival, for they are cut down for firewood faster than they can replace themselves.

Orchids enliven the high valleys from June through August, especially near lagos Llanganuco and Parón. Many varieties grow among low plants in the understory of the polylepis groves, and others find shelter among rocks and boulders.

The most distinctive smaller plants are bromeliads. They look like pineapple tops, and cling to trees, boulders, cliffs, bridges, and other unlikely spots. Their spiny outer leaves form a rosette that funnels water into the center of the plant, where it is stored against dry spells. Usually gray or dull green, with some in shades of pink, salmon, or scarlet, bromeliads look like misplaced holiday decorations. Although they appear to be parasitic plants, they are not. As epiphytes, the sole function of their roots is to provide secure anchorage. They extract the water and minerals they require directly from the atmosphere, and depend on the trees only for support.

Not all of the flora is exotic. Varieties familiar to North Americans—lupines, buttercups, forget-me-nots, and dandelions—bloom on open sunny slopes.

The Valle de Llanganuco is one of the more interesting and accessible areas of Huascarán. This classic hanging valley lies in the heart of the park, literally in the shadows of Pico Huascarán and its towering neighbor to the north, Huandoy.

A steep road climbs to the valley from the new townsite of Yungay, on the floor of the Callejón. The drive affords magnificent views of Pico Huascarán and, across the Callejón, the peaks of the Cordillera Negra. The scar left by the landslide that buried the old town of Yungay is clearly visible on the west face of Huascarán, a morbid reminder of the mountain's propensity for violence. The road enters a narrow slot, and winds back and forth across rickety bridges spanning a roaring mountain stream. The sheer walls of this intimidating defile loom thousands of feet over the road; ship-sized boulders overhang the roadbed, a narrow ledge hacked out of the cliff. The road finally eases into the Valle de Llanganuco, and the visitor is suddenly surrounded by gigantic snow-clad peaks.

A pair of small lakes, upper and lower Llanganuco lakes, occupy the valley floor, turquoise reflecting pools for the stunning alpine scenery.

Two trails leave the parking area at the west end of the lower lake. The first parallels the outlet stream and winds downhill to intersect the access road 1,000 feet down the mountain from the lake. An excellent mountain trail, it passes through a dense polylepis grove, down natural stone staircases, past caves, and through rock slides overgrown with bromeliads, grasses, mosses, and orchids. Not far from the lake, the trail passes a crude shrine set into a dim hollow beneath an immense overhanging boulder. A small Latin cross has been erected on a shrine in the hollow; passersby add small bits of bright yarns, feathers sewn into tight bunches, and amulets of bone and fur.

The second trail parallels the southern lakeshore for several hundred yards, ending abruptly at a lakeside cliff. Seagulls swoop over the lake—Andean gulls, *Larus serannus*. The only gull that frequents the high Andes, it is easy to recognize in summer with its jet-black head and wingtips, and white body. In winter, however, its head is all white. Black-crowned night herons or huacos (*Nycticorax nycticorax*) nest in shrubbery at the base of the cliffs that border the lake. Flamingos also frequent the lake, and the metallic purple puna ibis (*Plegadis ridgwayi*) occasionally forages in shallows along the shore.

Wet meadows between the two lakes provide habitat for the Andean goose (*Chloephaga melanoptera*). A white goose with black wingtips and tail, this bird cannot be mistaken for other geese, and like the Andean gull is common in marshes and on lakeshores and riverbanks throughout the Andean highlands.

East of Catác, a village in the south of the park, the Río Pochacoto is carving a valley into the *puna*. The upper valley is narrow, hemmed in by foothills and ridges wrinkling the bases of three snowcapped peaks. Cream, pink, and chocolate-colored talus slopes streak the hillsides, but the rest of the landscape is the straw-yellow color typical of Peruvian highlands. This is the Carpa Sector of Huascarán, and concentrated in these foothills is a rare and unusual plant of the high Andes: the puya or cunco.

Puyas are most contrary plants. They are bromeliads, but resemble 30-foot trees when mature. They lack woody tissue, so although they look like trees, technically they are enormous herbs. They live for a century or so, yet flower only once, then die. And though they flower but once, that single reproductive effort is spectacular, resulting in the appearance of a gigantic flower spike adorned with as many as 8,000 lime-green blossoms.

A living fossil, the puya has a unique evolutionary history. Paleobotanists believe that it flourished in the low subtropical swamps that existed in this park of South America long before the appearance of the Andes. When the earth underwent the protracted convulsions that forced up the Andes, the puyas rose with them, and adapted to a successful new life at high altitudes.

Mature puyas have a short thick trunk on top of which perches a spherical cluster of long, stiff leaves. In blooming puyas, a 15- to 20-foot flower spike, shaped like the pistil of an Easter lily, projects upward from the center of this cluster. Hard, sharp thorns, effective deterrents to would-be browsers and curious naturalists, line the puya's leaves.

Ornithologists make much of the fact that birds are found impaled amidst these thorny leaves. Perhaps more remarkable is that the hooks trap so few birds. Several species of birds utilize puyas, and many nest in the thicket of thorns between the leaves. For every puya that holds the dried remains of careless birds, fifty contain one or more nests.

Doves, passerines, and a few finch-like birds use puyas as nesting sites, perches, and hunting grounds. When the puyas bloom (July to September), the giant hummingbird (*Patagona gigas*) arrives. With respect to brilliance, this plain brown bird falls far short of its iridescent South American cousins, but it is by far the largest of the hummingbirds, some 8 inches long, and is easily recognized by its size and relatively slow wingbeats.

The first puyas come into view 0.5 mile (1 kilometer) past the park guard post. In the next few miles several hundred more puyas appear in various stages of development and inflorescence. The upper valley is of special interest because of the peculiar distribution of the puyas. They are strewn over the landscape in separate, family-like groups. Some are in full bloom, while others have bloomed, shriveled, and died. Spikeless immature plants are scattered around the adults like small children. Still other groups on hilltops lend the eerie impression of being arrayed in formation—immobile cadres of hillside sentries.

The group of puyas in this valley is the largest of several stands in the park. They grow elsewhere in isolated sections of the Andes as far south as Bolivia, but are in peril throughout their range. Where unprotected, they are cut for fuel or burned for amusement, and their numbers are dwindling.

Colorful springs well up in the upper valley. Near the park guard post, a group of cold sulfur springs streak roadside meadows with brilliant orange, red, and yellow deposits. Further east lies an *ojo de agua* (spring) called Pumashini, a complex series of cold seeps around a fluorescent-blue central pool reminiscent of the spring pools of Yellowstone. The spring feeds several ponds and the Río Pochacoto, which doubles back on itself in broad sluggish loops that attract ducks, geese, and flamingos. Tundra-like characteristics of the altiplano are conspicuous in the flats along the river: frost boils of churned clay and gravel, mat-like vegetation, and sodden, spongy cushion plants.

The Sector Carpa of Huascarán supports a small population of vicuñas. During the summer (June through August), however, they migrate to snowline at terrain even higher than the Valle Pochacoto, so only hikers with plenty of time and energy are likely to catch a glimpse of them. When the vicuñas descend to the valley in winter, access is difficult because of snow. Travelers determined to see vicuñas should put Pampa Galeras on their itinerary instead.

Visitor Facilities

Facilities at Huascarán include a central administrative office and several park guard posts. The park's headquarters are located in the building housing the Ministerio de Agricultura (Ministry of Agriculture) in the town of Huaraz. At this office, visitors can obtain maps of the park and informative folders, while climbers and hikers can study detailed topographical maps in the park office. Park personnel will point out areas of major interest, and on request show slides of the park.

Park guards at posts at Lago Llanganuco and in the Sector Carpa of the park assist and register visitors, and enforce park regulations. Visitors can make arrangements in the park office for overnight shelter at the guard post at Lago Llanganuco. Park maps show a number of mountain shelters (*albergues de montaña*) scattered throughout the park. Inquire at the park office before hiking to a particular shelter; some are still under construction or projected for future construction.

The major business center for the region if Huaraz, population 50,000. At the Ministerio de Industria y Turismo, visitors can obtain informative pamphlets, including a map of the town and vicinity, lists of hotels, restaurants, and useful addresses for travelers. It is possible to rent cars, arrange bus or taxi tours to many points of interest, or even rent horses by the day at reasonable rates.

The best overnight accommodations are in Huaraz or nearby. Camping is permitted throughout the park, although no special facilities are provided.

Recreation

Huascarán offers thermal areas, mountain climbing, good hiking trails, trout fishing, unusual flora, ancient ruins, and superb scenery.

The closest thermal areas to Huaraz are Chancos and Monterrey, developed hot springs. Bathing facilities at Monterrey are elaborate, but the waters of the rustic Chancos baths are rumored to have far superior therapeutic properties. To the north, there are thermals near the town of Carhuaz, Caraz, Mato, and the Baños Pacatquí near Corongo. On the eastern side of the Cordillera Blanca, thermals are found near Pomobamba and Chavín de Huantar; to the south of Huaraz, near Olleros and Lago Conococha.

The high peaks of Huascarán attract mountain climbers from all over the world. In response, the park service has organized a service to assist climbing expeditions in obtaining the services of experienced guides, porters, camp tenders, cooks, and other support personnel. All expeditions must obtain prior authorization from the park service. For information, write the Director, Parque Nacional Huascarán, Ministerio de Agricultura, Huaraz, Peru.

Lago Llanganuco is one of the few places in Peru to fish for trout. In the spring, trout up to 18 inches long spawn in small spring-fed ponds between the upper and lower lakes. Although fishing with nets is prohibited, Indians cast small nets into the lakes or adjoining waters. Locals ignore the 10-inch size limit, regardless of fishing method.

Backpackers will appreciate the established trails that follow ancient Indian paths connecting low-lying towns and villages to isolated settlements high in the Cordillera. Encounters with families walking along the trails with groups of heavily laden burros or llamas are routine.

One of the longest and most scenic trails starts at the village of Yungay, climbs to Lago Llanganuco, crosses the Cordillera Blanca, and traverses the Huaripampa area, then recrosses the Cordillera and follows the Valle de Santa Cruz to the village of Caraz. It passes both the highest and the "most beautiful" peaks in the park, Huascarán and Alpamayo. The trail is 42 miles (67 kilometers) long; the complete circuit takes about 5 days. An alternate return route descends to the town of Piscobamba rather than recrossing the Cordillera; from Piscobamba, one may return to Huaraz by bus.

A shorter trail from Olleros crosses the Cordillera to Chavín de Huantar, passing

A shorter trail from Olleros crosses the Cordillera to Chavín de Huantar, passing a stand of puyas as well as the noted ruins of Chavín. A popular 22-mile (35 kilometers) route, it requires about 3 days to hike.

Two of the trails entering the Cordillera from Huaraz are 2-day trails for most people. The first is a 17-mile (27 kilometers) trail that passes the ruins of Wilcahuaín and ends at a small lake, Lago Llaca; the other follows the drainage of the Río Quilcayhuanca for 11 miles (18 kilometers).

One trail leaves the village of Catác and follows the Río Pachacoto for about 18 miles (29 kilometers) into the Cordillera. A road follows this route for the first 12 miles (19 kilometers), going past the Sector Carpa guard post and several magnificent stands of puyas.

Shelter, food, fuel, and water may not be available along these routes.

Historical and Cultural Aspects

Quechua-speaking Indians inhabit the high mountain valleys of central Peru. In many respects, the life-style of these people is unchanged from that of their ancient ancestors. Some, but not all, speak Spanish, and many live within the park boundaries. Inevitably, conflicts of interest arise between those who wish to preserve the park's natural resources and those who need to utilize them to subsist. Visitors may see people grazing domestic livestock, fishing illegally, and cutting firewood—all prohibited activities. Park authorities do their best to enforce conservation measures, but in a region with a cultural legacy as ancient as that of Huascarán, significant changes in public attitudes evolve slowly.

Signs of the violent earthquakes that plague the Callejón are everywhere. Cracked walls, new bridges, heaved roadbeds, and piles of rubble are reminders that in the Andes the careful works of men are dramatically subject to the indifferent whims of nature. Restoration is proceeding slowly but steadily.

Crumbling traces of civilizations up to 2,500 years old are evident at archaeological sites throughout the park. Wilcahuaín is a popular site 2 hours by foot from Huaraz at the end of a trail that ascends the Quebrada Llaca (Llaca Gorge). The more spectacular ruins of Chavín, a temple dating from 800 B.C., lie near Chavín de Huantar, 6 hours by road from Huaraz. Other lesser-known ruins lie near Quebrada Cadros, Río Lucma, and Quebrada Quilcayhuanca.

Climate and Weather

Huascarán's climate is typical of mountainous Peru. The best time to visit the park is the dry season, June to August. From October to April the park receives from 10 to 40 inches of precipitation. During the wet season, snow is likely to cover the ground above 13,000 feet. Temperatures vary with elevation. For example, at 13,000 feet, visitors may expect a mild 45 to 55 degrees, but above 16,000 feet the mean average temperature is 30 degrees Fahrenheit.

Wide daily temperature fluctuations are the rule: warm jackets are indispensable in the chilly evenings. Winds can be severe. Afternoon temperatures are warm, but not hot. Those sensitive to sunlight should bring sunglasses, hat, and sunscreen lotion. Bring insect repellent; the blackflies, horseflies, and mosquitos are ravenous.

Location and Access

Huascarán is 216 miles (347 kilometers) northeast of Lima by road. Travelers arriving from the coast must cross the Cordillera Negra to reach the park. A paved highway (Ruta 034) leaves the Carretera Panamericana (Panamerican Highway) at Pativilca and crosses the Cordillera to reach Huaraz from the south via the Callejón de Huaylas. The trip from Lima takes 10 hours by bus, 6 hours by car.

Two more spectacular, but hair-raising routes approach the park from farther north. The first is Ruta 113, which leaves the Carretera Panamericana at Chimbote, follows the valley of the Río Santa to Huallanca, and from there leads south to Huaraz. This steep, winding road, frequently damaged by earthquakes, is a preferred route—for the adventurous—as the Valle del Río Santa is one of the most scenic routes through the central Andes.

The second approach is by Ruta 330, which leaves the Carretera Panamericana at Casma and leads directly across the Cordillera Negra to Huaraz. In many places the road is a single winding lane, but grades are gentle. The trip from Casma to Huaraz takes 4 hours.

Lago Llanganuco, the ruins of Chavín, and the Río Pachacoto are accessible by road. The road to Lago Llanganuco climbs into the Cordillera from Yungay, 2 hours of arduous mountain driving. The road to Chavín and the towns east of the Cordillera Blanca begins at Catác, and crosses the mountains via the Túnel Cahuish. A side road just south of Catác leads into the Valle Pachacoto. Turn east onto a gravel road at a small sign marked "Sector Carpa."

Glossary

baños	baths, sometimes hot springs
callejón	corridor
carretera	highway, main traveled road
lago	lake
nevado	snowcapped mountain
ojo de agua	spring of water
quebrada	ravine, gorge
termales	hot springs
túnel	tunnel

◧◡◪ 8
SURINAME

Note to Travelers: In mid-1986, a guerrilla campaign was mounted against the military government of Suriname that came to power in 1980, resulting in the closure of Suriname's parks and reserves. Government authorities cannot predict when these political problems will be resolved. The author has left the following description of Suriname's parks and reserves intact in the hope that these problems will be solved soon, and travelers will again be able to travel safely through Suriname's remarkable rain forests and savannas.

If this book has treasured spots to reveal to travelers, Suriname is first among them.

Suriname, one of South America's smallest countries, is about the size of Oklahoma. It has one of the smallest populations of any South American nation—400,000—about the population of Minneapolis, and is connected by road only to its tiny neighbors, Guyana and French Guiana. Because of its isolation, it is an off-the-beaten-path country; few travelers doing a grand tour of South America include Suriname in their itinerary. As a result, few people know much about this small nation. Yet with respect to facilities for the study and observation of neotropical natural history, Suriname is unsurpassed.

Few know, for example, that Suriname includes part of and is adjacent to the largest remaining expanse of uninhabited, undisturbed neotropical rain forest on earth—2.3 million square miles of jungle in which man is still an insignificant factor. Few know that from the perspective of visitors, Suriname has the most advanced system of national parks and reserves in South America. And few know that Suriname's government has made a systematic, deliberate effort to develop these parks and reserves in such manner as to maintain their essentially pristine character, yet permit visitors to enjoy their attractions.

LAST OF THE COLONIES. The last European colonies in South America were the Guianas: British, Dutch, and French. In the years following World War II, the first two of these colonies were granted independence from their parent nations and became Guyana and Suriname, respectively. (French Guiana is an overseas department of France.) Suriname became fully independent in 1975.

Suriname is a true melting pot. The children of slaves and indentured laborers brought to the country from all over the world during its colonial days have given the new nation a population with diverse ethnic characteristics. About a third of the Surinamese are East Indian, a third are black or Creole, and the remaining third comprises Indonesians, Chinese, Europeans, Jews, and Amerindians.

Ninety percent of these people live in the modern capital city, Paramaribo (pah-rah-MAH-ree-bo), and in smaller settlements along the narrow coastal plain. Suriname's backcountry is largely uninhabited. Dutch is the official language, although most people also speak a patois called taki-taki, an amalgam of Dutch and En-

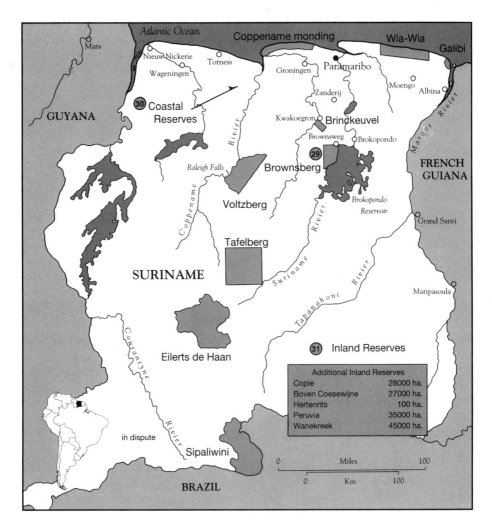

glish. Fortunately for North American visitors, English is spoken widely.

Suriname's physiography is diverse for a small country. The coastal fringe is a combination of sandy beaches, brackish mangroves, and muddy estuaries and deltas. Behind this fringe is a strip of fertile lowlands from 15 to 30 miles wide, largely given over to rice and sugarcane production. As the elevation increases, a narrow belt of grasslands appears, then gives way to the dense tropical forests and savannas that predominate in Suriname's interior highlands.

The coastal fringe and the interior forests and savannas are the country's biological treasure troves. Accordingly, Suriname's nature reserves fall into two categories: coastal and inland.

The coastal reserves have been established to protect enormous numbers of migratory and resident waterfowl, and to protect and regulate the major marine turtle nesting beaches of the entire Caribbean region. Three reserves occupy nearly 130,000 acres of these habitats, and over a third of Suriname's coastline: Coppename-mouth, Wia Wia, and Galibi Reserves.

Seven inland reserves have been established by the government primarily to protect and preserve representative cross-sections of the flora, fauna, and landscapes of Suriname. Because the forests and savannas of the interior are remote and sparsely populated, the wildlife of these reserves has not been exploited as relentlessly as in other South American countries. The reserves probably support a larger and more complete community of neotropical fauna than any similar system of reserves on the continent.

Casual visits to some reserves are discouraged in order to maximize protection of wildlife; most can be used for research purposes with the approval of government authorities. A few reserves from each category have been developed so as to fulfill educational purposes and to foster the interests of international tourists and students of natural history; one such reserve is Brownsberg Nature Park.

Suriname's venture into wildlife conservation began in 1942 with the creation of a small bird sanctuary on the coast intended to protect a number of nesting birds, among them the scarlet ibis. In 1948 a nature protection commission was formed, and in 1954 a nature protection law was enacted that provided for establishment of nature reserves. The same year a wildlife protection law was passed that protected all birds, mammals, and sea turtles except those specifically designated as game, domestic, or harmful species in the most populated third of the country. The same law has been revised and will soon apply to the entire country.

In 1969 Stichting Natuurbehoul Suriname or the Foundation for Nature Preservation in Surinam (STINASU), a semi-governmental organization, was established. The foundation assigned itself an ambitious set of objectives: to coordinate and finance scientific research in the reserves, to stimulate public awareness of nature preservation, to support educational purposes, and to encourage and facilitate tourism in the reserves.

Fortunately, the government and STINASU realized the value of the country's wildlife heritage, and soon established nine natural reserves and one park in order to preserve a representative cross-section of Suriname's flora, fauna, and landscapes. Plans were then made to administer these reserves on what was a truly revolutionary basis: that nature can support its own conservation by income derived from nature tourism.

In order to attract this type of tourist, facilities had to be constructed to facilitate their visits. Accordingly, funds were set aside to construct overnight accommodations at several reserves. STINASU staff carried out these plans in sophisticated fashion. By polling visitors, they discovered that tourists interested in natural history had no desire for luxurious accommodations; in fact, most such visitors indicated that such accommodations would be intrusive, and detrimental to their anticipated experience. STINASU decided to show city visitors the jungle, rather than take a piece of the city to the jungle. Instead of following the more typical and dubious South American practice of building luxurious and costly hotels in the wilderness, STINASU built modest, but practical and comfortable, bush camps, and kept prices for tourists at reasonable levels.

Much of Suriname's coast and most of its interior forests are so remote and primitive that they are far beyond reach of the ordinary tourist, but as a result of

STINASU's enlightened and far-sighted policy, Suriname now has several natural reserves in different regions that are interesting, accessible, and affordable.

Suriname's nature reserves are not subject to many of the chronic problems that plague parks and reserves in nearly every other South American country; all of its reserves are uninhabited, and the land in public ownership. No illegal settlers live in the reserves, and poaching is relatively rare.

⊡ BROWNSBERG:
Rain Forest School

About 80 miles (129 kilometers) from Paramaribo, on the Brownsberg Plateau, Brownsberg Nature Park lies smack in the middle of the rain forest at elevations that range from 700 to 1,400 feet. Facilities are comfortable, and simply strolling around camp is a modest jungle experience, but the real attraction of Brownsberg is its network of forest trails.

The park has by far the finest rain forest trails in South America. They are expertly laid out, well marked, and superbly maintained. Though only about 7 miles (11 kilometers) of trails weave through the park's 21,000 acres, they are designed to enable visitors to visit several sections of the park on long or short day hikes, and return to camp for a shower before dinner and darkness.

Names and numbers of seven different trails are prominently posted on signs at trailheads. The trails are color coded—blue diamonds for Koembe Valley, orange diamonds for the trail to Irene Vallen (Irene Falls), for example—and signs indicate destination, distance, and approximate hiking time. The signs are written in Dutch, of course, but visitors will have no problem deciphering them. Scientific and common names of many trees and prominent shrubs and lianas are posted on some trails. One interpretive trail has no fewer than forty-three stations, explaining such features as trees killed by strangler figs, nurse logs, ecological succession, buttress root systems, and so on.

Park managers have taken advantage of the terrain to design trails that provide a number of overlooks (*uitzicht* in Dutch), and have cut only enough foliage to maintain comfortably passable trails. Excellent trail maps are distributed to visitors on request. Even in the shade of the forest, it gets hot on the trails by midday, so hikers should try to do most of their hiking by 11 A.M.

The trails are well worth hiking. Visitors will definitely see typical rain forest flora, including a wide variety of climbing vines, lianas, epiphytes, bromeliads, orchids, and tall trees. Since the park is on a plateau, hikers can also look over broad expanses of trackless forest as well as Brokopondo-meer (Brokopondo Lake), an artificial but nonetheless wild lake formed by construction of a dam on the Suriname River. Look down to see inch-long ants that create their own 2-inch wide trails, giant morpho butterflies that flit silently across the path, and tracks made by jaguars the previous night (a pad mark and four toes, the whole track about 5 inches wide). Pacas, pumas, agoutis, brocket deer, peccaries, giant toads, jaguars, curassows, and some awfully big bugs can also be spotted. Keep an eye in the trees, home to toucans, macaws, jacamars, any of seven species of monkeys, and some more big bugs.

Oropendolas nest at the bush camp at Brownsberg Nature Park in order to discourage one of their main predators, toucans.

The rain forests of Brownsberg are filled with sound. Several bands of howler monkeys live in the park, and their hair-raising roars reverberate across the entire plateau. The white bellbird (*Procnias alba*) has a call that sounds like a bell tolling; other birds have gong-like songs. A low gurgling sound followed by three very loud bell-like notes or a modified wolf-whistle is the song of the screaming piha (*Lipaugus vociferans*). With the exception of howler monkeys, the quality of the sounds at Brownsberg lies not in volume but in persistence. One soon notices that not a great number of creatures make noise, but rather that something or other makes a loud noise consistently throughout the day—usually a few different birds with unusual calls.

The camp at Brownsberg is located atop a ridge that overlooks Brokopondomeer and a broad tract of forest that slopes to the lake. A half-dozen buildings are spread around a small clearing in the jungle, some with views of the lake, others tucked into the forest edge. The Dutch passion for cleanliness and order is apparent, for cabins are newly painted and scrubbed clean, and the grounds are trim and neat. The wooden buildings merge nicely with their surroundings, and are designated by appropriate Dutch names: Bellbird Cottage, Spider Monkey Lodge, Armadillo Bungalow, and so on. The complex songs of green oropendolas (*Psarocolius viridis*) add to the general jungle chorus, and their tear-shaped nests dangling from large shade trees at the side of the cabins enhance the jungle-like atmosphere of camp.

Visitors must bring and prepare their own food, but everything else is provided at modest cost: drinks, beer, tobacco, linen, blankets, cookware, dishes, and so on.

Beds, showers, and sanitary facilities are immaculate. A generator provides light for a few hours each evening.

The park is multipurpose; school groups as well as tourists visit regularly. If possible, time your visit to coincide with a regularly scheduled STINASU nature tour. The guides who accompany the tours are knowledgeable and often show excellent films at camp; many speak English.

Climate and Weather

The temperature in Suriname varies little—from 78 to 83 degrees Fahrenheit year-round. Annual mean temperature is 80 degrees. The warmest month is September, 83 degrees; coolest month is January, 78 degrees. Diurnal temperature variations are greater than annual variations. At night the temperature may fall below 70 degrees, and occasionally below 60 degrees. Prevailing sea winds keep the humidity high, but also help to cool sweltering tourists. Afternoon temperatures at Brownsberg are hot, but much cooler than in Paramaribo. It is cool and comfortable in the deep shade of the plateau's rain forest. Winter evenings can be cool enough for light sweaters.

Annual rainfall is 80 to 100 inches, but Suriname has a long and a short rainy season. The long season lasts from mid-April to mid-August, and unfortunately coincides with the nesting period of marine turtles. The short season is from mid-November to mid-February. The most pleasant season is usually the short dry season during February, March, and April.

Mosquitos are creatures of the seasons, and malaria and yellow fever are still endemic in some parts of Suriname. The coast and Brownsberg Nature Park, fortunately, are *not* in the danger zones, but some of the reserves deep in the interior are. Those who travel far into Suriname's interior should take preventive measures. A shot is all it takes to prevent yellow fever, and chloroquine is the usual drug taken for malaria, but adverse side effects can result from long-term use of the drug. Ask a physician to review current accepted practice for prevention, and follow his advice.

Mosquito nets are used in populated Suriname more for comfort than health reasons, but in remote areas they forestall disease-carrying insects as well as vampire bats, which can carry rabies.

Location and Access

At this writing, it is possible to fly to Paramaribo from Caracas, Venezuela; Belém, Brazil; Port of Spain, Trinidad; and Miami, Florida, but these schedules change frequently. Check with the airlines before making plans.

Brownsberg Nature Park can be reached from Paramaribo by car, bus, or with an organized tour. By car, it is a 2-hour drive from the capital, through the town of Brownsweg. Just follow the signs, and be sure to take enough fuel for the round trip.

Several buses a day go to Brownsweg, which lies 9 miles (14 kilometers) from the park. Travelers can get off in Brownsweg and hitchhike to the park or be picked up by a STINASU car if previously arranged.

Several travel agencies organize escorted tours to the park, but arrangements made through STINASU are cheaper, and just as good if not better.

Visits to any of Suriname's reserves should start with a stop at STINASU's office at Jongbawstraat 10 in Paramaribo. Staff speak English, are extremely helpful, have a rare abundance of printed material, and can arrange or coordinate trips to any of the reserves.

Glossary

beheerder	manager
boshut	forest hut
kantoor	office
meer	lake
meertje	pond
rivier	river
straat	street
uitzicht	viewpoint, abbreviated *uitz.*
val	waterfall
voetpad	footpath, trail

🔲 THE COASTAL RESERVES:
Wia Wia, Galibi, Coppename-mouth, Hertenrits, Peruvia, and Wanekreek

Wia Wia. Wia Wia Reservaat, a 33-mile (53 kilometers) stretch of coastline comprising mangroves, mud flats, and shoals, was created in 1961 to protect the nesting beaches of marine turtles. During the months March through June, thousands of green turtles and hundreds of huge (to 1,300 pounds) leatherback turtles arrive at the beaches (now completely outside the reserve because of shifting sands) to lay their eggs and return to sea. Somewhat less nesting activity can be observed in February and July. Wia Wia is also the site of nesting and feeding populations of such birds as storks, herons, egrets, skimmers, flamingos, scarlet ibises, roseate spoonbills, terns, kites, crab-eating hawks and other birds of prey, and many species of waterfowl. Take binoculars.

Visitors are housed in a comfortable, screened beach hut (*strandhut*) at Matapica. Drinking water, cooking facilities, kitchenware, and beds are provided. Visitors bring their own food and bedding or hammock.

Transportation involves travel by boat; total time from Paramaribo is about 4 hours. Travelers need to protect themselves from sunburn, and should bring insect repellent. Prices are reasonable. Make arrangements through STINASU.

Galibi. This reserve, a string of beaches at the mouth of the Marowijne River, was set aside in 1969. It is a small reserve (10,000 acres) but of international importance, for one of its beaches is the largest nesting site on either side of the Atlantic for the olive ridley sea turtle. On certain nights in June and July, up to 500 ridleys arrive and lay their eggs on 1,500-foot-long Eilanti Beach. Green and leatherback turtles also nest on these beaches.

Carib Indian villages are located nearby, and under some circumstances arrangements can be made to visit the infamous Devil's Island, just across the Marowijne River from the Indian village. **Note:** STINASU does not arrange these trips.

Visitors are accommodated in a beach hut at Baboensanti. As at Matapica, drinking water, cooking facilities and kitchenware, and beds or cots are provided. Visitors are expected to provide their own food, and sometimes bedding or hammock.

Transportation involves a 3-hour drive by bus or car to Albina, followed by a 3-hour boat ride down the Marowijne River to the reserve. Bring gear to protect yourself from spray, and plenty of insect repellent.

Coppename-mouth. This area at the mouth of the Coppename River has been protected since 1953 and has been a reserve since 1966. It was established primarily to protect nesting colonies of tricolored, little blue, night, and boat-billed herons; common and snowy egrets; scarlet ibises; and roseate spoonbills. The river estuary is also an important wintering area for at least 20 species of migratory North American wading birds. Hundreds of thousands of birds such as the lesser yellowleg, short-billed dowitcher, and semi-palmated sandpiper may be found in this and other coastal reserves in Suriname during winter months, feeding heavily to build fat reserves for the often nonstop return to North America.

At this writing, casual visits to the reserve are not encouraged; no accommodations are available. Check at the STINASU office on the status of the reserve.

Hertenrits. Established in 1971, Hertenrits is the smallest of Suriname's reserves, 250 acres that surround a mound in the middle of a swamp, an archaeological site of pre-Columbian Amerindian culture. No accommodations.

Peruvia. Peruvia, established in 1986, covers 86,000 acres of sand ridges, marsh forests, and swamp forests. Fauna includes large populations of blue and yellow macaws (*Ara ararauna*), tapirs (*Tapirus terrestris*), and capybaras (*Hydrochaeris hydrochaeris*). No accommodations.

Wanekreek. One of four reserves established in 1986, Wanekreek lies in the savannas of eastern Suriname. Like Herttenrits, the reserve is an archaeological site, protecting traces of pre-Columbian Amerindian culture. No accommodations.

ᵽᵂ THE INLAND RESERVES:
Raleighvallen/Voltzberg, Eilerts de Haan Gebergte, Brinckheuvel, Tafelberg, Sipaliwini Savanna, Copie, and Bovencoesewijne

Raleighvallen/Voltzberg. Raleighvallen Reservaat occupies 140,000 acres of pristine rain forest on the shores of the Coppename River in north-central Suriname. Among the reserve's features are granitic inselbergs (dome-shaped remnants of basement rock) that rise up to 400 feet above the forest and provide outstanding views of central Suriname. Raleighvallen (Raleigh Falls) is a series of cascades in the relatively clear Coppename River (safe for swimming), but the reserve's primary attractions are its birds and wildlife. Parrots, macaws, toucans, jacamars, and trogons are a few of the many species common in the park. Monkeys (eight species) are the most conspicuous mammals in the reserve, but it may be possible to sight pumas, jaguars, ocelots, giant and nine-banded armadillos, bushdogs, coatimundis, river otters, two-toed and three-toed sloths, collared and white-lipped peccaries, tapirs, squirrels, agoutis, brocket deer, and other wildlife.

Visitors stay in the Foengoe Island Lodge (*boshut*) or the more rustic Lolopasi Lodge. Facilities at Foengoe (overlooking the river) include complete kitchen, dishware and utensils, refrigerator, beds, shower, and generator-supplied electricity for four hours each evening. Linen and hammocks can be rented, and soft drinks and beer purchased. Bring food, bug dope, binoculars, and a light raincoat. Lolopasi Lodge, across the river from the main accommodations, is reached by boat and overlooks the rapids; a secluded beach borders the river below the lodge. Kitchen and dinnerware are provided, but there's no electricity (and therefore no noisy generator). A bush camp (hammocks only) is located at the foot of the Voltzberg Inselberg for hikers who wish to take a leisurely two days to make the trip to the dome.

Transportation to the reserve is by air (1 hour from Paramaribo) or by a far more scenic combination of car or bus and canoe. The trip by road from Paramaribo to Bitagron, a Bush Negro village, takes 3 to 4 hours, and is followed by a 4-hour boat ride from the village upstream to the reserve. Prices for all services are very reasonable.

Eilerts de Haan Gebergte. The largest of Suriname's reserves (544,000 acres), Eilerts comprises uninhabited, pristine lowland and lower montane rain forest. No accommodations are provided. An airstrip is located on the reserve. Eilerts is only for completely self-sufficient expeditions.

Brinckheuvel. This uninhabited reserve once contained prosperous villages. It is a mixture of savanna and brush communities not far from the coast. Of indifferent interest, it can be reached by means of the train that travels to Brownsberg Nature Park. No accommodations are provided.

Tafelberg. Tafelberg protects a representative example of the mesa-like tablelands characteristic of southern Guyana and southeastern Venezuela. Very little is known about the fauna of the area. There are no accommodations for visitors; Tafelberg is for self-sufficient expeditions only.

Sipaliwini Savanna. A large, uninhabited reserve in the extreme south of Suriname, on the border of Brazil, Sipaliwini is part of a large, undulating savanna. It has extensive, ungrazed grasslands, gallery forests along streams, and isolated forest patches. An airstrip permits access, but no visitor accommodations are provided. Expeditions only.

Copie. Established in 1986 and comprising 70,000 acres, Copie protects extensive tracts of wet clay savannas and marsh forest containing abandoned military paths, cannons, and cemeteries dating from the colonial years of the 17th and 18th centuries. Casewinica Creek harbors several species of caimans (*Caiman crocodiles, Paleosuchus palpebrosus,* and *Paleosuchus trigonatus*), and a small population of the rare giant river otter, *Pteronura brasiliensis.* No accommodations.

Bovencoesewijne. Also established in 1986, this reserve protects 67,000 acres of unbleached sand savanna. Freshwater swamps and riparian woodlands flourish along the banks of the Coesewijne River, a black-water stream of unusual beauty. Orchids are abundant in these riparian woodlands, and the river supports manatees (*Trichecus manatus*), giant river otters, and caimans. Birds are abundant in the reserve, which can be reached in 90 minutes by car from Paramaribo. Accommodations for tourists are planned for the near future.

Current information on all of these reserves is available at the following location: STINASU, Suriname Forest Service, Cornelis Jongbawstraat 10, Paramaribo, Suriname; mailing address: P.O. Box 436, Paramaribo, Suriname.

Almost as quickly as remnants of prior illegal occupation are removed, Morrocoy National Park returns to its unspoiled original condition.

⎯⎯ 9
VENEZUELA

In 1498, on his third voyage to the New World, Columbus discovered the northern coast of South America. One of his crew, probably the cartographer Amerigo Vespucci, noted the Indian houses built on stilts at a village near Lago Maracaibo. The houses reminded Vespucci of similar construction in Venice, so he named the settlement "Little Venice"—Venezuela.

The name persisted, and was given to a nation that was one of South America's poorest and sleepiest countries until 1914, when geologists discovered that the tiny stilt village lay atop an oil pool of immense proportions. That discovery launched the country into the modern age practically overnight, and today Venezuela is one of the wealthiest nations on the continent.

The country can be roughly divided into four regions: the mountains, the oil basin, the plains or *llanos,* and the mountainous southeast, called Guyana.

The Andes end in Venezuela, forming a rugged arc that extends from the Colombian border along the Caribbean coast nearly to the mouth of the Río Orinoco. Over

250

two thirds of Venezuela's population, most of its major cities, and Pico Bolívar, at 16,411 feet the country's highest peak, lie in this mountainous zone.

In the northwest corner of Venezuela lies the oil basin, a low-lying, arid region that is the primary source of the country's income, and the largest known oil reserve in South America.

Most of central Venezuela, a region corresponding to the watershed of the Orinoco—eighth-longest river in the world—is *llanos,* a steamy lowland of savanna and rain forest exceeded in size only by the Amazon Basin. The *llanos* are so flat and their clay soils so impermeable that during the rainy season vast areas become inundated to form broad, shallow inland seas.

The southeast region of Venezuela is called Guyana—not to be confused with the adjacent country of the same name. Guyana, like Patagonia, has a unique character that has attracted and fascinated explorers and adventurers for centuries. Remote, nearly inaccessible, and sparsely settled, this highland region is rich in minerals, timber resources, and legends. Guyana was long believed to be the site of the fabulously rich lost cities of El Dorado. Its most striking features, particularly in the area called La

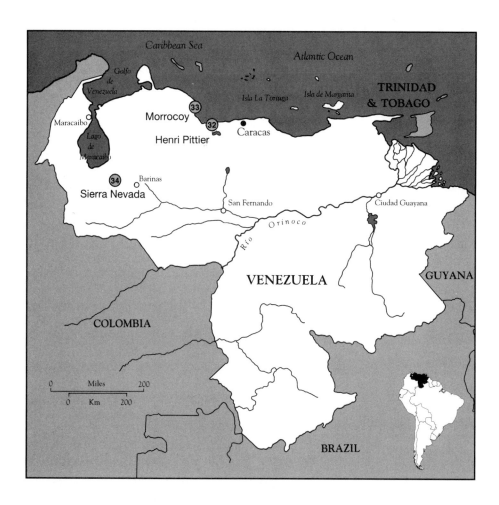

Gran Sabana, are the scattered, enormous mesas—*tepuis*—that jut from the flat savanna floor thousands of feet into the clouds. So high and sheer are the walls of the *tepuis* that the tops of many remain unexplored. The world's highest waterfall, Angel Falls, plunges 3,212 feet from a fissure near the top of one of these *tepuis* to a forested canyon in the floor of the savanna.

Each of these regions contain elements of the major biogeographical features of the northern half of the continent: Andean highlands, Amazonian rain forests, Guyanese savannas, and the warm Caribbean coast—fertile ground on which to develop diverse parks and reserves. Primarily because of its oil revenues, Venezuela has been able to do just that.

Venezuela's park system began with the establishment of Parque Nacional Henry Pittier, in 1937. By 1958, three more parks had been created, and the government formed a small office to administer them. Every few years a new park was added. In 1974 the idea of a national park system caught firm hold. Six new parks and three natural monuments were created that year, and the small park office was elevated to a section within the Ministerio del Ambiente y Recursos Renovables (Ministry of Environment and Renewable Resources). The new section wasted no time carrying out its mandate, and in 1978 seven more parks and four more natural monuments were added to the system.

Today, 8 percent of Venezuela's national territory—over 28,000 square miles—has been preserved; twenty-six parks and seven natural monuments protect representative examples of the flora, fauna, and landscapes of Venezuela's major biogeographical regions, fruits of a far-sighted conservation vision all too rare in the Third World.

🄿🅆 HENRI PITTIER:
Birds in the Clouds

Parks have been set aside in ten of the thirteen major biogeographical regions into which scientists divide Venezuela. One of these regions, Region Montañosa Centro-Occidental (the West-Central Mountains), contains several parks, of which the finest was created through the efforts of one determined man, Henri Pittier.

Pittier, a natural scientist, began to notice deterioration of the flora and fauna in a biologically diverse area along the coast just west of Caracas in about 1930. He began a one-man campaign to convince federal authorities to halt the depredations that were severely impacting these dense forests. From the perspective of the government, Pittier made a thorough nuisance of himself for nearly a decade, but he was tenacious, his arguments were compelling, and his campaign ended successfully on February 13, 1937, when the government set aside the area he fought for as Venezuela's first national park.

The park was originally called Parque Nacional Rancho Grande, but in 1953, three years after Pittier's death, the name of the park was changed to honor the memory of the man who had become known as the "Deacon" of Venezuela's park system.

The West-Central Mountains are the northernmost of the high peaks of the Andes. At Henri Pittier, these peaks literally drop into the sea. The area is therefore considered a transition zone between the Andean Cordillera and the Caribbean Sea, and has the wide habitat diversity characteristic of all transition zones.

The park is large—265,000 acres—and ranges in elevation from sea level to nearly 8,000 feet. This elevational range is responsible for the diversity of vegetational zones, and associated fauna, in the park. Mangrove swamps, spiny desert scrub, deciduous temperate forests, humid tropical forests, and dense cloud forests are all found surprisingly close to one another within the confines of the park. The most casual observer cannot fail to notice these zones, especially striking since the transitions from one to the next take place over such a short distance.

The two main roads through the park cross the mountains and link the interior town of Maracay with the coast. These roads pass through each of the vegetation zones in the space of about 20 miles. In effect, the visitor traveling these roads from the sea to Maracay first ascends, then descends a steep staircase of vegetation, each step representing a different zone.

At the edge of the sea, the flat landscape is dominated by mangroves and beaches lined with extensive coconut plantations (*cocoteros*). The lowest seaward hillsides are dry; cacti and spiny shrubs eke out precarious lives on the sere, brown slopes. Between about 600 and 1,300 feet of elevation, low deciduous trees predominate, leafless and stark during the dry season. A savanna-like zone lies between about 1,300 and 2,300 feet—grassy meadows through which are scattered clumps of trees and tall shrubs. A real forest takes over from about 2,300 to 2,800 feet, dense and deciduous. Mixed evergreen and deciduous forest appears at about 3,000 feet, an exuberant proliferation of tall trees and shrubs festooned with ferns, lianas, orchids, bromeliads, philodendrons, and epiphytes of every size and shape. Between 5,000 and 7,500 feet lies the eerie evergreen cloud forest, and in the few areas that are higher, small expanses of temperate forest.

For the visitor, the true gem among these zones is the cloud forest (*selva nublada*).

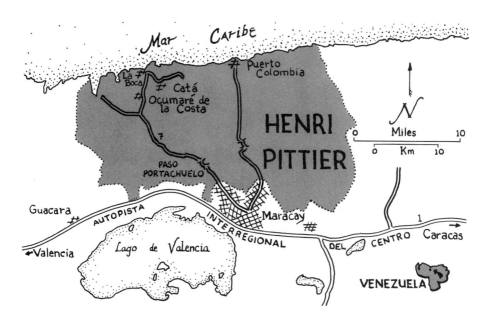

At Henri Pittier National Park, Venezuela, the Andes drop sharply into the sea.

(Only Parque Nacional Puracé in Colombia offers visitors equal accessibility to a true cloud forest.) Though the cloud forest zone begins at about 5,000 feet, you don't need an altimeter to tell when you have arrived. Indeed, as one drives through the park, the roadside is frequently obscured by swirling tendrils of the dense, cool fog that cloaks the forest in milky semidarkness. Vegetation overhangs and presses in from both sides of the road, creating a mountainside tunnel of greenery. Flowering shrubs—pink, yellow, blue, and purple—are particularly abundant in the cloud forest, but the real treasure is its birdlife.

Because of a long association with prominent natural scientists and the presence of a biological station designed to facilitate their work, the birds of Henri Pittier have been particularly well studied. Ornithologists estimate that of the 8,000 species of birds known in the world and the 1,250 so far discovered in Venezuela, over 520 are found in Henri Pittier National Park. That means that representatives of nearly 7 percent of the birds in the world, and 42 percent of the birds in Venezuela have been found in this single park! And more bird species are found in the cloud forest—about 200—than in any other of the park's vegetation zones.

Enumeration of these birds is far beyond the scope of this book, but among those that visitors are most likely to see or hear are the bearded bellbird (*Procnias averano*), whose gong-like call reinforces the eerie character of the mist-shrouded forest; the large (16 inches long) black and white owl (*Ciccaba nigrolineata*); the small lilac par-rotlet (*Touit batavica*), so colorful that Venezuelans call it the seven-colored parakeet; and the foot-long orange-winged parrot (*Amazona amazonica*). Keep an eye on the for-est floor for a glimpse of the bizarre helmeted curassow (*Pauxi pauxi*), a turkey-sized shiny black bird with a bony, clam-shaped crest above its eyes. Another turkey-sized bird, usually found roosting in branches of the forest canopy, is the brown crested guan (*Penelope purpurascens*). Visitors will also see tyrant flycatchers, for more than sixty species of this bird alone have been identified in the park. Look in tall trees for the woven hanging nests of oropendola birds.

The park's fauna is also diverse, but as in all tropical forests, populations are low and the animals difficult to see, a drawback complicated in Henri Pittier by rugged terrain. Visitors who hike the trails described below or who bushwhack along water-courses might see tapirs, opossums (*Chironectes* sp.), agoutis, and arboreal puer-coespíns (*Coendou prehensilis*), which are odd, squirrel-sized porcupines with a naked, prehensile tail.

Butterflies are abundant in the cloud forest, but the creature that most persis-tently makes its presence known to the world is neither bird, mammal, nor insect, but the giant marsupial frog, *Gastrotheca ovifera*. These frogs are called marsupials because the females carry their young in small pouches on their backs, but they should have been named *Stentorius*, for they begin their loud chorus of croaking at dusk and don't falter until dawn.

One of the most noticeable plants throughout Henri Pittier is Tillandsia—the long strands, hoary when dry, that we call Spanish moss and South Americans call old man's beard (barba del viejo). Plants of the genus Tillandsia are neither mosses, nor as once thought, lichens, but rather bromeliads, related to the pineapple-top epiphytes so proliferous in the tropics. Several hundred species of Tillandsia have been identi-fied, and the plants are extremely widespread in South America (and the southern United States), from the rain forests of the Caribbean coast to the beech forests of Tierra del Fuego. In Henri Pittier, Tillandsia may appear to smother the trees to which it clings in enormous masses, but it is a true epiphyte, dependent upon other plants only for secure anchorage; it obtains the water and nutrients it requires directly from the atmosphere. Many of the park's birds use Tillandsia to construct or line their nests.

Note: Several species of highly poisonous snakes inhabit the forests and savannas of Henri Pittier. They are seen only rarely, but hikers should take appropriate precau-tions.

Visitor Facilities

A wide range of restaurants and visitor accommodations is available in Maracay or at any of several villages along the coast. Because the park is so close to Caracas, roads, trails, and beaches can become very crowded on weekends. Most weekend visi-tors crowd into one of the following towns and their nearby beaches: Ocumaré de la Costa, Catá (site of a public beach resort), Choroní, and Puerto Colombia. Cabins, hotels, and guesthouses are available in the villages.

The park service has constructed a recreation center (*nucleo recreacional*) on each of the two roads into the park. The first of these, Guamita, lies 9 miles from Maracay on the road to Ocumaré (Ruta 7), where picnic areas, swimming holes in the Río Limón, rest rooms, and dressing rooms (*vestuarios*) have been constructed. Camping is permitted. The second site, Las Coquizas, lies 4 miles from Maracay on the road to Puerto Colombia. Both sites are designed more for family recreation than for nature study. They tend to be boisterous on weekends.

Serious wildlife observers should visit the Estación Biológica (Biological Station) de Rancho Grande, near Paso Portachuelo on Ruta 7. The station, proposed by Pittier in 1948 and established in 1950, lies at a comfortable elevation. A small museum at the station houses specimens of the park's fauna, with especially good displays of birds and their nests, and an enormous collection of bizarre insect life. Simple but cheap living accommodations for visiting scientists are sometimes made available to serious visiting naturalists.

Two trails near the station are good for day hikes and bird-watching. The more interesting of these climbs goes to Cerro Periquito (4,900 feet) and on to Pico Paraíso (5,900 feet). Take along a light sweater and raingear. The longer trail, recommended only for experienced hikers, leads to Pico Guacamaya (6,700 feet) and then northward down a long ridge to Cuyagua, near the sea. The trails are not well marked; ask for information, including the condition of these and other trails, at the station.

Recreation

Henri Pittier is an ideal park for bird-watching and studying several types of tropical vegetation; hiking is the best way to achieve both objectives, and the park's roads and trails facilitate visitors' efforts.

Swimming, snorkeling, and other beach activities are popular on the park's coast. Unfortunately, Venezuela's beaches tend to be badly littered. Wise travelers should look for boat operators who take advantage of this situation by offering cheap, often exciting rides to isolated, cleaner beaches.

Climate and Weather

The relationship between altitude, temperature, and rainfall (and vegetation) is very strict in Parque Nacional Henri Pittier. At the highest elevations, temperatures range from 42 to 54 degrees Fahrenheit. The humidity is always high, although warm sweaters or jackets may be needed at night. Below 3,200 feet, normal temperatures range from 54 to 95 degrees; midafternoons in Maracay or on the beach can be torrid.

Rainfall also varies widely according to elevation. At low elevations, annual rainfall can be as low as 30 inches. At the biological station—about 3,500 feet—annual rainfall reaches 42 inches, but the humid tropical forests on the seaward side of the mountains can receive as much as 158 inches every year, mostly in the form of torrential, drumming rainstorms.

The best time to visit the park is the dry season, from January to March. The rainiest season, called winter (*invierno*) by the Venezuelans, lasts from April to September.

Location and Access

Henri Pittier is located between the Caribbean coast and the city of Maracay, about 60 miles west of Caracas via Carretera 1. The two cities are connected by several daily buses, a trip of 1½ to 2 hours.

Two separate roads enter the park from Maracay. The first road, Ruta 7, which passes Guamita and the Estación Biológica de Rancho Grande, leads to Ocumaré, and is paved. The second road, to Choroní and Puerto Colombia, is a poor dirt road that crosses higher passes than Ruta 7. Beaches near Puerto Colombia are consequently less crowded than those in the vicinity of Ocumaré.

Because gasoline is so cheap in Venezuela, taxi service is also cheap in most cities. With a bit of bargaining, it is possible to rent a taxi for a day's tour of the park for a few dollars. Hitchhiking is possible, but competition is intense on weekends and holidays.

Glossary

barba de palo	Tillandsia, spanish moss
cocotero	coconut plantation
conoto	oropendola bird
nido colgante	hanging nest, usually woven nest of oropendola birds
puercoespín	porcupine
selva nublada	cloud forest
vestuario	dressing room

🄵 MORROCOY: A Park Reclaimed

Venezuela's western coastal region is the driest section of northern South America; some areas receive as little as 15 inches of annual rainfall. Few creeks or rivers carry sediment to the Caribbean Sea from these parched plains. As a result, the sea is extremely clear along these shores. A steady, gentle northeast wind prevails, rustling the fronds of palm trees at the edges of glistening white beaches of fine coral that border the crystalline waters. The inland plains are dusty wastelands of cactus and spiny shrubs, but the coastline is a succession of tropical scenes of the sort that adorn the walls of travel agencies the world over.

Along this coast lies a park whose terrestrial, marine, and submarine resources have been saved from almost certain destruction: Parque Nacional Morrocoy.

Morrocoy is a large polygon—80,000 acres—that includes a long, narrow strip of shoreline, thousands of acres of ocean and reefs, a dozen small islands, and scores of islets and salt flats. The area is extremely attractive, and for decades prior to 1974,

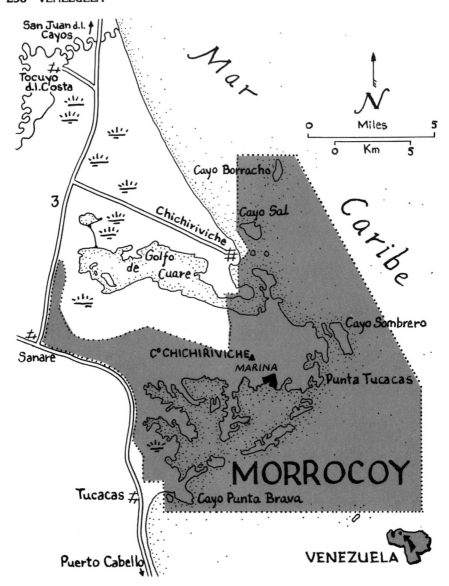

whomsoever wanted to have a dock, cabaña, or house on the beach or hidden away on a deserted offshore island for summer use simply built one . . . no questions asked.

Over the years, seasonal settlement accelerated. Before long, 1,500 simple shacks on stilts (*palafitos*) had been built over the beaches and reefs, and another 1,500 houses had been constructed on the islands and keys. Soon the inevitable results of unplanned, illegal occupation of desirable but fragile property began to appear. Beaches began to erode, the once-clear waters became severely polluted, tons of garbage accumulated, fish and wildlife began to disappear, and mangroves and coral reefs began to die.

In 1974 the government stepped in and turned 124 square miles of the area into a national park, and began the monumental task of dismantling all of these structures and restoring the area to its original, near-pristine condition. The job was immense, perhaps greater than the government had itself anticipated. The *palafitos* could be burned and their ashes would blow away, but many of the docks, foundations, and houses were constructed of concrete and had to be buried or blown up and the pieces trucked off or dropped into the sea. The government painfully learned that prevention is much cheaper than remediation.

The results, however, have been spectacular. Signs of prior habitation are still visible in the park as reclamation continues: old foundations, unnatural clearings, concrete pilings, mounds of rubbish. But unmistakable signs of healthy recovery are also evident: the water is clear again, beaches are stable, mangroves are green and vigorous, and the park teems with birds and other wildlife.

Morrocoy is proof positive that if a fragile ecosystem can be protected in time, it can recover, and enjoyment of its resources can be returned to the general public.

Morrocoy, a coastal park ranging in elevation from sea level to 900 feet, can be divided into four distinct habitat types: the keys, salt flats, dry forests, and mangroves.

The keys (*cayos*) are low, 3 to 5 feet above the sea, and formed by accumulations of sand and finely ground, clean, white coral and shellfish remains. They are stabilized by three species of mangroves—black (*Avicennia germinans*), white (*Laguncularia germinans*), and yellow (*Conocarpus erectus*)—and several species of salt-tolerant plants, and abound with hidden coves and tiny trackless beaches.

The extensive salt flats (*bajíos de sal*) are dry most of the year, but sometimes flood during the rainiest months, November and December. Bordered by low-growing mats of ice plants (*Batis maritima*), which Venezuelans call hierba de vidrio (glass plants), the salt flats are favored feeding grounds for thousands of wading birds.

The dry forests (*bosques secos*) are located on the slopes of the park's only hill, Cerro Chichiriviche, a low prominence near a town of the same name. Its slopes are dry, but it is capped by a small semideciduous forest that supports a small population of howler monkeys (*Alouatta seniculus*).

The seaward slopes of Cerro Chichiriviche tip into yellow limestone cliffs that contain a number of grottos and small caves. Local legend holds that pirates once sheltered themselves in these caves. Today some of the caves shelter guácharos or oil birds (*Steatornis caripensis*). These dark brown, nocturnal birds are large—18 inches long—and nest exclusively in caves. Scientists have proven that they navigate through the dark like bats, making use of echoes to determine their location. They feed on palm fruits, and their young, which grow enormously fat on this diet, were once rendered by Indians into cooking oil. Hence the name oil bird.

Stands of mangroves (*manglares*) line much of the coast, but have also taken root offshore throughout the park and are steadily advancing seaward. The mangroves and offshore reefs protect the many miles of placid channels that wind through the keys, and permit visitors to explore most of the park in sheltered waters. Magnificent pure stands of red mangroves (*Rhizophora mangle*) that reach nearly 50 feet predominate in the southern part of the park.

Most of the mammals in the park are found in the vicinity of Cerro Chichiriviche: the howler monkeys; a few deer; fox-sized arboreal collared anteaters

Magnificent frigate birds in flight, Morrocoy National Park, Venezuela

(*Tamandua tetradactyla*), which South Americans call oso melero or honey bear; pacas; and a few others. They are not easy to see.

One mammal that does live near the mangroves and salt flats is the crab-eating raccoon (*Procyon cancrivorus*). This animal, which looks just like the familiar North American raccoon, mask and all, is also difficult to spot, for it sleeps by day and hunts at night. Its dainty tracks crisscross nearly every mud flat in the park. South Americans do not call them raccoons, but rather zorros cangrejos, or crab foxes.

What is visible at Morrocoy, however, are waterfowl, shorebirds, and wading birds—thousands of them. They first appear from miles away, flocks wheeling over the mangroves, flying to and fro like busy commuters: herons and egrets, pelicans and gulls, ducks and flamingos.

At Morrocoy, it is not the variety of birds that is so striking, but rather their numbers. Venezuela is on a major migratory pathway for ducks, for example, and it is estimated that over 70 percent of the ducks that pass through Venezuela visit this park.

In this teeming cornucopia of birds, two species invariably attract more attention than the others—the scarlet ibis (*Eudocimus ruber*) and the magnificent frigate bird (*Fregata magnificens*). The scarlet ibis, corocora roja, is one of nature's most colorful creatures. Except for barely visible smudges of black at the tip of its primaries, the entire bird is the color of arterial blood. Mere tomatoes pale by comparison, and for all their spectacle, flamingos are rendered pallid next to a scarlet ibis. The brilliant plumage of the scarlet ibis has delighted and puzzled bird-watchers for centuries. It is now known that carotenid pigments in the marine organisms that ibises eat is primarily responsible for their coloration, for populations of ibises that live on the *llanos* of interior

Venezuela are dull red or orange, wan imitations of their coastal cousins. The function of the bright coloration is less well understood. Ibises are extremely colonial birds, however; they are almost never observed alone. Current theory holds that the color simply helps the birds to keep one another in easy sight.

Usually seen soaring or hovering immobile above the mangroves and channels, magnificent frigate birds can exceed 3 feet in length; their wings, angled like those of terns, can span 8 feet. They have slender, deeply forked tails and long, sharply hooked bills. Males are entirely black most of the time, but females have a white breast. During breeding season, the male's gular pouch—a small, bright-red, sac-like organ below its bill—inflates dramatically. The bird's chest becomes so puffed-up that it can rest its head and bill on this taut, scarlet balloon with which it seeks to attract females.

The magnificent frigate bird is a strong and efficient flier and a fierce-looking creature. It obtains its meals by forcing other birds in flight to drop their food, which it then steals. Although magnificent frigate birds always live near the ocean, they never stray far from land, for they are poorly adapted to water and do not land on the sea.

Visitor Facilities

Stop first at park headquarters in the town of Tucacas, at the southern end of the park. Staff are friendly and helpful, and will orient visitors to the park and suggest sites for campers. About a half-dozen beach campsites are available. One is accessible from land, a short walk from Tucacas; the others are easily reached by small boats that can be rented in Tucacas near the park office. Ask if permits are required for campsites on the islets near Chichiriviche. Take food, bug dope, and plenty of water or beer. Pick a breezy site to temper the midday heat, and, more important, to keep away the tiny biting sand flies (puripuri, or simply *la plaga*—"the plague"), which appear the instant the breeze dies and can make life miserable.

Note: Now that the park is recovering, caimans are once again on the increase. They are so shy that they are seen rarely; often only a distant splash reveals their presence. Visitors who explore beaches and sandy points in late evening or at night should nevertheless keep their eyes open and their wits about them.

Tucacas has two small hotels; Chichiriviche, the larger town at the northern end of the park, has four more hotels and several restaurants. Boats may also be rented at Chichiriviche in order to reach additional beach campsites on the keys at the northern end of the park.

Recreation

The park is popular for ocean recreation of all sorts: fishing, waterskiing, swimming, snorkeling and scuba diving, boating, windsurfing (in Spanish, *windsurf*), and beach camping. Spearfishing and collecting of marine organisms of any kind is strictly prohibited.

Climate and Weather

Seasonal variations at Morrocoy are insignificant; the weather is hot but pleasant all year. The average annual temperature is about 80 degrees. Afternoons can be blistering if the wind dies down. Take plenty of sun screen. Average annual rainfall is about 48 inches, mostly from quick rainstorms.

Location and Access

Morrocoy is located about 155 miles (250 kilometers) west of Caracas, on the west shore of the Golfo Triste. To reach the park by road from Caracas, proceed on Carretera 1 west to Valencia, then north toward Morón. Turn west at the coast on Carretera 3, and proceed to the park. There are no buses direct to the park, but buses from Caracas serve Valencia and Puerto Cabello. From either city, collective long-distance taxicabs, called *por puestos* in Venezuela, travel to Tucacas or Chichiriviche. The Venezuelan term for hitchhiking is *la cola*.

Glossary

albufera	saltwater lagoon
arrecife coralino	coral reef
bajío de sal	salt flat or marsh
bosque seco	dry forest
cayo	key, islet
corocora roja	scarlet ibis
manglar	mangrove
morrocoy	small turtle
puripuri	biting sand flies
tijereta, fragata	magnificent frigate bird

SIERRA NEVADA:
Roof of Venezuela

In the far west of Venezuela, south of the Lago Maracaibo oil basin, lies what scientists call the Región Montañosa Occidental or Mountainous West Region. Its principal subregions are the foothills, highlands, and *páramos*.

Most of the foothills in this region are semiarid; some are in dry rainshadows that receive as little as 30 inches of annual rainfall and are clad in forests of scrubby, xerophytic vegetation. The highlands, which generally range from 6,000 to 10,000 feet, are cooled by extremely humid winds that blow in from the Caribbean; these mountains support a variety of mixed forests, from subtropical rain forests to open pine forests to clammy, dripping cloud forests. Above about 10,000 feet, the forest cover begins to give way, to be replaced by alpine meadows, brush, herbaceous plants, and scattered trees of species well adapted to higher elevations. At about 12,000 feet appear the first frailejones (*Espeletia* sp.), the tall, gray-leaved plants characteristic of the moist *páramos.*

The mountains have been glaciated, and the high terrain is rugged; many of the peaks are perpetually snowcapped. Not far from the warm waters of the Caribbean, a few glaciers persist in the wrinkles near the top of the highest peaks. One would expect such a region to be scenic as well as interesting, and it is. Venezuela has established five national parks in the Mountainous West Region, of which the most interesting and best developed is Parque Nacional Sierra Nevada.

The extension of the Andes that penetrates western Venezuela is the Cordillera de los Andes. A separate range of this cordillera, the Sierra Nevada de Mérida, is the only extensive area in Venezuela characterized by high snow-clad peaks, and Parque Nacional Sierra Nevada occupies the heart of it. The park is large (470,000 acres), and though set aside relatively recently, it is Venezuela's second-oldest national park, dedicated in 1952.

Pico Bolívar, 16,411 feet, is the highest mountain in the country, a chief objective of Venezuelan mountaineers, but it is by no means the only notable mountain in the park. The twin peaks Humboldt (16,215 feet) and Bompland (16,021), plus La Concha (16,143 feet), El Toro (15,601 feet), and El León (15,552 feet) all lie within the boundaries of the park.

Most of these peaks lie within full view of Mérida, a pleasant university city of about 130,000 inhabitants that lies on the northern border of the park. The strategic location of the city with respect to the park and its scenery is largely responsible for the presence of the installation that draws tourists from all over the country to Parque Nacional Sierra Nevada: a gondola cable-car system claimed by Venezuela to be the longest and highest in the world. Whether it is truly highest or longest does not really

matter; the ride is unquestionably spectacular. The gondola system, *teleférico,* is of practical use to park visitors, but in any case should not be missed.

About thirty clear, cold lakes, the majority glacial in origin and characteristically tinted with rock flour, are scattered through the park. Most lie tucked into the shoulders of the highest mountains at elevations between 10,000 and 15,000 feet. Most are accessible by trail, and those on the road system have developed campsites. Rainbow trout have been planted, and the lakes, notably *lagunas* Verde, Negra, Victoria, and Mucubají, are popular fishing spots during the season (May through October).

Although the park has fauna typical of the northern Andes, including spectacled bears, tapirs, mountain lions, jaguars, deer, opossums, coatis, and even howler monkeys, the populations are low and the animals shy. Most live on the remote lower and more heavily forested southeastern slopes of the mountains, where they are less likely to come into contact with humans. Similarly, birdlife is relatively sparse in the higher portions of the park. The cloud forest zone has plenty of birds, of course, but except for an occasional passing raptor or passerine, the *páramos* are curiously silent and empty. Visitors should not come to this park in search of easily observed wildlife.

The scenery and the hiking opportunities, however, more than make up for the lack of wildlife.

Visitor Facilities

For sheer excitement, the feature of paramount interest to most visitors is the *teleférico,* French-built and 49 percent privately owned. Nearly 8 miles (12.5 kilometers) long, the *teleférico* rises from Mérida to 15,634-foot Pico Espejo, a granitic giant that lies between the even higher *picos* Bolívar and El León. The trip to the top takes 1½ hours in four stages, and is something of an adventure in itself, so some planning and precautions are required, as described below.

First, the vertical ascent of about 10,500 feet (3,200 meters) into oxygen-poor air is too sudden for normal acclimatization; some visitors suffer symptoms of altitude sickness such as headache, breathlessness, and nausea. Young children, who find it difficult to curb their energy, seem to be particularly vulnerable. Travelers who are susceptible to altitude sickness would be wise to take most of a day to make the ascent, spending an hour or so at each of the stop-off points between stages. People with serious heart or respiratory problems should pass this trip up.

Second, even though it may be shirtsleeve weather in Mérida, the temperature can be below freezing at the top, especially early in the morning, the best time to make the ascent. Travelers *must* take warm clothes, including a good windbreaker, to the top, or they will be far too cold to enjoy the views. (August is the coldest month in these mountains.) A hat that will shelter one's face from the sun plus sunglasses are also recommended. Ultraviolet radiation is intense at 15,634 feet, so visitors who intend to spend the entire day at the top or plan a hike from one of the stop-overs, must take sun-block face cream to avoid parboiling instantly. Hikers need to get a permit (and topographical map) from the park service office next to the *teleférico* station in Mérida. Permits for solo hikers are not issued; a party must comprise a minimum of two hikers. Plan accordingly.

Third, make reservations for the *teleférico* upon arriving in Mérida. Even though the *teleférico* runs six days a week and has a capacity of over 800 persons per day, tickets are often booked for several days in advance during holiday seasons. Lines for tickets start to form at 6:00 A.M., so if possible, avoid a long wait in a long line by getting a ticket through a hotel or travel agency. The station is located at the end of Calle 24, south of Avenida 8.

Finally, unless you intend to spend at least one night high in the mountains, do not ride the *teleférico* at any hour of the day; the ride might not be worth the trouble. On rides that leave Mérida much later than 8:30 A.M., clouds are likely to obscure many of the views, and travelers will spend most of the day wandering about in a freezing mist. The best months for views with respect to cloud cover are November through June. During summer (July through October) the peaks are likely to be snowy and shrouded with clouds. Photographers and visitors who want to catch a glimpse of the distant *llanos* to the southeast take special note.

The trip itself is accomplished in four stages. All stations have rest rooms and a coffee shop (*cafetín*).

Stage 1. Mérida to La Montaña (elevation 8,000 feet). The *teleférico* ascends a canyon, passing over cultivated fields of sugarcane and coffee bushes, and enters the lower levels of a cloud forest. La Montaña offers splendid views of Mérida and neighboring towns, and the Chama Valley.

Stage 2. La Montaña to La Aguada (elevation 11,326 feet). The vertical rise of this stage approximates the cloud forest zone. The trees, garbed in incredible numbers of mosses, ferns, lichens, bromeliads, orchids, and lianas, grow shorter as you rise up the mountainside. This is also the elevational zone of the pine forests of the Sierra Nevada de Mérida, seen somewhat better elsewhere in the park or from nearby trails. The most prominent tree is a straight, showy, five-needled pine the Venezuelans call pino aparrado (*Podocarpus oleifolius*). Picos Bolívar and El Toro come into view. Look for bright green splashes of parrot wings over the foliage below.

Stage 3. La Aguada to Loma Redonda (elevation 13,272 feet). This stage leaves the cloud forest behind and rises to the lower level of the *páramos;* most of the trees are left behind. Three glaciers (*ventisqueros*) come into view, two on Pico Bolívar, one on Pico La Concha. Waterfalls appear below every snowfield. A trail leads from Loma Redonda station north to one of the high-country *refugios* owned by the park and maintained by a climbing club. Another recommended destination from Loma Redonda is Los Nevados, a 5-hour downhill hike from the station. A small inn that serves food is located at Los Nevados.

Stage 4. Loma Redonda to Pico Espejo (elevation 15,634 feet). This final stage is nearly 2 miles long (3 kilometers), and rises 2,369 feet into the *páramos,* zone of flowers and frailejones. During the months from September to December, the frailejones will be decorated with bright yellow flowers; gentians, geraniums, heather, avens, and a host of other tundra flowers will also be in bloom. A few scattered clumps of hardy trees appear at this elevation. They are the familiar polylepis trees, called coloraditos by Venezuelans and *Polylepis sericea* by botanists. Well adapted to harsh conditions, they are able to grow at higher elevations than any other trees. The polylepis stands of the Parque Nacional Sierra Nevada are believed to be among the highest in South America.

Several glacial tarns and the major peaks of the Sierra Nevada de Mérida are now in sight. To the north is the crest of Pico Bolívar, on which has been erected a barely visible bronze bust of the Venezuelan-born liberator Simón Bolívar, the warrior-politician who freed most of northern South America from Spanish rule and is as revered on much of the continent as George Washington is in the United States. To the northwest lie Pico La Concha and the twin peaks Humboldt and Bompland. Pico El León is to the southwest, and to the southeast—early on a clear day—are the humid tropical forests of the *llanos,* which merge, well beyond the eye's ken, into the jungles of the Amazon Basin.

A visitor center, *cafetín,* and small infirmary (oxygen is available) are located near the Pico Espejo station. A concrete path leads to the tall white statue of *La Virgen de las Nieves* (Our Lady of the Snows), an excellent photo point.

The Pico Espejo station is also the jump-off point for trails that lead to some of the dozen or so *refugios* in the park. Inquire at the *teleférico* station for the Club Andino, where guides and information are available. Many of the trails are difficult, and not intended for inexperienced hikers. A permit and climb plan are required of mountaineers; at least fifteen climbers have died during the past several decades, and park authorities may require that climbing parties clear their plans with local civil-defense authorities. Nonclimbing backpackers and day hikers are reminded that permits are required to leave the *teleférico* stations or to overnight at the *refugios,* which are free, basic, and adequate. The topographical maps available at the park office only indicate general locations of trails and *refugios.* Ask a park ranger to mark your map.

Two *refugios* are located near El Espejo station, one between picos Humboldt and Bompland, and four more widely scattered to the northeast of El Espejo. A group of four *refugios* is concentrated in the vicinity of *lagunas* Negra and Mucubají, in the northeastern corner of the park.

Among the well-established trails are:

◆ Pico Espejo to Loma Redonda. A knee-jarring downhill hike from Pico Espejo station.

◆ Pico Espejo to Refugio Albornoz to Pico Bolívar. This hike, for experienced hikers only, reaches Ventisquero Timoncito. Ropes are required at some points. The round-trip hike can be completed in 1 long day.

◆ Pico Espejo to Timoncito to Pico La Concha. A 2-day hike that begins at Pico Espejo, leads to Refugio Albornoz (overnight), and on to *picos* La Concha and La Garza.

◆ Loma Redonda to Pico El Toro. An 8-hour round-trip hike to the Páramo Media Luna (Half-moon Páramo) from the Loma Redonda station.

◆ Loma Redonda to north flank of Pico Bolívar. A 2- to 3-day round trip for climbers only.

◆ La Aguada to El Paramito. A 3-day trip to a glacier on the flank of Pico Bolívar.

◆ El Vértigo. A very difficult climb up a portion of Ventisquero Timoncito. Climbers only.

Gray-haired friars of the páramos: frailejones or espeletias, Sierra Nevada National Park, Venezuela

◆ La Mucuy to Laguna Coronota to Laguna Verde to *picos* Humboldt and Bompland. A difficult but interesting 3-day hike through the heart of the Sierra Nevada.

◆ Laguna Mucubají to Pico Mucunuque. A very difficult 2-day trip in the northeast section of the park, for experienced hikers. The higher portions of this trail are steep and treacherous, but the lower sections, near Laguna Negra, are good for day hiking or establishing a base camp from which to explore or fish.

For a detailed written guide to these and other trails, see *Backpacking in Venezuela, Colombia, and Ecuador* by Hilary and George Bradt, available from Bradt Enterprises, 409 Beacon Street, Boston, Massachusetts, 02115.

Mérida has scores of hotels and restaurants. Overnight accommodations for noncampers are also available at several other towns and quaint villages along the northern border of the park: Apartaderos (close to Lagunas Mucubají and Negra), Mucuchíes, La Mucuy, Jají, and Santo Domingo.

Recreational centers have been established in several park locations. The most popular are at La Mucuy, just up the hill from Tabay, a village 10 miles (16 kilometers) east of Mérida, and at Laguna Mucubají, 30 miles (50 kilometers) east of Mérida. A visitor center, large public dormitory, cabins, park ranger station, and picnic sites have been constructed at La Mucuy. At Laguna Mucubají are campsites, picnic sites, a park information center, and access to several trails and park *refugios*.

Recreation

Sierra Nevada is principally a mountain hiking park, but because of the *teleférico*, visitors do not have to hike to enjoy the wonderful scenery. The trail network is appropriate for day hikes, and the *refugios* facilitate short or long backpacks. Mountaineering, including rock climbing and ice climbing, is popular, and gear, guides, and reliable information are available locally. Trout fishing is good in the high lakes.

Climate

Sierra Nevada has two distinct rainy and dry seasons. The two rainy periods are January to February and August to September; if possible, avoid visiting the park during these months, when it clouds up and rains nearly every afternoon. From July to September, snowstorms are common in the mountains. Seasonal temperature variations in the higher portions of the park range from 32 degrees to 70 degrees Fahrenheit.

Location and Access

Parque Nacional Sierra Nevada is south of Lago Maracaibo, in the extreme western section of Venezuela, adjacent to the town of Mérida.

The park is easy to reach. Several daily flights link Mérida with Caracas. Several buses a day also connect Mérida with all cities in western Venezuela. The bus ride from Caracas to Mérida requires about 12 hours. *Por puestos* cost twice as much as buses, but are quicker and usually more comfortable.

Glossary

cuerdo	climbing rope
por puesto	long-distance taxi, shared with several riders
teleférico	gondola cable car system
trucha	trout
ventisquero	glacier

ꔮ GLOSSARY

SPANISH

agua dulce	fresh water
aguas termales	hot springs
aguti	agouti
albufera	saltwater lagoon
alfarería	ceramic pottery
alojamiento	lodging
altura	altitude, high place
andarivel	ski lift
andinismo	climbing
andinista	climber
anfiteatro	amphitheater
apachetá	road, trail, or pass marker (cairn)
apague su cigarillo	put out your cigarette
arrecife	reef
arrecife coralino	coral reef
azufrada	sulphurous
babilla	cayman
bahía	bay
bajío de sal	salt flat or marsh
balcón	viewpoint, balcony
ballena	whale
baños	baths, sometimes hot springs
barba de palo	Tillandsia, spanish moss
blanquillo	crested grebe
bosque	forest
bosque galería	gallery forest
bosque seco	dry forest
brazo	arm, including arm of a body of water
buceo de observación	skin diving, snorkeling
cabalgata	horseback ride
cabeza de acero	steelhead
caimán	cayman
caití	Andean avocet
callejón	corridor
calzada lítica	stone pathway
caminata	hike
camino	road, highway
campo de lava	lava flow
caña	rod, usually fly rod; also sugarcane
cañadón	steep, usually deep canyon
caño	canal or channel

carpincho	capybara
capitanía del puerto	port authority
carpintero negro	Magellanic woodpecker
carretera	highway, main road
caseta de control	control station, entrance
cayo	key, islet
centro de visitantes	visitor center
cerro	hill, mountain
chaco	vicuña trap
ciénaga	brackish lagoon
cimientos viviendas	house foundations
coati	coatimundi
cocotero	coconut palm grove, coconut plantation
confitería	snack bar
cono cinérico	cinder cone
conoto	oropendola bird
cormorán	cormorant
corocora roja	scarlet ibis
cría	young animal, usually nursing
cuerdo	climbing rope
cuervo	cormorant
cuervo de pántano	Puna or Andean ibis
cuide al bosque	take care of the forest
cumbre	peak, summit
cuy	guinea pig
danta	tapir
delfín	dolphin
escalador	climber
escorpión	scorpion
estancia	large ranch
evite incendios	avoid fires; i.e., prevent forest fires, a common sign
fogón	fire ring or barbecue pit
fósil	fossil
fragata	magnificent frigate bird
gallo de roca	cock-of-the-rock
Garganta del Diablo	Devil's Throat
garúa	coastal fogbanks, common along the Atacama desert
garza	ibis, heron, or egret
garza real	great egret
gavilán	hawk
gaviota	gull
gaviota Andina	Andean gull
gaviotín	tern
glaciar	glacier
goce del paisaje	enjoy the landscape or scenery

grupo familiar	family group
guardaparque	park ranger
guardería	ranger station
helechos	ferns
hembra	female animal
hoja	leaf
hongos	fungi, mushrooms
huala	great grebe
huella	trail
intendencia	headquarters
jabalí	wild boar
la caza está prohibida	hunting prohibited
lago	lake
laguna	lake
leña	firewood
lengal	grove of lenga trees
león	mountain lion
letrina	latrine
lobería	sea lion colony
lobito de río	river otter
lobo marino	sea lion
loro	parrot
macho	male animal
madera	wood
manatí	manatee
manglar	mangrove forest or swamp
mangle	mangrove
mangle amarillo	white mangrove
mangle rojo	red mangrove
mangle salado	black mangrove
Mapuche	descendant of Araucarian Indian tribes of southern Chile and Argentina
martín pescador	kingfisher
mirador	overlook, observation point
mochila	backpack
mochilería	backpacking
mochilero, -a	backpacker
mono	monkey
mono aullador	howler monkey
mono caí	capuchin monkey
montañeros	mountaineers
morrocoy	small turtle
mosca	fishing fly, as well as the insect
museo	museum
musgos	mosses
ñandú	lesser or Darwin's rhea

nevado	snowcapped mountain
nido colgante	hanging nest, usually of oropendola birds
nieve	snow
no grabe	don't carve on (the trees)
ojo de agua	spring of water
paca	paca, a large rodent
parina	Quechua word for flamingo
pasarela	raised walkway
paseo	walk, stroll
pato anteojillo	spectacled duck
pato cuervo	cormorant
pato jergón	Chilean pintail duck
pecarí	peccary
perdido	intermittent cataract
pesca vedada	fishing forbidden
pescar	to fish
petrificado	petrified
picada	trail
picadero	Indian tool-making site
piedra del sol	stone of the sun alter
pingüinera	penguin colony
pingüino	penguin
piscina techada	covered pool
plazoleta ceremonial	ceremonial square
población	village, small town
por puesto	long distance taxi, shared with several riders
portería	entrance, access
proteja la fauna	take care of the animals
proveeduría	grocery store, place for provisions
puercoespín	porcupine
puesto de vigilancia	ranger station
puma	mountain lion
punta de flecha	arrowhead
puripuri	biting sand flies
quebrada	ravine, gorge
Quechua	Indian language commonly spoken in Peru, Bolivia, and Ecuador
raíz	root
raspador	scraper
salmón encerrado	landlocked salmon (*salar sebago*)
salto	falls, cataract
se prohibe la caza	hunting prohibited
sede	headquarters
sede administrativa	administrative headquarters
selva nublada	cloud forest

senda	trail
sendero	trail
sendero de historia natural	natural history trail
siempreverde	evergreen
tambo incaico	Inca house (ruin)
tapir	tapir
Tehuelche	pre-Columbia Indian tribe of Patagonia, now extinct
teleférico	gondola cable car system
témpano	iceberg
termales	hot springs
termas	hot springs
tigre	jaguar
tijereta	magnificent frigate bird
tortuga marina	marine turtle
tramo	trail
tronco	trunk
tropilla de solteros	bachelor herd
trucha	trout
trucha arco-iris	rainbow trout (*Salmo gairdneri*)
trucha de arroyo	brook trout (*Salvelinus fontinalis*)
trucha fontanilis	brook trout
trucha marrón	brown trout (*Salmo fario*)
túnel	tunnel
venado	deer
vencejo	swift, swallow
ventisquero	glacier
vestuario	dressing room
vida silvestre	wildlife
viento	wind
volcán	volcano
zorro	fox

PORTUGUESE

abrigo	hostel, shelter
agulhas negras	black needles
andorinha	swift, swallow
animais	animals
anta	tapir
aparado	precipice, abyss
arara	macaw
árvore	tree
aves	birds
beijaflor	hummingbird, literally flower-kisser
borboleta	butterfly
borracha	latex rubber

bugio ou guariba	howler monkey
cabeceiras	headwaters
caboclo	subsistence settler of the Amazon Basin, peasant
cachoeira	small cascading stream, river rapids
caitetu	peccary
caminho	trail
capivara	capybara
carrapato	tick, chigger
cascatinha	cascade
catarata	falls, cataract
cerrado	savanna
chuva	rain
coati	coatimundi
cotia	agouti
cupineiro	termite nest
escorpião	scorpion
estrada	road, highway
fazenda	farm, plantation, or ranch
floresta	forest, woods
Garganta do Diabo	Devil's Throat
grama	grass
guarda florestal	park guard
guía	guide
igapó	flooded forest
igarapé	stream
jaguar ou onça	jaguar
maça	apple
macaco	monkey
macaco-prego	capuchin monkey
mata	forest, woods
mata ciliar	gallery forest
mata galería	gallery forest
mirante	viewpoint
morro	hill
museu	museum
paca	paca, a large rodent
palmero	palm
pántano	marsh, swamp
papagaio	parrot
pássaro	bird
passeio	walk, stroll
pedra	rock
pegada	animal track
peixe	fish
picada	trail
picapau	woodpecker

pico	peak
pinheiro	pine, pine tree
pinho	pine, pine tree
piquenique	picnic
pium	biting blackfly
planalto	high plateau
portão	gate
prateleira	shelf
raia	stingray
ramal	long trail
rodovía	freeway
sede	headquarters
sucuarana	mountain lion
tamanduá bandeira	giant anteater
tamanduá mirím	lesser anteater
tartaruga	turtle
tatú bola	three-banded armadillo
tatú canastra	giant armadillo
tatú galinha	nine-banded armadillo
trilha	trail
tucano	toucan
veado, cervo	deer
vereda de Buriti	grove of Buriti palms
véu da noiva	bride's veil

DUTCH

beheerder	manager
boshut	forest hut
kantoor	office
meer	lake
meertje	pond
rivier	river
straat	street
val	waterfall
voetpad	footpath, trail

◪ SELECTED BIBLIOGRAPHY

Andrews, Michael A. *The Flight of the Condor.* Boston: Little, Brown, and Company, 1982. Fauna of South America.

Bates, Marston. *The Land and Wildlife of South America.* New York: Time-Life Books, 1964 (revised 1975). Overview of South American landforms. Sections on primates and several other mammal groups, birds, reptiles, amphibians, fish, and insects. Well illustrated.

Box, Ben, ed. *The South American Handbook.* London: Trade and Travel Publications, revised annually. North American distribution by Rand McNally & Co. The most reliable and complete travel guide to South America available.

Bradt, George and Hilary. *Backpacking in Venezuela, Colombia, and Ecuador.* Boston: Bradt Enterprises, 1980.

Corporación Nacional Forestal, Departamento de Conservación. *Parques Nacionales de Chile.* Santiago.

Daciuk, Juan. *La Fauna del Parque Nacional Laguna Blanca.* Anales de Parques Nacionales, tomo XI. Buenos Aires, 1968.

Darwin, Charles. *The Voyage of the Beagle.* 1836. Though first published in 1836, this classic account of a young naturalist's wanderings in South America is still useful.

Dimitri, Milan. *Aspectos fitogeográficos del Parque Nacional Lanín.* Anales de Parques Nacionales, tomo VIII. Buenos Aires, 1959.

———. *Pequeña Flora Ilustrada de los Parques Nacionales Andino-Patagónicos.* Anales de Parques Nacionales, tomo XIII. Buenos Aires, 1974. Available only in Spanish. Illustrated technical description of the major trees, shrubs, and forbs of the Andean parks of Patagonia.

División de Parques Nacionales, Ministerio de Agricultura y Cría. *Parques Nacionales.* Caracas, 1975.

División Parques Nacionales y Vida Silvestre, Instituto Nacional de los Recursos Naturales Renovables y del Ambiente. *Parques Nacionales y Reservaciones.* Bogotá, 1976.

Dorst, Jean. *South and Central America: A Natural History.* New York: Random House, 1967. The most comprehensive description of the natural history of the continent available today. Well illustrated.

Durrell, Gerald. *The Drunken Forest.* London: Rupert Hart-Davis, 1956. Flora and fauna of the Gran Chaco and Rio de la Plata region.

———. *Three Singles to Adventure.* London: Rupert Hart-Davis, 1954. Flora and fauna of Guyana.

———. *The Whispering Land.* London: Rupert Hart-Davis, 1961. Flora and fauna of Patagonia and northwestern Argentina.

Etchichury, María. *Petrografía de Algunas Rocas Características del Parque y Reserva Nacional Los Alerces.* Anales de Parques Nacionales, tomo XIII. Buenos Aires, 1974.

Fundación de Educación Ambiental. *Los Parques Nacionales de Venezuela.* Caracas, 1983.

Goodall, Natalie P. *Tierra del Fuego.* Buenos Aires: Ediciones Shananaiim, 1970 (revised 1975). A bilingual edition that describes flora, fauna, land, history, and tourism in Tierra del Fuego and the Falkland Islands.

Harroy, Jean-Paul, F. Tassi, F. Pratesi, and C. Humphries. *National Parks of the World.* London: Orbis Publishing, 1974. Global view of the national park movement. Contains sections on the history and distribution of parks of the world, and essays on animal and plant conservation.

Instituto Brasiliero de Desenvolvimento Florestal. *Encontro Nacional Sobre Conservacāo da Fauna e Recursos Faunistícos.* Brasilia: Ministerio da Agricultura, 1977.

————. *Parques Nacionais e Reservas Equivalentes.* Brasilia. Ministerio da Agricultura. n.d.

Instituto Nacional de Parques Nacionales. *Parques Nacionales y Monumentos Naturales de Venezuela.* Caracas: Ministerio del Ambiente y de los Recursos Naturales Renovables. 1978.

International Union for the Conservation of Nature and Natural Resources. *Conservar el Patrimonio Natural de América Latina y del Caribe.* Morges, Switzerland, 1981.

————. *1982 United Nations List of National Parks and Protected Areas.* Morges, Switzerland, 1982.

————. *United Nations List of National Parks and Equivalent Reserves.* Morges, Switzerland, 1971 and 1975.

Keopcke, María. *Las Aves del Departmento de Lima.* Lima, 1964. An illustrated description of more than 300 Peruvian birds. Also useful in other parts of South America. English translation available in large bookstores in Lima, Peru.

Luna, H. C. *La Conservacíon de la Naturaleza: Parques Nacionales Argentinos.* Buenos Aires: Servicio Nacional de Parques Nacionales, 1976. Available only in Spanish, this book describes Argentine national parks: flora, fauna, climate, and so on. Essays on the history of conservation in Argentina, and phytogeographic and zoogeographic regions.

Macinnes, Hamish. *Climb to the Lost World.* London: Hodder and Stoughton, 1974. Account of a mountaineering expedition to Mount Roraima, in the Guiana highlands.

Marcolin, Arrigo. *Estudio Geológico Preliminar del Parque Nacional Laguna Blanca.* Anales de Parques Nacionales, tomo XI. Buenos Aires, 1968.

Matthiessen, Peter. *The Cloud Forest.* New York: Viking Press, 1961. Lucid account of a naturalist's trip in Amazonia, Tierra del Fuego, Mato Grosso, and the Peruvian highlands.

Morrison, Tony. *The Andes.* New York: Time-Life Books, 1975. Descriptions of the flora, fauna, and landforms of the Andes Range. Well illustrated.

————. *Land Above the Clouds.* London: Andre Deutsch, 1974. Descriptions of flora and fauna of the Altiplano and nearby regions.

Oficina Regional de la FAO para América Latina y el Caribe. *Sistemas Nacionales de Areas Silvestres Protegidas en América Latina.* Santiago, 1988.

Padua, María Tereza Jorge. *Os Parques Nacionais e Reservas Biológicas do Brasil.* Brasilia: Instituto Brasileiro de Desenvolvimento Florestal, 1983.

Perry, Roger. *Patagonia: Windswept Land of the South.* New York: Dodd, Mead, 1974. Descriptions of flora, fauna, and indigenous peoples of Patagonia and Tierra del Fuego.

Roquero, Maimonides. *La Vegetación del Parque Nacional Laguna Blanca.* Anales de Parques Nacionales, tomo XI. Buenos Aires, 1968.

de Schauensee, Rodolphe Meyer. *The Birds of South America.* Philadelphia: Livingston Publishing, 1970. Technical descriptions of more than 3,000 species of South American birds. A good resource book, but difficult for beginners.

Schulz, Joop, R. Mittermeier, and H. Reichart. *Nature Reserves and Wildlife Status in Suriname.* Paramaribo: Foundation for Nature Preservation in Suriname.

Shipton, Eric. *Tierra del Fuego: The Fatal Lodestone.* London: Chas. Knight and Co., 1973.

Shuttleworth, Dorothy. *The Wildlife of South America.* New York: Hastings House, 1966. Descriptions of fauna for juvenile readers.

Theroux, Paul. *The Old Patagonian Express.* Boston: Houghton Mifflin Co., 1979.

⊡ ADDITIONAL INFORMATION

Addresses of park service offices for the parks described in this book and a selection of useful pamphlets are listed below alphabetically, by country. Most are printed in Spanish or Portuguese; none are dated. Readers are reminded that when supplies of these materials are exhausted, they may not be replenished.

Argentina

Park Service Office:
Servicio Nacional de Parques Nacionales
Avda. Santa Fe 690
Buenos Aires
Capital Federal
Rep. de Argentina

Pamphlets:
- *Flora del Nahuel Huapi.* Published by the Sociedad de Horticultura de Bariloche, San Carlos de Bariloche, Río Negro, Rep. de Argentina. Small booklet with colored photos and short description of common wildflowers of Nahuel Huapi National Park.
- *Nahuel Huapi National Park, Argentina.* Brief description in English.
- *Parque Nacional Iguazú.* Pamphlet describing flora and fauna.
- *Parque Nacional Nahuel Huapi.* A small, descriptive handout.
- *Parques Nacionales Argentinos.* A 60-page booklet describing the geology flora, fauna, and other characteristics of twelve Argentine parks.
- *Parques Nacionales: Iguazú, El Palmar, El Rey, Río Pilcomayo, Chaco, Reserva Natural Formosa.* Short descriptions of each park.
- *Parques Nacionales Lanín y Laguna Blanca.* Brief descriptions of each park.
- *Parques Nacionales: Los Glaciares, Tierra del Fuego, Perito Moreno, Monumento Natural de los Bosques Petrificados.* Small handout.
- *Parques Nacionales: Nahuel Huapi, Los Arrayanes, Laguna Blanca, Lanín, Los Alerces, Puelo.* Brief descriptions of six parks.
- *Parque y Reserva Nacional El Palmar.* Small pamphlet and map.

Brazil

Park Service Office:
Instituto Brasileiro de Desenvolvimento Florestal
SAIN
Avenida L-4 Norte
Brasilia, Distrito Federal
Brasil

Pamphlets:

◆*Parques Nacionais e Reservas Equivalentes.* Pamphlet with very brief descriptions of Brazil's national parks and reserves.

Chile

Park Service Office:
Corporación Nacional Forestal
General Bulnes 285
Santiago
Chile

Pamphlets:

◆*Parque Nacional Fray Jorge.* Excellent small booklet describes flora, ecology, geology, and history of park.

◆*Parque Nacional Puyehue.* Small handout.

◆*Parque Nacional Torres del Paine.* Excellent pamphlet with descriptions of flora and fauna, plus map.

◆*Parque Nacional Vicente Pérez Rosales.* Small folder with map.

◆*Parques Nacionales Los Paraguas y Conguillío.* Small pamphlet.

Colombia

Park Service Office:
División de Parques Nacionales y Vida Silvestre
Ministerio de Agricultura
Avda. Caracas, No. 25A - 66
Bogotá, Colombia

Pamphlets:

◆*Parques Nacionales Naturales y Reservaciones.* Brief descriptions of several parks and reserves.

Ecuador

Park Service Office:
Sección de Parques Nacionales y Vida Silvestre
Dirección General de Desarrollo Forestal
Ministerio de Agricultura y Ganadería
Quito, Ecuador

Pamphlets:

◆*Parque Nacional de Altura—Cotopaxi.* Excellent booklet on park, with history and lists of flora and fauna.

Peru

Park Service Office:
Dirección General Forestal y de Fauna
Ministerio de Agricultura
Natalio Sánchez 220—Oficina 907
Jesús María, Lima, Peru

Pamphlets:
- ◆*Ordeza, Parque Nacional Huascarán.* Informative pamphlet, with map.
- ◆*Parque Nacional Huascarán.* Pamphlet with brief descriptions of flora and fauna of the park.
- ◆*Proyecto para la Utilizacíon Racional de la Vicuña Silvestre.* Leaflet describing Vicuña Project at Pampa Galeras.
- ◆*Proyecto Utilización Racional de la Vicuña.* Complete description of Vicuña Project at Pampa Galeras.

Suriname

Park Service Office:
Foundation for Nature Preservation in Suriname
Suriname Forest Service
Dept. of Nature Preservation
P. O. Box 436
Cornelis Jongbawstraat 10
Paramaribo, Suriname

Pamphlets:
- ◆*Nature Reserves and Wildlife Status in Suriname.* Brief descriptions of reserves in Suriname.

Venezuela

Park Service Office:
Oficina Nacional de Parques Nacionales
Dirección General de Recursos Naturales Renovables
Ministerio de Agricultura y Cría
Caracas, Rep. de Venezuela

Pamphlets:
- ◆*Parques Nacionales.* Booklet with short descriptions of Venezuelan parks and reserves.

🔲 INDEX

(Boldfaced names are national parks.)

BILL LEITCH's interest in South American parks stems from his education as a biologist and his experience as a Peace Corps volunteer in Colombia. He has spent several years exploring parks in all the republics of South America. He now lives and writes in Livingston, Montana, with his wife and daughter. Leitch is the author of several books and articles and is currently working on a guide to trout fishing in Argentina. He returns to South America every other year.

Other Books From The Mountaineers:

A Guide to Trekking in Nepal, 5th Ed., by Stephen Bezruchka. Extensively detailed guide covers the most rewarding trekking routes, permits, maps, health care, language, natural history, trip preparations. 352 pp, paper; $12.95

The Galapagos Islands: The Essential Handbook for Exploring, Enjoying and Understanding Darwin's Enchanted Islands, by Marylee Stephenson. Only complete, practical guide to touring this isolated archipelago off Ecuador. Includes history, necessary travel information, and descriptions of plants' and animals' unique adaptations to environment. 160 pp, paper; $12.95

The Best of Britain's Countryside: Northern England & Scotland—A Walking & Driving Itinerary, by Bill & Gwen North. Two-week, customized itinerary to the most rewarding places in Great Britain and Scotland. Day-by-day route information includes directions, distance, and "daily bread and bed" advice. 272 pp, paper; $12.95

Walking Switzerland—The Swiss Way, by Phil Lieberman. Covers 10 different areas in the Alps. Route descriptions include access, trail distances, times, technical difficulty, and details on mountain huts, inns, and hotels. 272 pp, paper; $12.95

The Pocket Doctor: Your Ticket to Good Health While Traveling, by Stephen Bezruchka. Covers jet lag, water, food, hygiene, health in different environments, treatments for common illnesses and bites, sprains, scrapes, infections, and much more. 96 pp, paper; $3.95

Alaska's Parklands—The Complete Guide, by Nancy Simmerman. Covers every state and national park and wild area—location, terrain, scenery, wildlife, outdoor activities available, camping, weather, facilities, access. 336 pp, paper; $15.95

Glacier Bay National Park, by Jim DuFresne. Only complete backcountry-use guide to the Park via foot or kayak. Describes weather, bears, fishing, wilderness camping, route information. 160 pp, paper; $8.95

Ask for these at your local book or outdoor store, or phone order toll-free at 1-800-553-HIKE with VISA/MasterCard. Mail order by sending check or money order (add $2.00 per order for shipping and handling) to:

The Mountaineers Books
306 2nd Avenue West, Seattle, WA 98119
Ask for free catalog